CONFLICT MANAGEMENT

CONFLICT MANAGEMENT

A Communication Skills Approach

DEBORAH BORISOFF

*Department of Communication
Arts and Sciences
New York University*

DAVID A. VICTOR

*Department of Management
Eastern Michigan University*

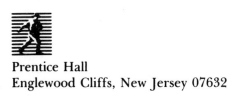

Prentice Hall
Englewood Cliffs, New Jersey 07632

LIBRARY OF CONGRESS
Library of Congress Cataloging-in-Publication Data

Borisoff, Deborah.
  Conflict management : a communication skills approach / Deborah
Borisoff, David A. Victor.
      p.   cm.
  Bibliography: p.
  ISBN 0-13-167503-6
  1. Interpersonal conflict. 2. Conflict management.
3. Interpersonal communication.   I. Victor, David A.
II. Title.
HM136.B597 1989
303.6--dc19   88-20944
                                                          CIP

Editorial/production supervision and
    interior design: Joy Moore/Gail Morey Hudson
Cover design: Lundgren Graphics, Ltd.
Manufacturing buyer: Ed O'Dougherty

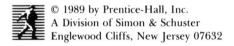 © 1989 by Prentice-Hall, Inc.
A Division of Simon & Schuster
Englewood Cliffs, New Jersey 07632

Printed in the United States of America
10 9 8 7 6 5

ISBN 0-13-167503-6

Prentice-Hall International (UK) Limited, *London*
Prentice-Hall of Australia Pty. Limited, *Sydney*
Prentice-Hall Canada Inc., *Toronto*
Prentice-Hall Hispanoamericana, S.A., *Mexico*
Prentice-Hall of India Private Limited, *New Delhi*
Prentice-Hall of Japan, Inc., *Tokyo*
Simon & Schuster Asia Pte. Ltd., *Singapore*
Editora Prentice-Hall do Brasil, Ltda., *Rio de Janeiro*

To
Cindy, Megan, Sandy, and Alec

CONTENTS

CHAPTER FIVE   CROSS-CULTURAL AWARENESS IN CONFLICT MANAGEMENT, 120

PREFACE

This book provides a communication skills approach to managing interpersonal conflict. The first three chapters focus on defining conflict and on the communication skills required for effective conflict management. Chapter 1 explores the nature of conflict and provides a five-step model for conflict management. Chapters 2 and 3 delineate the principles and techniques of verbal and nonverbal communication that facilitate conflict handling behavior.

The second three chapters explore conflict in specific contexts—contexts not included in works that address other aspects of conflict. Chapter 4 addresses gender differences in communication and explains how the communicative behavior of both sexes may contribute to the ways in which women and men regard, express, and manage conflict. Chapter 5 considers the pseudoconflicts that often result from interacting with individuals from other cultures and explores how these cultural differences can be anticipated, assessed, and avoided. Chapter 6 addresses the act of writing as an often overlooked contributor to conflict and explores how to avoid the unnecessary misunderstandings that frequently result from written communication.

Each chapter is followed by several exercises that target the intervention strategies and communication skills essential for effective conflict management.

Our intention is to familiarize the readers with the many factors that can lead to interpersonal conflict and to provide readers with appropriate communication skills to manage these differences effectively. We hope that those who read this book will no longer regard conflict negatively but will instead consider conflict as an opportunity for development, creativity, and change.

We wish to thank especially Michael L. Rosenberg and to gratefully acknowledge the Michael L. Rosenberg Fund in Speech Communication at New York University for helping to make possible the completion of this work. In addition, we wish to thank those who reviewed the book and provided invaluable insight at various stages of its development: Paul A. Argenti, Amos Tuck School, Dartmouth College; Judythe Isserlis, Department of Speech Communication, Iona College; Maria F. Loffredo, Speech and Theatre Department, St. John's University; Ralph Webb, Department of Communication, Purdue University; and Virginia Eman Wheeless, Department of Communication Studies, West Virginia University.

INTRODUCTION

Conflicts are broadly defined as disagreements between and among individuals. While this definition does not denote a pejorative meaning, many societies— including that of the United States—have imbued the term *conflict* with a negative connotation.

Although disagreements occur routinely, many people regard conflict as a battle to win or an encounter to avoid. People who engage in conflict are often considered aggressive, belligerent, and inflexible. Consequently, many individuals experience anxiety when faced with a situation that may produce a conflict. They want neither to enter into what they consider a negative encounter nor to be regarded in a negative light. They are therefore ill prepared to deal with conflicts, which inevitably arise.

Not every difference, however, need be so debilitating. Rather than accepting and perpetuating the negative stereotypes that surround conflict, it is important for individuals to recognize its positive aspects.

The prospect of change can be a compelling and highly motivating force. It is difficult, however, for people to achieve the changes required for managing differences without damaging relationships. The purpose of this book is to help people understand (1) the nature of conflict, (2) the appropriate communication skills for managing conflict, and (3) how gender differences, cross-cultural differences, and writing styles can be sources of conflict. Much of the literature on conflict and on the various contexts of interpersonal communication addressed in this book come from diverse disciplines. Consequently, the references cited reflect the works of noted anthropologists, linguists, psychologists, sociologists, and speech-communication specialists.

The first aim of the book, to enhance the reader's knowledge of the nature and dynamics of conflict, is presented in Chapter 1. This chapter introduces the concept of conflict and conflict-managing behavior. Moreover, it provides a five-step model—assessment, acknowledgment, attitude action, analysis—to enable individuals to effectively handle disagreements.

Chapters 2 and 3 address the second intention of this work: to provide the reader with an understanding of the appropriate communication skills for productive conflict management. These chapters address the action stage of conflict management and detail the communication strategies conducive to a supportive communication environment.

Chapter 2 explores verbal communication: the words we choose to express ourselves and the syntactic structures we select to deliver these messages. These aspects of verbal communication influence our listener's reactions to us. We must therefore develop an awareness of and sensitivity to the potential negative effect our verbal assertions can convey.

Oral communication, however, is not the only source of conflict; nonverbal behavior is often a more potent indicator of how we truly feel. This forms the core of Chapter 3. Our tone of voice, the way we use our eyes, facial expressions, and body movement reflect aspects of nonverbal communication. The unspoken messages we send can speak volumes in a business meeting, in a courtroom, in the classroom, and in the home. Thus, the effect of nonverbal communication in preventing, initiating, and managing a conflict is enormous.

The third aim of this book is to address specific sources of conflict. Three major sources have been selected for exploration: (1) the effect of gender differences on communication, (2) the effect of cross-cultural differences on interaction, and (3) the effect of writing on creating interpersonal conflict.

Recent social changes exacerbate the potential for conflict. For example, women and men are working together in greater numbers than ever before. When men and women work as colleagues, their different styles of communication may lead to conflict because each sex's communicative behavior reflects distinct acculturation processes and behavioral expectations. Chapter 4 reviews the stereotypical and discernible communication behavior patterns of women and men in the United States and explores how this behavior can be channeled toward constructive conflict management.

International politics and global economics also have brought nations closer together. But, as we see in chapter 5, proximity does not necessarily result in mutual understanding, especially when members of different cultures are required to negotiate with one another. To manage cultural differences—differences that often turn out to be pseudoconflicts—it is important for individuals to extend beyond their ethnocentric view of the world and to understand how people from other cultures feel and think.

Pseudoconflicts do not occur only in cross-cultural communication. In Chapter 6 we explore the potential and often avoidable differences that arise from written communication. Much of our daily interaction is handled through the written memo, letter, and report. Because the writer is not usually present to respond to the reader's interpretation of the message, however, careful writing strategies can be extremely useful in averting possible conflict.

Conflict will not vanish just because individuals are reluctant to deal with disagreements. Those who have grown up in an environment in which conflict was ostensibly absent are often ill prepared to deal with others under adverse circumstances. They lack experience handling disagreements productively. Those who have been raised to regard conflict as a direct clash are often equally ill equipped to manage productively the give-and-take characteristic of interpersonal relationships.

Individuals will be better prepared to deal with the problems that conflict can create if they are able to replace the notion of conflict as solely a hostile encounter with the more positive attitude of approaching disagreements as a challenge. When people embroiled in conflict are able to convey a cooperative attitude toward handling disagreements and to demonstrate the communication skills required for effective conflict management, they will embody the best qualities of the empathic, open-minded, and cooperative communicator.

CONFLICT MANAGEMENT

ONE
THE NATURE OF CONFLICT

"In my civilization, he who is different from me does not impoverish me—
he enriches me" (Saint-Exupery 1939). There are several definitions for
the term conflict. Coser (1956, p. 8) introduced the conflict perspective into
American sociology with his definition of conflict as "a struggle over values
and claims to scarce status, power, and resources in which the aims of the
opponents are to neutralize, injure, or eliminate their rivals." Cross,
Names, and Beck (1979, p. v) define it as "differences between and among
individuals." These differences are created by the nature of the conflict, for
example, over goals, values, motives, ideas, and resources. Thomas (1976)
provides a process definition of conflict — a process that originates when
one individual perceives that another party has frustrated, or is about to
frustrate, some goal or concern of his or hers. Deutsch (1971a) distin-
guishes five types of conflict: intrapersonal (within the self), interpersonal
(between individuals), intragroup (within a group), intergroup (between
groups), and international (between nations).

Deutsch (1971a, p. 51) further elaborates the term by stating that
"conflict exists whenever incompatible activities occur. . . . An action which
is incompatible with another action prevents, obstructs, interferes with, or
injures, or in some way makes it less likely or less effective." Finally, Hocker
and Wilmot (1985, p. 23) provide a communication perspective for the

term conflict: "Conflict is an expressed struggle between at least two interdependent parties who perceive incompatible goals, scarce rewards, and interference from the other party in achieving their goals."

The common elements to these definitions include the terms *differences, expressed struggle, incompatible, frustration, interference, perception,* and *interdependence.* Part of the difficulty U.S. culture has heretofore experienced in dealing with conflict stems from the pejorative connotation any type of discord conveys in a society that values harmony, compatibility, satisfaction, and independence. Because of these values, there has been a tendency in the past to avoid conflict.

In recent years, however, we have come to recognize and to acknowledge the benefits dealing with conflict affords. Because of our differences, we communicate, we are challenged, we are driven to find creative solutions to problems. Barnlund (1968, p. 9) cautions that were we all to agree with one another on every topic, conversation would come to a grinding halt, for "Where men see and feel alike there is nothing to share. Talk is primarily a means of confronting and exploring differences."

Regardless of the variations in how theorists define conflict, one attribute of conflict management remains consistent, that is, that conflict-handling behavior is not a static procedure; rather it is a process that requires flexibility and constant evaluation to be truly productive and effective.

Fisher and Ury (1981), Hocker and Wilmot (1985), Stuart (1980) and Wehr (1979) are among those who present step-by-step procedures for effective conflict intervention and conflict management. We believe that examining steps for communication can also provide an interesting vehicle for presenting and evaluating notable theorists and traits and skills required for effective conflict management. In contrast to providing conflict-management techniques as the culmination of understanding, we will use the process of conflict management itself to discuss the issues of conflict, for the process of management or resolution depends on the effective integration of theory and interpersonal communication skills.[1]

Our model for conflict management consists of five steps: assessment, acknowledgment, attitude, action, and analysis. A thorough understanding

---

[1]Arguably, the result of conflict is not always resolution. In fact, there are occasions when individuals feel it is appropriate to instigate a conflict, to escalate one that already exists, or to refuse to engage in conflict. Regardless of the intent of the disagreement, however, all conflict needs to be managed. An extreme example of violent conflict includes the country that feels it must retaliate with a military strike for a perceived transgression. In direct contrast to this agressive act is the use of interpersonal nonviolence to refuse to engage in conflict (as Hocker and Wilmot [1985], for example, assess Gandhi's pacifist stance). In this book, we do not advocate one style of conflict-managing behavior. Rather, we advise individuals to become sufficiently familiar with the different types of conflict-handling behavior and with the appropriate interpersonal communication skills that will allow them to productively manage differences when they occur.

of each of these components will result in both heightened awareness of the dimensions of conflict and, hopefully, in a greater ability for conflict-handling behavior.[2]

ASSESSMENT

Two department heads disagree about how their limited budget should be allocated. A worker is deeply offended because he feels he has been unjustly passed over for an important promotion. He wants to confront his boss. A couple has two distinct views of each other's responsibilities for household tasks. Parents have divergent positions on the freedom they feel their teenage daughter should have. In each of these examples, the individuals are cognizant of their opposing viewpoints. How they choose to deal with these expressed differences will likely affect the quality of their relationship.

Assessment is an important initial step in managing differences, for it provides each party with an initial understanding about the nature of the relationship, the course of the conflict, and the appropriate communication strategies used in addressing the differences. Five aspects of the communication environment should be assessed during this first stage: (1) the individual traits of the participants and the nature of the relationship, (2) the nature and cause of the conflict, (3) the clarification of each party's goals, (4) an examination of the communication environment climate, and (5) a preliminary determination of the appropriate conflict-handling behavior.

Individual Traits

Consider the individual traits of the participants and their relationship with one another. These two factors, according to Deutsch (1971), affect both the development and course of the dispute, for it is in the relationship, not within the individual, that the conflict resides. For example, a cordial relationship between the president and vice-president of a firm is qualified by virtue of the fact that the president controls their professional relationship. In the event of conflict, the power imbalance between the two is exacerbated by the discrepancy in their roles.

According to Watzlawick, Beavin, and Jackson (1967), the two elements in any communicative act are the content of the communication and the relationship that mediates the content. Consequently, in the conflict

---

[2] While the five steps for managing conflict are designed especially as strategies to be used before differences erupt into full-blown conflict, they also provide a vehicle for individuals already embroiled in a conflict to step back, evaluate, and hopefully ameliorate the communication between themselves.

design described by Deutsch, we would include in our assessment consideration of the status of the parties involved, the nature of their prior relationship, how they communicate (style), the perceived threat of loss or change engendered by the relationship, and the communication environment in which the conflict occurs.

Nature and Cause of the Conflict

Different belief or value systems are likely to produce a conflict when individuals harboring these fundamental differences vie for goals in such a way that they perceive that one goal only can emerge. An example of a difference in belief may emerge when two colleagues disagree over which type of computer will best service the needs of their division, or when a couple dispute whether to save or invest a substantial amount of money.

A difference in values can be illustrated if we consider the example of two directors competing for how to spend their limited $60,000 budget: One wants to put money into student scholarships; the other believes the department cannot function adequately without sorely needed equipment. The key in this example is in the term *limited*, for it is the perceived (as opposed to the actual) scarcity of resources that may produce a conflict. It is important to bear in mind that one's definition of the term *limited* is in itself a matter of individual interpretation.

Depending upon whether we are dealing with a conflict of values, ideas, belief systems, or resources will ultimately determine the approach in managing the conflict. The more we feel that personal identity and basic values are compromised, the more likely a conflict will ensue and the more difficult it becomes to resolve such differences. Thus, debates over religious issues, ethical dilemmas, and basic values—such as pro-life versus pro-choice, capital punishment, and capitalism as opposed to communism—are not easily resolved.

Individuals who find themselves embroiled in an argument over such issues are not likely to compromise or cede those beliefs they hold strongly. In contrast, when individuals hold certain goals in common but differ in how to achieve these goals, managing differences is far more likely. For example, while two professors may share the same goal of increased student enrollment, one faculty member might favor scholarships as a means to attract qualified students; the other may believe improving the quality of existing equipment will enhance the department's reputation. In the event that funds could be applied to either scholarships or equipment, even though one faculty member would be disappointed, at least his or her goal of hoping to recruit students would not be compromised.

Clarification of Goals

Related to determining the nature of the conflict is the need to clarify one's goals. This is often a difficult step because our goals are frequently more than merely the ostensible issue at hand.

In the case of the aforementioned directors, while the superficial problem may appear to be a matter of priority, that is, of whether funds should be spent on equipment or on scholarships, the root of the conflict may lie deeper. Perhaps the director who wants the equipment is adamant in her position because the other director has received funds for scholarships over the past several years. The director in favor of scholarships may be similarly positioned in his view because while granting agencies continue to provide for equipment, the amount of available scholarships has been reduced drastically during the past decade, thereby preventing otherwise qualified students from pursuing an education. Thus the issues may be joined due to the practical matter of how to spend limited resources, but of equal importance, because of philosophical divergence, and the perception by both directors that the other has or could receive the desired funds by means other than the money at hand.

As long as the underlying issues remain buried, it will be extremely difficult, if not impossible, for the participants in this conflict to reach a satisfactory agreement, for each will adhere strongly to her or his point of view without being clear why they are fighting so strenuously. Only when the unarticulated issues are acknowledged can the parties involved begin to resolve their conflict productively.

Examination of Climate

A fourth step in the assessment process is the examination of the communication environment. It is impossible to deal effectively with a problem unless we know that our efforts and our approach will be appropriate within the structure. In their book *Managing Job Stress,* Brief, Schuler, and Van Sell (1981) observe that the type of institution, the stress factor, and the precedents for dealing with conflict are important variables that determine how problem solving can be handled effectively within an organization. Consequently, as part of the initial assessment, it is important to ask the following.

1. Does the environment facilitate or discourage open communication?
2. Are there established and fair procedures for addressing and resolving problems effectively (appeals and grievance procedures, for example)?
3. Are there designated channels and personnel who are empowered to deal with problems?

4. Is the problem typical of the kinds of difficulties that arise in the institution or organization?
5. Have similar problems been resolved satisfactorily in the past?

If we consider the aforementioned conflict between the two directors, it is obvious that they will be unable to proceed in reconciling their differences until they know they can do so openly in an environment that allows for expressed divergence of opinions without reprisal.

Preliminary Determination of Conflict-Handling Behavior

Once the nature of the conflict has been defined and clarified and the climate of the communication environment has been examined, the parties involved can begin to determine the proper approach for dealing with the problem.

Blake and Mouton (1964) are credited with identifying five conflict-solving strategies: smoothing, compromising, forcing, withdrawal, and problem solving. Thomas and Kilmann (1974) later developed a conflict-mode instrument designed to determine managerial conflict-handling behavior and labeled their approaches accommodating (smoothing), compromising, competing (forcing), avoidance (withdrawal), and collaborating (problem solving).

While labels for these strategies may have been altered, the essential aspects of each of these approaches have remained consistent and the basic dimensions of each of these modes are important to consider when dealing with conflict. According to Blake and Mouton (1964), the five conflict-handling modes represent a degree of cooperation or willingness to satisfy another's needs and assertiveness or need to satisfy one's own needs (see Table 1-1).

TABLE 1-1   Conflict-Handling Modes

MODE	LEVEL OF ASSERTIVENESS	LEVEL OF COOPERATION
Competing	High	Low
Compromising	Moderate	Moderate
Collaborating	High	High
Avoiding	Low	Low
Accommodating	Low	High

Summary of Thomas and Kilmann's (1974) communication styles of conflict-handling behavior based on Blake and Mouton's (1964) categories of conflict style.

Competing behavior reflects the extreme example of concern for one's needs at the expense of the other party. Identified with win-lose behavior, all-out competition may be appropriate in such contexts as a sporting event, a battle, or when a company is trying to beat out the competition.

When dominance, or win-lose strategies are employed in interpersonal relationships, however, the effect on the party who has lost can be frustration or dissatisfaction. Filley (1977), for example, reports that in corporate settings the least effective managers rely on win-lose strategies when dealing with subordinates. Similarly, as evidenced by the extensive research on relationships between women and men in U.S. culture, personal settings are also an arena for dissatisfaction when one party dominates the other (Bernard, 1981; Henley, 1977; Kramarae, 1981; Stockard and Johnson, 1980).

While competing may not be suitable for bolstering interpersonal relationships, if the goal is to win at all costs, then competition may be the appropriate technique. An actor trying out for a part, a dean determined to get the biggest budget for his school, or a major company fending off the competition will feel justified in employing any means necessary to accomplish their goals.

At the other extreme of competing behavior is avoidance. Identified with withdrawal from or denial of a problem or conflict, the inability or unwillingness to deal with a problem can be "a painful, disconfirming experience," according to Hocker and Wilmot (1985, p. 113) because avoiding a problem may convey that one person's needs or goals are unimportant.

It is essential during the assessment stage to determine if the conflict should be acknowledged at all. For example, a coworker might decide not to confront his colleague about regularly coming in late because he knows his coworker will be leaving the firm at the end of the month. He therefore does not wish to create a tense environment and will avoid the issue during this brief period.

On the other hand, if an employee resents the fact that her supervisor keeps passing over her for special assignments and promotion, avoiding the issue will only sustain, if not exacerbate, the employee's bad feelings toward her boss.

Compromise is considered the middle-ground position on the conflict grid, and certainly it is one of the easier tactics to employ. If we return to the example of the two directors pursuing the $60,000, an ostensibly simple method to resolve the issue would be to divide the money evenly. While on the surface this would solve the problem, both parties may in fact lose: that is, half of the money may be insufficient either to purchase adequate equipment or to provide for meaningful scholarships.

In other circumstances, however, a compromise might be indicated. For example, a secretary might be induced to work late for several nights if she is allowed to come in later for work on these days. Or, in the aforementioned example, one director might be willing to forego the money this year if he can be persuaded that an equal amount will be allocated to his program the following year. Although compromising often leaves one or both parties dissatisfied (Filley, 1977), Jamieson and Thomas (1974) have found that compromise is often a highly viable approach when time and resources are limited.

Accommodation, the fourth mode of conflict-handling behavior, reflects the highest degree of cooperation on the part of one of the parties but the lowest amount of assertiveness. Associated with smoothing behavior or ceding to the other party's wishes, as with avoidance behavior, accommodation satisfies only one party's concerns and fails to consider the needs and feelings of the person who is seeking to establish harmony.

As with other modes, however, the situation and parties involved often require accommodation. A wife or husband may be especially accommodating to her or his spouse's needs if the latter has recently been laid off from work. A manager might accommodate his colleague's wishes to select her office first because having a window facing in a particular direction is not that important to him.

The willingness or ability of an individual to act in an accommodating way over a period of time is highly individual. Depending upon whether one is concerned with relational or task-oriented goals, accommodating may or may not satisfy the needs of the accommodating party. If a group of people are concerned about the quality of a relationship, they may find accommodating others rewarding, while those who are less concerned with the nature and quality of interpersonal relationships may find this approach to problem solving unsatisfactory. (In Chapters 4 and 5, which deal with gender differences and cross-cultural issues and conflict management, this concept will be further explored.)

Collaboration is the conflict-handling behavior that requires a high level of both assertiveness and cooperation. Recognized as a "win-win" mode by Thomas and Kilmann (1977), it is the most integrative method of problem solving, for it acknowledges the concerns of the parties involved and identifies clearly their motives and goals. Although generally recognized as the most productive conflict-handling behavior because a collaborative approach requires a great deal of energy, creative thinking, empathy, and activity, all conflicts may not warrant such intensity. For example, a collaborative approach may not be necessary when a couple given a gift of $100 disagrees on how to spend the money. Such an issue may be resolved simply by dividing the gift in half.

If we return to the initial dilemma of the two directors, however, the most effective way to solve their problem might be a collaborative approach. One way to address the problem, for example, would be to analyze carefully the health of each program. The program seeking equipment may lease/purchase the equipment, thereby reducing an initial outlay of funds and allowing for scholarship support.

A second way of approaching the problem might be an integration of programs. Perhaps scholarships could be awarded to students in one program, who in turn would contribute certain hours to working in the lab, thereby reducing personnel costs in the other program. This would allow the savings to be invested in equipment. Certainly, an approach such as this is at best difficult and requires both commitment and cooperation from both parties. This approach may also, however, allow most fully that both programs get what they are seeking.

As we have seen, the effectiveness of the five conflict modes depends on the circumstances and conditions underlying the ostensible conflict. Only through an accurate assessment of the situation can we preliminarily select the most appropriate conflict-handling behavior for dealing with a problem.

ACKNOWLEDGMENT

Although all the steps designated in the assessment phase are important, these are essentially ineffective unless we acknowledge the other party involved. A key concept in Deutsch's (1971) social psychological approach to conflict management is that we are dealing with an individual's perceptions, which may or may not correspond to an objective assessment of the situation. Yet, unless we are able to demonstrate an awareness, and to articulate fully the beliefs, goals, ideals, and personality traits, of the other party involved, it will be unlikely that the conflict can be handled productively.

A useful process for understanding and acknowledging others is to follow the ideas proposed by cross-cultural experts Hall (1961; 1966) and Triandis (1976), for the works of both rely on the ability to understand and to acknowledge the similarities and differences between people.

A crucial issue in cultural evaluation stems from the fact that most of us behave in ways Hall calls "out-of-awareness." That is, we make certain assumptions based on our own backgrounds, experiences, and culture about how we behave and about how others behave. When our expectations are violated or intruded upon, we experience discomfort and anxiety. Hall illustrates the concept with the example of how time communicates. For example, if a U.S. businessperson arrives for an appointment in certain Latin American countries approximately 10 minutes ahead of the scheduled appointment, the individual will become extremely irritated if forced to wait for more than 20 minutes beyond the time scheduled. The reason for this response, according to Hall, is that Americans value time and view it as a commodity that should not be wasted. The other culture, in contrast, may not have such a restricted view of time, and being late for an appointment may not demonstrate rudeness or disregard for others. Therefore, two individuals may regard the same objective fact from diametrically opposed positions.

To illustrate this concept from a monocultural perspective, consider the vice-president who always sets "rush" deadlines for her director. To meet the constantly "urgent" deadlines, the director would have to submit incomplete materials. To avoid this, she consistently turns in complete and accurate documents—but they are inevitably late. The director is frustrated by her inability to function well under pressure, as attested by the fact that she is always late with urgently needed materials.

A conflict will inevitably erupt if the vice-president and the director do not acknowledge the following information: When the vice-president demands urgent material, she does not expect a perfect document; for the director, "crucial," "urgent" materials also mean totally correct. Once the vice-president and director are able to recognize and acknowledge each other's expectations, a frustrating situation for both can be turned into a productive relationship.

Therefore, during the acknowledgment phase, it is incumbent upon each party to recognize that the other individual's concepts and precepts may differ from his or her own. Without such awareness, the ability to deal with a problem is thwarted. Concepts related to language use, time, proxemics, kinesics, and haptics are particularly vulnerable to misperceptions and should be clearly and accurately defined and explained. (Chapters 2 and 3 address more fully the verbal and nonverbal communication required for effective conflict management to occur.

ATTITUDE

To assure productive conflict management, it is not sufficient to assess the situation and to acknowledge the other parties involved. Simply acknowledging another person's beliefs, goals, and values does not necessarily imply that our attitude toward the other party will be conducive to dealing with the problem.

For conflict to be productively managed, it is important that the participants demonstrate their willingness to engage in a mutually dependent exchange that includes rather than excludes the parties involved. In fact, research indicates that individuals who demonstrate conciliation, compassion, concern, those who are willing to take risks, who take reponsibility for their own actions, and who are able to trust are more effectively able to deal with conflict than individuals who do not evidence these qualities (Cummings, Harnett, and Stevens, 1971). Thus, one's attitude toward others becomes a crucial dimension in effective conflict management.

To create an atmosphere that generates trust and cooperation, individuals must address their attributions of behavior (or comparing their own behavior to the behavior of others) that can serve as barriers to conflict management. Consequently, in addition to acknowledging the other individual's perspective, our attitude toward that individual needs to be a willingness to engage in a productive communication exchange.

As individuals, we develop perceptions about ourselves and form opinions about others. This, Hall (1961) observes, is the result of cultural experiences. But our socialization also causes us to apply labels to our own as well as to others' behavior (Knapp, 1980; Williams and Best, 1982).

We can illustrate this concept if we consider our cultural expectations of ectomorphic, or thin, men to include mistrustfulness (Knapp, 1980). By linking appearance to expected behavior, we may therefore ascribe certain behavioral responses to a thin man and adjust our own behavior to that person in anticipation of his responses. In other words, if we anticipate the thin man's response to be unfriendly and/or suspicious, we are likely to act in a mistrustful and suspicious way toward this person, thus eliciting a mistrustful or negative response, even if it is not in this person's nature to act unfriendly.

The implications of our assumptions about others for conflict management are clear: to deal effectively and productively with others, it is essential to suspend stereotyped assumptions and to enter into an encounter with an attitude of open-mindedness and a willingness to evaluate the communicative behavior of the other party when it occurs. Certainly we are aware of the debilitating effects of stereotyping behavior and the danger of attributing a trait to others based on our own assumptions even when the other party does not possess this characteristic. Labels about ethnicity, gender, and religion attest eloquently to the damage that can result from attitudinal attributions.

In addition to examining our own stereotyping behavior, it is important to explore how we perceive our own behavior compared with the other party's behavior. This process will also influence directly our attitude toward the other individual in a conflict situation. Thomas and Pondy (1977) postulate four reasons why in a conflict situation individuals are inclined to regard their own behavior as reasonable and appropriate while they view the other party's behavior as just the opposite.

First, we often fail to understand fully why the other party is acting or feeling as she or he does. Our attitude thus becomes an assumption that the other individual is being unreasonable in contrast to our own reasonable actions. A manager who states, "I am always bending over backwards to meet his deadlines," in response to a supervisor's criticisms may be unaware that his boss is equally pressured to meet her own unit's schedules. To effectively prevent escalation of a conflict or to manage an already evident problem, one's attitude should be willingness to suspend judgment of the other party's behavior until all sides of the issue have been articulated.

A second reason why an individual will regard his or her own behavior as reasonable or fair in contrast to how the other party behaves is that people are often unaware of how their own behavior is perceived and interpreted by others. Because we are often unable to monitor our own nonverbal behavior, a woman, for example, may be unaware that her frowning and lip biting is communicating unhappiness and nervousness, thereby contradicting her verbal assertions that everything is fine in a relationship. Because nonverbal behavior is regarded as a more accurate measure of how an individual actually feels than what is said (Birdwhistell, 1970), it is reasonable to assume that the individual in conflict with the woman in the above example will respond to her gestures instead of to her words. Because constructive conflict requires open and honest communication, one's attitude toward the other party should include monitoring one's own behavior so that verbal behavior is consistent with what is being communicated nonverbally.

Related to how we manifest our own nonverbal behavior is how we interpret others' behavior. The third reason that attitude affects a relationship in a conflict situation is due to the implicit threat of losing to the other party. This makes us particularly sensitive to another's communicative behavior. Such sensitivity may also result in misperception and in misinterpretation. A worker, for example, might be suspicious of her boss's affirmation of a need to resolve a problem if the worker's attitude toward management in general is negative. Two colleagues pursuing a promotion to the same position may regard each other's behavior with skepticism and as a means of solely furthering their own chances for getting ahead. Such negative positions belie an attitude that can prevent productive resolutions to problems and that make it difficult to maintain satisfactory relationships. In the above examples, to turn destructive conflicts into productive ones, attitudes need to change. The worker needs to suspend judgment of her boss and to react on the merits of the interaction rather than on the basis of their positions within the company. In the second example, for the two colleagues to work productively, they need to acknowledge their individual aspirations, but they also need to place the demands and well-being of the organization above their personal pursuits.

A fourth barrier to creating a trusting environment is the pressure on both parties in a conflict to regard themselves positively and to view the other individual negatively. A couple experiencing marital difficulties may consider their own contribution to the problem as minimal, placing the blame for their difficulties on the other partner. The husband, feeling his wife wants to talk everything to death, turns off (justifiably so, in his opinion) many of his wife's attempts to discuss their problems. The wife, seeing her husband turn her off, accuses him of not wanting to listen to her and of not caring sufficiently about the relationship. As long as both parties remain defensive about their own behavior and critical of their partner's actions, their negative attitudes will likely make untenable any satisfactory resolution.

Assessment of a conflict or potential conflict situation is a crucial first step, for it enables the individual to consider the nature of the conflict, to clarify individual goals, and to preliminarily plan how each will interact with the other. Acknowledging the other party's concerns and outlook is a second stage that will undoubtedly affect how an individual will bring the other party's perspectives to bear on his or her own behavior. This third step, examining one's attitudes toward the other party, engenders an encounter with an open and, hopefully, unbiased perspective. Having completed the assessment, acknowledgment, and attitude phases, one is ready to proceed to the fourth stage, action.

ACTION

The ultimate aim of conflict management is to take productive action toward achieving one's goals. Anyone who has ever been involved in emotionally fraught conflict situations recognizes how difficult it can be to control consciously one's actions and how potentially destructive such a lack of control may be. A crucial stage of the conflict-management process is to integrate the assessment, acknowledgment, and attitude dimensions into the most appropriate action for the particular situation.

The primary manifestations of action are in the participants' choice of verbal and nonverbal cues. As noted by Gibb (1961), communication strategies are the central factors in the creation of either defensive or supportive climates. Verbal choices can create defensiveness when statements sound evaluative rather than descriptive, controlling rather than problem oriented, strategic rather than spontaneous, neutral rather than empathic, or superior rather than equal. Nonverbally, body position and orientation, distance between participants, and facial expressions such as frowning may put the other party on the defensive, thereby either exacerbating the conflict or even creating conflict where none necessarily exists.

Clearly, the parties in conflict must be conscious of their actions and should work to become skilled at using various communication techniques. On the verabl level, a conflict participant must make active choices regarding a variety of issues. Language style must be appropriate to the situation. A conflict participant may sound condescending in certain instances by his or her selection of language style, which may contribute to conflict escalation. Slang, jargon, or obfuscation may also cause unnecessary problems, whereas thoughtful word selection may assist participants in achieving their goals more efficiently.

Besides language style, decisions must be made regarding asking questions. Too many and poorly timed questions may be harmful, whereas judiciously asked questions may indicate attentive listening and caring and may enhance effective communication when in conflict. Incorporating techniques such as dating (noting clearly when something occurred or how long ago observations were made), indexing (pinpointing the uniqueness of specific individuals or situations—avoiding stereotyping), and "to-me-ness" (a means by which a speaker indicates that his or her perceptions are not etched in stone by making statements such as "it seems to me . . .") in one's language may also be helpful.

On the nonverbal level there is an equally broad range of choices. Participants must carefully select the setting of the confrontation. Would it be best to interact on home territory, on a neutral front, or on your opponent's home court? What kind of object language should participants choose for their encounter? It may be more appropriate to dress down for some conflicts and to dress up for others. Whether it is appropriate to touch fellow interactants is an important question about nonverbal behavior in conflict. A touch from a subordinate of one's boss may indicate insubordination when in conflict and may contribute to punitive measures, whereas touch between a battling couple may be the right choice to move communication in a productive direction. Appropriate facial expressions, decisions regarding eye contact, and tone of voice are also crucial to productive conflict management. Smiling may indicate that you do not take the conflict seriously, staring may appear to be a challenge, and sounding hesitant may bring sincerity into question.

The work of researchers such as Dean Barnlund (1968), Jon Condon (1965), and Jack Gibb (1961) exploring semantics and verbal coding; Ray L. Birdwhistell (1970), Mark L. Knapp (1980), and Albert Mehrabian (1972) investigating nonverbal cues; psychologists Paul Watzlawick, Janet Beavin, and Don Jackson (1967) studying human interaction; and sociologist Erving Goffman (1959) discussing the nature of the situation all provide insight into the action dimension of communication strategies that are crucial for effective conflict management. Although the work of most of these scholars focuses primarily on interpersonal theory in general terms, specific applications to the field of conflict studies can be made. Conflict management is, after all, effected through communication. To take productive action in conflict situations one must therefore develop both an understanding of communication techniques and the ability to put these techniques to work.

Using the aforementioned verbal and nonverbal communication strategies in an environment conducive to rather than inhibitive of interpersonal exchange, participants in a conflict should attend to the following transactional stages:

1. Establish credibility with the other party. According to Gahagan and Tedeschi (1968), compliance depends upon the credibility of one's opponent.
2. Early on in the encounter establish a level of trust so that the transaction can proceed toward a resolution of differences. Zand (1972, p. 178) defines trust as "the conscious regulation of one's dependence on another that will vary with the task, the situation, and the other person."
3. Articulate the problem from both points of view so that all parties have a clear understanding of the other person's position and motivation.
4. Use accurate and appropriate verbal and nonverbal communication. (See Chapters 2 and 3.)
5. Ascribe equal status to the participants during the exchange. Watson and Johnson (1972) observe that only when both parties are empowered to articulate their goals and feelings can productive conflict management occur.
6. Early on during the exchange, establish common goals. For example, if a strike is pending, to thwart an actual work stoppage both labor and management will have to agree that preventing or ending a strike is a mutual goal.
7. Try to anticipate the concerns of others so that communication is not one-sided.
8. Seek continual feedback. The only way to ascertain that one's statements and concerns are clearly understood is to elicit questions and information from others. Fisher and Ury observe that while statements often generate resistance, questions can be a powerful tool to encourage answers (1981, p. 117).
9. Demonstrate willingness to modify one's communication behavior. Because conflict management reflects a process and not a static procedure, it is important to reevaluate one's conflict-handling behavior and to adapt one's behavior according to the needs of the interaction.
10. Generate as many potential options or solutions as possible that integrate both sides of the issue. In their study on effective leadership, Maier and Sashkin (1971) propose that a combination of integration of needs and proposition of creative solutions is a highly desirable and successful conflict-management strategy.
11. Keep the channels of communication open in an atmosphere that supports interaction. It will be extremely difficult to achieve satisfactory solutions to a problem if one's needs, ideas, and feelings are continually misinterpreted or denied a voice. Barnlund (1968) contends that those who are impervious to the words of others, while staunchly defending their right to assert their concerns, serve only to deny individuals any meaningful role in the transaction.
12. Review and summarize the expectations and decisions of all parties.

ANALYSIS

The final step in our conflict-management model is analysis. It should be clear that analysis is employed throughout the conflict-management process as part of the assessment, acknowledgment, attitudinal, and action stages. It is important, however, to designate analysis also as a separate, culminating step.

Once the decisions have been reviewed and summarized, it is important to consider:

1. If the concerns of all parties have been met as adequately as possible;
2. If the decisions can be implemented swiftly and/or effectively;
3. If the short- or long-term effects of the solution are viable; and
4. If the relationship between the conflicting parties has been modified productively.

Hocker and Wilmot (1985, p. 34) observe that conflict brings both danger and opportunity. While certainly the notions of frustration, loss, and threat represent undeniable dimensions of conflict, as Deutsch (1971) notes, the potential value of conflict should be neither ignored nor denied. We can propose that the value in conflict emerges from the fact that through conflict, stagnation can be ended. Also, conflict can provide a vehicle for presenting and solving problems. Equally important, social and personal change, and hopefully growth, can result from addressing differences. Finally, we can generate creative approaches to problem solving through how effectively we manage conflict.

If indeed we are living in an era that supports and requires communication, conflict can, as Hocker and Wilmot (1985) observe, bring about a great deal of opportunity. No longer subjected to subjugating our needs and concerns, ours is now an environment that encourages open and honest, albeit at times painful, exchange. Yet it is through such exchange that we can truly avail ourselves of the opportunity to grow. Conflict assuredly is a part of our culture. How we choose to deal with it, however, belies the changes and strides emerging today.

THIRD-PARTY INTERVENTION

In the box on page 17 a summary of the five steps to managing integrative conflict is presented. In some situations however, individuals are unable to manage conflict on their own. In such instances, it may be appropriate to recommend an outsider, someone skilled in bargaining or problem solving.

Mediation

Mediation is essentially the art of persuasion. This type of intervention aims to persuade individuals or groups of people in a conflict to resolve their differences. Mediation is a part of our everyday lives. In some instances we become mediators; in other cases we require the assistance of an individual to mediate our differences. Examples of people who need or become mediators include a department head who is asked to help two

STEPS TO INTEGRATIVE CONFLICT MANAGEMENT

ASSESSMENT: Allow yourself time to calm down and to evaluate the situation
Gather appropriate information or documentation
Assess the points you are willing or unwilling to compromise on
Assess what the other party wants
Make a preliminary determination of the appropriate conflict-handling behavior for the situation; for the relationship; for the environment

ACKNOWLEDGMENT: Listen to the other party's concerns
Try to understand his or her viewpoint

ATTITUDE: Avoid stereotyping and making predeterminations
Try to remain objective
Remain as flexible and open as possible

ACTION: Watch your own use of language
Watch your nonverbal communication
Observe how the other party communicates verbally and nonverbally
Stick to the issues; don't go off on tangents
Don't make promises you can't keep
Don't present issues in a win-lose context
Don't sidestep the issues
Be sincere and trustworthy
Try to remain open-minded and flexible
Use the conflict-handling behavior appropriate for the situation and be able to revise your behavior according to how the transaction progresses
Listen, repeat, clarify information

ANALYSIS: Make sure all parties' concerns have been articulated and considered
Summarize and clarify decisions
Review procedures for implementing any changes

committees resolve their differences about how to allocate their annual budget, a marriage counselor who is hired to help a couple learn to communicate their needs to one another, or a parent who is called in to help the children resolve which program to watch on television.

Because mediation is often not binding, it becomes incumbent upon the mediator to assure both sides that he or she will address all the concerns fairly and openly. In addition to following the points presented in the box on page 17, a good mediator must additionally demonstrate the following abilities and characteristics:

1. Establish and maintain credibility;
2. Demonstrate neutrality toward both sides;
3. Manage effective contact and communication between the parties;
4. Help both parties determine, analyze, and understand all the facts;
5. Listen for clues to a settlement;
6. Convey accurately information from and to both sides;
7. Try to keep the channels of communication open between the parties;
8. Maintain discretion about what is said and how it is communicated.

Arbitration

In cases when individuals or groups of individuals are unable to resolve or manage their differences through negotiation, they may determine that their differences can best be ameliorated by having a third party hear both positions and determine which side has the best case. Both sides would agree that such a determination would be binding.

Like mediation, which can occur in both the simple and complex levels of everyday life, arbitration is similarly evident. Children might go to their parents to settle a disagreement. Lawyers might take their clients' cases to court. Labor and management might resort to arbitration to resolve a contract dispute.

Presenting a case to an arbitrator requires that the disputing parties prove their case. Toulmin's (1958) model of argument provides an epistemological framework for justifying a position. Although Brockriede and Ehninger (1960) provide a comprehensive interpretation, analysis, and application of Toulmin's model, Toulmin's stages for any justificatory argument can be summarized as a basic three-step process:

1. Data—evidence presented in an argument. Facts, opinions, examples, statistics, testimony are common examples of evidence.
2. Claim—conclusion being supported.
3. Warrant—what allows individuals to make a mental leap from the data to the claim

An example of this process is diagrammed in Figure 1-1.

The aforementioned basic steps for an argument are often sufficient

FIGURE 1-1   Toulmin Model

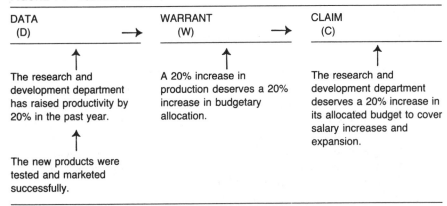

to make a case. Three secondary steps in Toulmin's model may be required, however, to further substantiate a claim:

1. Backing—additional support for the warrant.
2. Rebuttal—acknowledgment of conditions that might contradict or restrict the claim.
3. Qualifier—indication of the degree of force behind a claim characterized by such terms as *probably, likely, possibly.*

FIGURE 1-2   Six-Step Process to Toulmin Model

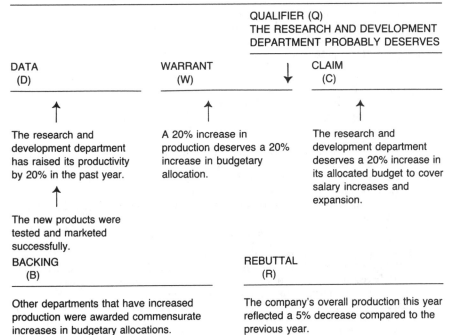

Using the example in Figure 1-1, the secondary steps may be added as shown in Figure 1-2.

EXPLAINING: THE RHETORIC OF APOLOGY

Up to this point, the dimensions of conflict management presented have dealt with advocating and defending one's case. Frequently, however, problems arise because events have gone awry, or mistakes have been made. How these events or mistakes are explained can have an enormous impact on the situation. Failure to acknowledge or to address a situation or occurrence adequately can exacerbate difficulties between individuals.

An often-heard excuse for not submitting a paper or report on time is that "the computer was down." While many faculty members or administrators have accepted such explanations in the past, in many instances further elaboration such as "I have taken my material to an outside company. The report will be to you within 36 hours" or "My computer is being repaired today. I'll have the data ready this evening" would be warranted.

Although the communication skills required for effective conflict management are addressed in the next chapter, according to Goodman (1983), some basic steps for explaining or apologizing for a situation include:

1. *Acknowledging and explaining your role in the situation.*

   EXAMPLES: "I realize we will not be able to meet the order because of equipment breakdown, and I am aware that this is my responsibility"; "I know I am in charge of this unit and the severe absenteeism of personnel has seriously hampered our ability to function."

2. *Explain the problem in general terms.*

   EXAMPLES: "Our department has been experiencing many problems with these machines. They have been breaking down on the average of twice a month"; "Apparently there has been an outbreak of the flu in our community—our department, unfortunately, has not been spared."

3. *Offer a solution to the immediate problem.*

   EXAMPLES: "I have already contacted a manufacturer who makes the same equipment we have, only their machines have a superior performance record. We have arranged to lease their equipment on a short-term basis with an option to purchase"; "I have contacted several local placement firms. They are sending over temps to cover our office until our employees are able to return to work."

4. *Explain controls and make assurances.*

   EXAMPLES: "I have begun to take steps to assure that this type of situation will not happen again. I am negotiating a contract with the other manufacturer to include regular equipment inspections that will prevent breakdowns"; "I have set up a system with our personnel department to inform me when three cases of the same illness are reported so that I can either make arrangements to borrow personnel from other units or contact temporary agencies before absenteeism reaches crisis proportions."

5. *Explain the impact of the situation.*

EXAMPLES: "I realize that while this breakdown cost the company several thousands of dollars, I have assessed the productivity we will be able to handle with the new equipment. My estimation is that we will be able to increase sales by 10% next year, an increase that will far surpass this loss"; "We were fortunate that because this is a relatively slow period for us, frayed nerves and inconvenience seemed to be the greatest impact."

SUMMARY

The term conflict has many definitions. Common elements among these definitions include conflict as an expressed struggle between individuals over perceived incompatible goals, resources, or rewards. Moreover, effective conflict management requires a positive attitude toward appropriate interpersonal communication and toward conflict itself. Rather than regard all conflict as a threat or negative condition, individuals need to consider expressed differences as the potential for creativity and growth.

We propose a five-step model for conflict management that encourages a flexible attitude toward managing differences. This model integrates both conflict theory and interpersonal communication skills.

During the initial or assessment stage, individuals are encouraged to examine the context of the communication environment. They must first consider the participants engaged in conflict and their relationship to each other. Second, they need to identify the ostensible areas of contention along with the communication climate in which these issues are expressed. Only after these initial assessments can people make a preliminary determination of the appropriate conflict-handling behavior, choosing from the five styles—competition, avoidance, accommodation, compromise, and collaboration—initially identified by Blake and Mouton (1964).

The second step, acknowledgment, involves the ability to understand and to articulate both sides' views. The ability to manage differences productively is greatly impeded if individuals lack fundamental information about each side's perspectives regarding issues of contention.

The third step in the conflict-management process is for individuals to develop and display an attitude conducive to productive interaction. An appropriate attitude includes the ability to trust in the other party, or at least in the process of communication, and to enter a communication exchange unencumbered by negative stereotypes, pejorative attributions of intent, or erroneous assumptions about the other party.

Action comprises the fourth step in our conflict-management model. This step encompasses interpersonal communication skills, for it is through communication that we are able to effect conflict management. Accurate communication, appropriate verbal and nonverbal behavior, flexibility of communication style, and the ability to keep the channels of communication open reflect in part aspects of productive action.

The fifth and final stage of our model is analysis. While analysis is in fact an ongoing process of transactional communication, conflict participants need to consider the feasibility and effectiveness of implementing mutually agreed upon decisions.

In many instances, individuals engaged in conflict are unable or unwilling to manage their disputes on their own. When an impasse occurs, conflict participants often resort to third-party intervention. Through mediation, individuals are encouraged to work out their disagreements. Where negotiation fails, conflict parties may resort to arbitration as a means to resolve differences.

Elaborate procedures are not always required for disagreements. In some cases, differences can be appropriately handled through an apology. By acknowledging their role in and responsibility for a situation or event, communicators demonstrate their willingness to address and manage conflict constructively.

SUGGESTED ACTIVITIES

The following activities focus on various aspects of conflict management.

A. Focus on Conflict Management: Self-Evaluation

At the beginning of the course or workshop each participant is asked to begin a journal aimed to follow his or her conflict-handling behavior over a period of time. Each entry should include the following information:

Date: _____

1. Assessment
   a. Describe briefly the conflict in an objective manner.
   b. Who were the participants in the conflict?
   c. What is their relationship to one another?
2. Acknowledgment
   a. Describe the conflict from your perspective.
   b. Describe the conflict as well as possible from the other individual's viewpoint.
3. Attitude
   a. In your opinion, were you being reasonable?
   b. In your opinion, was the other individual acting reasonably?
   c. Specify why or why not for a) and b).

4. Action
   a. What conflict-handling behavior(s) did you employ?
   b. Describe your verbal and nonverbal communication strategies.
5. Analysis
   a. Was the conflict successfully resolved?
   b. What was the outcome?
   c. If you were not satisfied with the outcome, what steps might have been taken that would have led to a different solution?

At the end of a designated period, individuals should review their overall development in their ability to assess and manage conflict and set goals for continued improvement. Individual cases may be used as a basis for open discussion.

B. Focus on Conflict: Mediation and Arbitration

Divide the participants into small groups of approximately five. Consider the following situations:

1. An 18-year-old wants to spend the summer following his high school graduation working abroad. His parents feel he is too young to be on his own for so long.
   a. One group will present the son's case.
   b. One group will represent the parents' feelings.
   c. One group will portray an arbitrating body that will determine if the son should be allowed to spend the summer abroad.
2. Students should be assigned and asked to role play the following situation:

Employee's Side: The employee contends that the employer "dumps" work on him. Frequently, the employer gives the employee work and says it is urgent. The employee believes he is trying to get the work done: he likes the office and his coworkers, but he cannot cope with the overbearing and demanding employer. After working for 8 months in this position, the employee has been cautioned by the employer that he may be let go if his job performance does not improve.

Employer's Side: The employer contends that after 8 months, the employee should know the job and not have to be told what is important. In fact, there are a lot of important materials and many items that are urgent. Somehow the employee always manages to find time to take a coffee break in the morning and in the afternoon. If that time were spent working, perhaps the job would get done.

As the mediator called in, what questions would you ask? What recommendations would you make?
The remainder of the group should address the following issues:
   a. What were the attitudes of the employee and the employer toward the situation; toward each other?
   b. What traits of an effective negotiator were demonstrated by the mediator?

   c. What conflict-handling behavior(s) were employed?
   d. Assess the outcome of the interaction.
3. Consider the following situation. A new manager has been hired to oversee a unit composed of seven employees. After a few months, it becomes evident that the manager's organizational style conflicts sharply with the communication environment to which the employees were accustomed. The employees were used to an informally run office where interaction among colleagues and feedback to and from the former director were encouraged. They are therefore resentful of the more formal attitude and expectations of their new supervisor. The employees have communicated their frustrations to the vice-president. The new director has also related concern about the employees' poor attitude and lack of cooperation to the vice-president. The vice-president has determined the need to mediate the conflict between the two sides before productivity is negatively affected.

The class or seminar group should be divided so that there are approximately three groups, each composed of two directors, two employees, two vice-presidents, and one observer. Each group works independently to address the issues from the perspectives of both the employer and the employee. The vice-president will listen to each side and endeavor to mediate the conflict. One member of each group will act as "observer" and will record what transpires within each group.

The entire group reassembles and each "observer" presents what occurred in his or her group. A discussion and assessment of the effectiveness of each mediator's actions/decisions should follow.

C. Focus on Conflict: Competition and Collaboration

A major company is moving from the East to the West Coast and plans on moving only one of its four divisions. The entire group determines the nature of the company, the four divisions (that is, product development, marketing, sales, personnel, advertising, and others), and divides into these four groups. Two or three class members volunteer to act as the company's CEOs.

Each group wants very much to be selected. Since only one can be chosen, however, the officers decide to allow each group to present its case about why it should be chosen. Each group will have about 10 minutes to present the following:
   a. Each member will be able to introduce him - or herself and explain his/her qualifications;
   b. The entire group will present what it has accomplished/can accomplish for the company and explain why it should be selected to relocate.

The groups should be allowed time to work together so that they can determine the salient facts and have ample opportunity to rehearse their individual and group presentations. If possible, each of the presentations should be taped and played back for the entire group to review.
   c. Following the presentations by the four groups, the CEOs will determine which group will be selected to relocate and why.

D. Focus on Flexible Conflict-Handling Behavior

Consider the following situations:

1. A wife wants to develop a career after spending 8 years raising two young children who are now in school. The husband believes he should provide their income; she is needed to attend to the family's needs.

2. A young man has been invited back for a second interview at a major accounting firm. The partners he has met seem impressed with his credentials. He is equally impressed with their reputation and with what they can offer him in terms of experience and remuneration. Toward the end of the interview, the partner casually states to the candidate, "Our policy is that no mustaches or beards are allowed. You will, of course, need to shave your mustache when you start to work here." The candidate has had a mustache for several years; it is a part of his identity.

3. Two directors who have worked in the same corporation for 1 year are having lunch. One director mentions his ideas to help increase productivity at no additional cost to the company. The other director asks questions about this idea. Two weeks later at their monthly divisional meeting, the vice-president proudly announces that the company will be adopting the plan presented by one of the directors and asks the director to present her ideas. She proceeds to describe in detail the plan that her colleague presented to her over lunch. The director who conceived of the initial plan is outraged by the fact that the colleague whom he trusted "stole" and claimed full credit for his ideas.

4. Two coworkers have been with a company for 3 years and have developed a positive and productive professional relationship. A new supervisor has recently been hired. After a few months it becomes evident to one of the workers that the supervisor favors his colleague. He receives what she considers "plum" assignments, is praised more often, and is granted preferential treatment in general. When she raises her concerns with her colleague, he tells her she is imagining differences in the way they are treated. The colleague, however, is convinced that she is being treated neither equally nor fairly.

5. A husband and wife have had the following relationship for the past 12 years: He has run his family's business and provided the primary monetary support; she has taken care of the children and now works part-time as a nurse. The husband admits he has been unhappy with his work. He wants to change careers and become an attorney. The wife believes he has too many responsibilities and commitments to start making a costly career change at this time in their lives.

Different members of the class or seminar group should be assigned a role in one of the above situations. Participants should determine which conflict-handling behavior they feel will best serve dealing with the situation (accommodating, avoiding, competing, compromising, or collaborating). Each situation should then be role-played. The rest of the group should assess the effectiveness of the conflict-handling behavior selected. If the group feels a different approach would be either more effective or appropriate, the individuals enacting the roles will re-do the encounter using a different conflict-handling mode.

E. Focus on Apology

Consider the following situations:

1. You are in charge of a foreign exchange program for a university, bringing foreign students to your university for 6 weeks. Thirty students are scheduled to arrive on Friday. Apparently, the dormitory space was never confirmed by your office, and now space is available for only half the group. This means that your office will have to pick up the tab for hotel accommodations for 15 students for 6 weeks. This terribly overextends the approved budget for the program. What do you tell the dean in charge?

2. You are in charge of publicity for a major manufacturing firm. Brochures were supposed to be mailed out by June 1 to stores on the coast showing your fall line. It is now 1 month later and the brochures have not yet gone out. The president of the firm anticipates an enormous loss in orders because of this delay. He or she calls you in for an explanation. What do you say?

3. You are co-chairing a local fund-raising event for a charitable cause. For several months many volunteers have been soliciting donations and selling raffles. A great deal of money has been collected, and you are scheduled to make a financial report at a meeting with all the volunteers. A few days before you are to make your report, you discover that $60,000 (of the $80,000 collected) is missing. An executive committee of five had access to the safe. What report do you make to the volunteers?

Divide the class or seminar group into six small groups. Each group will be assigned one of the above situations. Half the members of each group will prepare a statement that they will deliver orally. The other half of each group will prepare a written explanation. In addition to discussing how effectively each situation was handled, note what differences appear in the oral and written statements.

TWO
THE LANGUAGES
OF CONFLICT
MANAGEMENT
Verbal Strategies
for a Supportive
Communication Environment

In the preceding chapter, we addressed the nature of conflict and presented a five-step model for effective conflict management. While understanding each stage is important to the overall effectiveness of dealing with conflict, it is during the action phase that transactional communication occurs and where it is important to demonstrate the requisite communication skills for productive conflict-handling behavior.

Individuals embroiled in a conflict are likely to focus on their own concerns and interests (Blake and Mouton, 1962). This tendency toward self-absorption often results in the inability to attend fully to those individuals who hold differing ideas, concerns and views. For example, in a dispute over wages, employees are apt to consider the impact of insufficient wages on their lifestyles. If their attention is focused primarily on what they regard as the dire consequences an insufficient wage hike will produce, it is unlikely that they will be prepared to acknowledge sufficiently the problems that a wage increase will create from management's perspective.

Because of this tendency to focus intrapersonally rather than interpersonally, the participants are likely to ignore any similarities among the opposing parties. In the aforementioned example between management and the employees, the workers might overlook the fact that they stand to benefit by the company's increasing expenditures to raise profits—profits that would ultimately translate into earnings for them. Instead, their focus on the employer's decision to step up production as a direct barrier to their own need for more money makes the management of their differences untenable.

To manage conflict productively, it is important for the participants to be able to communicate. In their work on intergroup conflict, Watson and Johnson (1972) elaborate the four kinds of communication required for effective conflict management. First, it is important for the conflict participants to have a clear perception of the other's underlying motivations and position. This, we acknowledged earlier, is a difficult process because individuals tend to focus on their own concerns. Second, accurate communication is essential for true understanding between individuals. Third, an attitude of trust must be conveyed for productive interaction. Fourth, a shared assessment of the conflict as a mutual problem is needed to motivate participants to attempt to ameliorate their differences.

The kind of communication posited by Watson and Johnson (1972) represents the need to engage both parties in managing the conflict. Furthermore, the prescribed attempts to achieve mutual understanding and to acknowledge the concerns of all parties also reflect efforts to integrate the needs of both sides into the process of handling the conflict. Considering both parties' concerns and viewing the conflict-management process as a "win-win" situation enables individuals to establish a collaborative style.

Blake and Mouton (1964) initially identified five types of conflict-handling behavior: competing, withdrawing, smoothing, compromising, and collaborating. Of these five types of behavior, conflict theorists maintain that collaboration may be highly effective in managing differences (Blake and Mouton, 1964; Filley, 1975; 1977; Folger and Poole, 1984; Putnam and Wilson, 1982; Thomas and Kilmann, 1977). Because collaboration requires the effort, effective communication, and open-minded attitude needed to ensure that the concerns of both sides are fully articulated and addressed, the likelihood of arriving at solutions acceptable to both sides is greatly enhanced.

It was observed in Chapter 1 that not all differences merit the effort and energy that characterize collaboration. Because collaboration can only be achieved by employing the basic verbal and nonverbal communication skills that reflect effective interpersonal communication, however, we will focus on the types of environments that enhance the productive communication strategies required of collaborating behavior.

Barnlund (1968) has observed that misunderstanding, alienation, and frustration often result when people do not listen to one another and are quick to interrupt or disregard what has been said. He portrays in this instance interpersonal communication at its worst. The inadequacies, misunderstanding, and alienation to which he points can be avoided if one can interact in an environment characterized by trust. Gibb's (1961) seminal

TABLE 2-1   Traits of Contrasting Communication Climates

DEFENSIVE	SUPPORTIVE
Evaluation	Description
Control	Problem orientation
Strategy	Spontaneity
Neutrality	Empathy
Superiority	Equality
Certainty	Provisionalism

Summary of Gibb's (1961) behavioral traits for supportive and defensive communication environments.

work on communication defines the nature of such a supportive communication environment.

Gibb posits two opposing climates and describes the effects of each climate on communication. One type of climate he describes is defensive and threatening. A defensive climate is characterized by communication that is evaluative, controlling, strategic, neutral, superior, and certain.

The other climate Gibb presents is supportive and provides an atmosphere conducive to mutual trust, openness, and cooperation. In contrast to the defensive climate, the supportive climate is characterized by communication that is descriptive, problem oriented, spontaneous, empathic, equal, and provisional. (See Table 2-1.)

Although Gibb's work addresses communication climates in general, his observations apply to the communication evidenced in conflict-managing behavior. The defensive climate reflects the type of atmosphere characteristic of competition—an atmosphere that Deutsch (1973 a and b) notes inhibits the mutual trust required for effective conflict management. The supportive climate presented by Gibb characterizes the type of environment reflective of collaboration—an environment that Filley (1975) observes leads to mutual trust and to an atmosphere conducive to managing differences.

Therefore, if we consider the interpersonal communication skills reflective of the supportive communication climate described by Gibb, we are also providing skills that facilitate a willingness to engage in a cooperative and integrative approach to conflict management.

DESCRIPTIVE SPEECH

Gibb (1961, p. 144) defines descriptive speech as that which "tends to arouse a minimum of uncertainty. Speech acts which the listener perceives as genuine requests for information or as materials with neutral loadings is descriptive." In an environment characterized by dissension, it is not so easy to decrease uncertainty and to gather information. According to Rogers (1961), individuals tend naturally to be judgmental and evaluative of others. They therefore create barriers to productive interpersonal communication. If Rogers's claim belies a natural tendency, then individuals who want to communicate in nonjudgmental, nonevaluative, and nonthreatening ways need quite consciously to employ verbal strategies that will result in disclosure, comprehension, and information sharing free from pejorative connotations. The following five verbal strategies are intended to enable parties embroiled in a conflict to participate in the supportive descriptive environment that Gibb proposes.

Admitting One's Assertions

In conflict situations it is often difficult to remove barriers to effective interaction between participants. Barriers are especially resistant to change when individuals are reluctant to acknowledge their own feelings and ideas about a problem.

According to Mehrabian (1972), it is far easier to ascribe blame to a third party, and therefore to distance ourselves from the other party, than it is to admit our position about a situation. For example, a manager lashes out at his colleague with a statement such as, "Everyone thinks you're not pulling your weight in this company." By claiming that *everyone* shares this perception, he is likely to provoke defensiveness, for his colleague will become concerned with who has made these statements.

If participants in a conflict want to open rather than impede a dialogue, they will find it more productive to admit and to acknowledge their own ideas. The manager might open the conversation with a statement such as, "It seems to me" or, "I believe you are not pulling your weight in the company." By owning his own assertions, the manager has enabled his colleague to respond directly to the individual who holds these views rather than to some anonymous other.

Stating Issues Clearly and Specifically

How clearly and specifically individuals articulate their ideas and concerns will have an enormous impact on the way individuals respond in a conflict. Deutsch (1971) cautions against employing generalities. Generalities occur when individuals resort to abstract, ambiguous, or exaggerated, rather than concrete, terms when describing feelings, events, and situations.

The attorney who tells her associate, "Jim, I'd like to talk to you about your performance," creates, according to Mehrabian (1972), a negative effect. This occurs because she has excluded substantive information about Jim's performance. Until she clarifies her statement (for example, "You have not been bringing in sufficient clients to merit your salary," or, "We are delighted with the number of clients you have brought to the firm"), Jim will be unable to respond appropriately to the term *performance*.

Similarly, exaggerations are often employed when trying to substantiate claims. The administrator who accuses her employee of "always" making personal telephone calls on company time or of "never" being on time opens herself up to criticism unless, of course, literally every telephone conversation is of a personal nature and the employee has never actually been punctual.

If individuals are concerned with how others respond to them, it is incumbent upon them to articulate their concerns as clearly and as accurately as possible. Thus, the administrator who states, "I have observed that you made 12 calls in the past two days" has provided specific information to which the employee can respond. By avoiding the accusatory sweeping claim (such as "You are always making personal calls!"), the administrator does not put the employee totally on the defensive. Perhaps making personal calls is habitual and is therefore a problem. But it is also possible that extenuating circumstances, such as an illness in the family, have necessitated these actions. By being specific and concrete rather than general and unclear, the administrator has opened the channels to a productive exchange.

Semantic Selection: Word Choice

A dual-career couple has spent considerable time and energy negotiating what they believe is an equitable plan for executing household tasks. Within a short period, however, they become critical of the arrangement. Each individual claims that he or she has more to do than the other partner. The couple's ability to manage their disagreement will be unlikely if they are unable to agree on their perceptions of the facts. For example, they may disagree over how much time constitutes too much time spent weekly on tasks. Agreement may also be untenable if they have divergent perspectives. For instance, one task is considered either easier or harder, more menial or meaningful, depending on one's orientation.

Many writers suggest that individuals' experiences, identities, roles, and cultures serve to shape their *Zeitgeist*, or world view (Barnlund, 1968; Barry, 1970; Goffman, 1959; Hall, 1961; 1966; Rogers, 1961; Simmons and McCall, 1966). Yet when individuals, in Barnlund's terms, "project private significance into the world" (1968, p. 7), the potential for managing conflicts productively diminishes because these individuals hold values significant only unto themselves.

Perspectives are highly personal. This notion conflicts directly with the idea that definitions of problems as well as information conveyed must be understood by all the participants in a conflict (Blake and Mouton, 1962; Deutsch, 1973 [a and b]). The semantic, or word choices each individual makes consequently will affect the quality of a communicative exchange.

Denotative Meaning of Words

The denotative, or dictionary, definition of words is normally clear and readily understood. The vice-president tells her director, for example, "I need the report next Monday." If this statement is made on Wednesday, the director knows he has 5 days before he must submit the report to his boss.

Ostensibly, there is no difficulty understanding both the intent and content of the message: The report is needed by the vice-president on Monday. Indeed, if this type of request is routinely made, a minimal chance exists for a misunderstanding.

Connotative Meaning of Words

In contrast to the clearly defined denotative meaning of words, the connotative meaning reflects individual interpretation and is highly personal. As indicated earlier, our experiences serve to shape how we react to certain words. For example, two men reading the statement, "The boy was hungry" may have quite different responses. One may accept the statement at face value, assuming the boy will satisfy his hunger shortly. The other man, however, may react quite strongly to the same sentence, recalling with trepidation his own hunger as a child growing up during the Depression.

In a conflict situation the intention of individuals may be to select carefully words that both parties understand clearly. As the above example indicates, however, the potential to use words that produce divergent reactions among individuals may create a real barrier to managing a conflict. (The possibility for misunderstanding created by connotative interpretations of words is exacerbated further if one introduces gender and culture as variables. These ideas are further elaborated in Chapters 4 and 5.)

It is impossible for individuals to be fully acquainted with every person with whom they interact. Thus, individuals cannot be expected to avoid using all the words that may unintentionally provoke adverse reactions.

Additionally, words may become highly charged when they reflect current problems or especially debatable issues. The words "conscientious objector," for example, had a highly subjective meaning in the mid to late 1960's. More recently, the terms *surrogate mother* or *AIDS* may be highly provocative terms.

To the extent that individuals embroiled in a conflict need to be sensitive to the other party's concerns, it is important to try to anticipate what words are likely to increase the difficulties between individuals and to avoid these words if possible. Thus, in a labor dispute, if the goals of management and labor are truly to ameliorate differences, it would behoove the labor representative to avoid using the term *strike*, just as the management representative might judiciously avoid the words *lay off*.

Semantic Obstacles to Communication: The Use of Slang, Stereotypes, and Automatic Phrasing

If supportive communication climates employ descriptive rather than prescriptive communication, individuals engaged in a conflict should avoid using verbal conventions that aim to hurt others or that exacerbate differences between people. Slang and stereotypes reflect overt examples of language intended to damage interaction. The incorporation of what Mehrabian (1972) terms *automatic phrasing* into one's verbal expressions reflects subtler forms of avoiding open communication.

Slang

In contrast to the accidental use of words that may create differences between people, conflicting parties often resort to slang expressions to make their point. In other instances, individuals intentionally employ words to provoke others, for example, expletives, purposefully incorrect grammatical statements, or mispronunciation. This differs from the unintentional language misusage discussed in Chapter 6, as the communicator is aware of the effect he or she creates. By breaking from societal norms, or what Goffman terms *situational propriety* (1959), individuals distance themselves from the other party.

Thus, the ordinarily articulate supervisor who, in response to his colleague's request for a report responds, "There ain't no way in hell that you'll have the report by Friday!" is challenging his coworker through the language he chooses. He intentionally conveys a negative message that would not have occurred had he instead responded, "I'm sorry, but I won't be able to have the report ready by Friday."

Stereotyping

Stereotypes to substantiate one's beliefs all too often convey misinformation. Rather than conveying descriptive communication, asserting opinions that belie stereotypical assumptions creates a defensive atmosphere. Although it is a normal and even helpful (Casmir, 1985) part of our information-coding process to attempt to categorize information and people, Knapp (1980) and Simmons and McCall (1966) caution that in the process of ascribing or excluding certain traits to groups of people, we are apt to make errors of commission or of omission.

It is not necessary to look too far to observe the damaging effects stereotypes can have on certain groups. Opposing sides in a conflict are not likely to move closer to one another if one or both parties resort to stereotyping behavior. For example, a personnel director proposes new hiring policies to reflect ethnic diversity and gender equality in the organization.

Her plan may be met with stereotyping comments, such as, "Those people can't be trusted" or, "Women are too emotional to hold positions of responsibility." These derisive responses are apt to produce anger and increase the distance between her and her supervisor.

Automatic Phrasing

In contrast to the use of slang or stereotyping remarks as intentional strategies to distance people from one another, often individuals unintentionally employ verbal forms that can convey suspicion or doubt. Mehrabian (1972) identifies three types of automatic phrasing that may serve as barriers to descriptive communication: fillers, tags, and pauses.

Fillers   Fillers, words that are linguistically unnecessary to the content of the message, (such as, "um," "you know," "just") serve to minimize the speaker's association with the message, thereby diminishing its impact.

Examples of statements that reflect the inclusion of fillers are, "I, um, want you to listen to me," or "It's just a few dollars we're talking about." If the speaker wants to own his or her words, the more assertive "I want you to listen to me," or "It's a matter of a few dollars" would be more appropriate.

Tags   The addition of tags to statements is the second type of automatic phrasing Mehrabian (1972) identifies. Although there are examples of appropriate use of tags (see Chapter 4), when individuals employ tags when their intention is to assert their opinions, the use of the tag may be construed as seeking approval or verification of their assertions from the listener. For example, "I believe the director has made the correct decision," becomes less assertive when "don't you?" is tagged onto the end.

Pauses   The third example of automatic phrasing is the overuse of pauses when speaking. Certainly the thoughtful pause as conveyed by the example, "Uh . . . let me think about your suggestion for a few minutes," is appropriate. When individuals employ pauses to convey that they don't wish to discuss a topic further, however, this strategy conveys uncertainty and ambivalence.

When two parties are in conflict, the likelihood of managing differences is impeded when pauses are employed. For example, a person may say, "Let's discuss the areas where we are at odds with each other." If the other party responds, "I, er . . . don't, uh . . . want to discuss this now," this statement may be interpreted as attempting to avoid the issue.

Mehrabian's (1972) description of automatic phrasing reveals that the three examples he describes—fillers, tags, and pauses—all serve to distance individuals. Such distance often creates barriers to open, honest, and disclosing communication, which is the type of communication characteristic of Gibb's (1961) supportive communication climate. If conflict participants are truly concerned with managing the differences between them, such management will be facilitated by choosing their words with care and by paying attention to the little slips, or automatic phrasing, that may contradict productive efforts.

Syntactic Selection: The Impact of Threats, Hostile Joking and Sarcasm, and Hostile Questioning on Managing Conflict

Selecting words carefully and appropriately is essential for achieving the supportive communication climate characteristic of collaboration. Semantic tactics form only part of the communication, however. Syntax, or how these words are formulated into phrases and sentences, also affects the ability to manage conflict productively.

Threatening Statements

Several types of statements inhibit the flow of ideas between individuals (Barnlund, 1968; Deutsch, 1973; Hocker and Wilmot, 1985). The use of threats is but one example. Threats may be direct, as reflected by the example, "If you don't meet this deadline, you will be fired." In other situations threats may be veiled. The following example is, for instance, not so overtly obvious, "The organization does not look kindly on individuals who are unwilling to travel."

Both Gibb (1961) and Hocker and Wilmot (1985) observe that threatening behavior presents the most obvious barrier to creating a supportive environment. This is because threatening behavior creates defensiveness in those who are the object of the threat.

That threats can serve as effective deterrents has been documented (Watson and Johnson, 1972). For example, in the arena of international politics, the implied threat of nuclear retaliation keeps many countries' aspirations in check. Yet scant empirical support appears to substantiate that the results of threatening postures are as productive a strategy as collaborative attempts to manage differences (Watson and Johnson, 1972).

Rather than resorting to the coercion that results from threatening tactics, a far more effective compliance-gaining strategy is to explain clearly the rationale for certain behaviors and the implications a lack of cooperation or defiance engenders. These strategies form a part of the intent model for impression management described by Thomas and Pondy (1977) and are particularly effective for productive conflict management. For example, a manager who explains, "This position requires that individuals must be willing to work under tremendous pressure and time constraints," or who expresses her reservations about a subordinate by saying,

"I am concerned that you will not be able to meet the established deadlines" is asserting the organization's and her own expectations while allowing the other party to participate in the communication exchange.

Hostile Joking and Sarcasm

Although threatening behavior creates discomfort, at least individuals are clear about the intention of the message. If a person does not perform a certain task, then some type of punitive action will be taken.

In contrast to the direct use of threats, the use of hostile joking and sarcasm represents insidious tactics for opposing or criticizing others. A manager, for example, says to her department head, "I'm upset that you went ahead and implemented these policies without consulting us." The department head responds with the statement, "Oh, come on, now, Carole. Don't get so nervous about a couple of tiny, little procedural changes. You've already got enough important matters to worry about." By teasing Carole about the relative importance of the procedural changes, the department head attempts to defend her actions by trivializing the manager's concerns.

Using the same example, the department head might also react sarcastically, as conveyed by the response, "If I could ever get this department together at the same time, perhaps we could meet." The explicit message is that it is difficult to convene the group. The implicit communication, however, may be interpreted as follows: The department members are not where they are supposed to be. Otherwise it would not be so difficult to bring them together.

Both of these responses serve to silence the manager. Both serve to diminish the ability for the two parties to participate in an honest communication exchange. Both responses, in sum, increase the distance between these two individuals who presumably need to work together.

To turn a defensive exchange into a productive encounter, the recipient of defensive communication tactics must avoid escalating further the destructive communication cycle that has been initiated. In the previous examples, the manager needs to articulate clearly her feelings about the procedural changes. For example, she might say, "I feel that the changes you implemented will have a major impact on how the organization functions." Further, she might suggest ways to rectify the department head's perception about the members of the department. To do this, she might state, "I will be happy to convene the group so that we will all have an opportunity to consider the changes you have implemented."

Hostile Questioning

When individuals employ questions to accuse or to find fault with the other party's behavior, such actions are also likely to create defensiveness.

For example, when management fails to approve what the workers regard as an equitable cost-of-living wage increase, a union representative might feel justified in asking the management representative, "Don't you care at all about the quality of life of your employees?" Because the union representative has attempted to link care about employees solely to a wage increase, the employer must guard his or her response. To admit that the company cares about its employees is likely to invite further criticism about the way it deals with those about whom the organization presumably cares. Thus, a countering statement, such as, "Of course we care about our employees,"may be met with further accusations. A likely union response to this might be, "If you admit that you care about your workers, then how can you deny them the basic necessities they need to survive?"

By using hostile, and therefore accusatory, questions, the labor representative has put management on the defensive. In such a situation, apparently any answer offered will provoke additional accusatory lines of questioning.

For management to prevent this conflict from escalating further, the representative might enumerate specifically the ways it has demonstrated the company's positive attitude toward its employees. For example, the management representative could say something to the effect that "our company has initiated the following plans that reflect our concern and commitment to our employees. . . ."

PROBLEM ORIENTATION

A primary aim of communication is to persuade or enable another individual to share our perceptions and view of reality. We either consciously or unconsciously initiate communication to change the other party. As Barnlund observes, "If difference is the raw material of conversation, influence is its intent" (1968, p. 10). This inclination toward control, however, is likely to create a defensive environment, especially if the attempts to regulate others are indirect or hidden. When this occurs, managing conflict can be thwarted because the ability to trust others is in part dependent upon openness (Zand, 1972).

In contrast, a cooperative conflict-management process is characterized by openly acknowledging the views of both parties. Gibb (1961) observes that listeners are more likely to cooperate when they perceive that speakers are similarly cooperative. Speakers may demonstrate their willingness to work jointly by communicating their desire to work together to define the problem, to generate viable solutions, and to refrain from purporting preconceived agendas or solutions. Consequently, it is essential for participants engaged in conflict to assure each other of their intentions and efforts to work together towards managing the differences that exist between them. Further, they must endeavor to separate the people from the problem (Fisher and Ury, 1980).

If we consider the aforementioned example of the couple who are dissatisfied with the way they have allocated household responsibilities, we can compare how effective the different processes of problem versus solution orientation will be in managing their differences. It is rather simple to seemingly resolve the problem of sharing chores by merely dividing up the tasks. For example, the wife may assume the responsibility for taking and picking up clothes from the cleaners; the husband may agree to do the wash. This solution will not be satisfactory, however, if either party believes that the other has manipulated him or her into agreeing to the solution. Nor will the couple be satisfied if problems related to the solutions have not been addressed. In this example, maybe the wife resents having to alter her work schedule so that she can get to the cleaners before it closes.

Maier and Solem (1962) and Maier (1963) propose a three step plan that not only considers solutions to problems but also emphasizes the process of uncovering the basic problems from which conflict has originated. They propose that individuals initially need to identify the problem. Second, persons engaged in a conflict must attempt to generate as many viable and appropriate solutions as possible. The third and final step in the process is assessing the quality of the solutions generated.

Identifying the Problem

An important first step is to acknowledge the problems. In the example of the couple, several areas of disagreement may lie below the surface relationship. The wife, for example, may believe she works harder than her husband and therefore feels strongly that an equal amount of household duties should not be required of her. The husband may feel that his position is more important than his wife's and therefore he should not be asked to perform what he considers menial tasks.

Rogers's (1961) contention about the tendency of individuals to make judgmental assertions would create, in this instance, a highly defensive and destructive communication environment. One party might assert, for example, "Your job isn't nearly as important as mine. I don't see why I should have to be bothered with housework." These comments connote an evaluation about the other party's work and about the other party's relative importance within the relationship.

Without acknowledging the fundamental issues of each party's status within the relationship, managing differences will be greatly impeded. Employing the descriptive language characterized by Gibb (1961), however, will enable both parties to express their differences without offending one another. Thus, the husband may assert, "I have worked very hard to achieve my position. I don't want to perform the same task I was doing when I first started out." Similarly, the wife may express, "I work extremely long hours. I am too tired to perform many of the household duties as well." These statements reflect attempts to bring out into the open feelings both parties have about certain tasks. Equally important, neither side has made judgments about the other partner.

Proposing Solutions

Once problems have been acknowledged, individuals can attempt to propose solutions. Important to the process of managing conflict cooperatively is that these solutions reflect the concerns of both parties. Furthermore, these tentative solutions should be articulated in an open yet nonevaluative manner.

For example, the husband who is adamant about doing the laundry may not be staunchly positioned about preparing meals or cleaning dishes. Similarly, the wife may be willing to stop at the cleaners if on those days she brings home dinner. If, as Barnlund (1968) has observed, there are neither perceived hidden attempts to control each other nor overt power struggles over whose time, job, or role is more valuable, then reaching solutions that have addressed the couple's attitude toward doing housework is possible. If, as Maier and Sashkin (1971) have posited, both parties have generated as many solutions as possible that integrate the needs of both sides (the husband's need for recognition, the wife's need for a lighter work load), then reaching solutions acceptable to both sides is also more likely.

Assessing Solutions

Conflict management does not end merely because an agreement has been reached. Of equal importance is how individuals choose to deal with solutions to problems that have failed to meet their expectations or needs.

Dissatisfied parties who resort to defensive communication tactics as, for example, accusations ("You did this on purpose!"), negative judgments ("Your idea was stupid!"), threats ("If you ever force me to do this again, I'll leave!"), or stereotypes ("It's typical of people like you to act this way") are apt to find their verbal assaults met with equal resistance and defiance. In contrast, individuals who include descriptive communication strategies when asserting their feelings are likely to find their concerns responded to. Thus, a wife might say, "When I agreed to bring home dinner, I didn't anticipate the impact it would have on our budget. Let's talk about what we can do." By acknowledging the source of the problem (the cost of dinner) and a willingness to work jointly toward a new solution, she is far more likely to initiate a more productive interaction than would be possible in an atmosphere charged by accusations and defensiveness.

Pruitt has defined negotiation as "a process by which a joint decision is made by two or more parties" (1981, p. 1). We contend that assessing the quality and viability of decisions is also a process, for effective interaction with others and integration of the needs of both parties does not cease once a decision has been reached. Assessment is merely a continuation of the conflict-management process. Consequently, it is subject to the same variables that allow for productive or destructive communication.

SPONTANEITY

Gibb (1961) explains the difference between strategy and spontaneity as the difference between deliberate manipulation (through feigned guilelessness and other forms of pretense or deception) and genuine responsiveness and openness to a communication exchange. Strategic behavior often results in defensive behavior in the other party. In contrast, spontaneous communication encourages mutuality and cooperation.

Zand (1972) has postulated that an essential factor in effective conflict management is the extent to which individuals have confidence in or trust each others' assertions. The ability to trust is possible in a communication environment that is unfettered by deception and that is characterized by co-orientation.

While manipulative individuals do not typically verbalize their intention to control or to deceive, we are all too familiar with the strategies that belie manipulation. For example, we are able to sense when the other party withholds relevant or important information by use of automatic phrases, especially fillers and inappropriate pauses. We are often able to detect another person's lack of genuine interest in our concerns, for example, when he or she changes the topic or does not provide appropriate feedback. (The topic of feedback is addressed in the next section.) We become aware of hidden agendas by the way in which ideas or propositions initially not evident in the negotiation are brought to the forefront. And we are loathe to confide in others if we fear that our comments will be either divulged or used against us at a future time.

In contrast to the defensive environment that can result from manipulation or deception, a supportive environment is possible when communication is open and spontaneous. Conflict theorists Maier and Sashkin (1971) encourage an exhaustive search for ideas and solutions to problems. Filley (1975) adds to this process when he proposes using choices between solutions to generate new problem statements.

The technique of brainstorming—defined as "literally bombarding a problem and generating as many ideas as possible" (DeVito, 1986, p. 48)—allows for the spontaneous exchange of views in a nonevaluative atmosphere. Although brainstorming as a problem-solving technique is generally employed among cohesive groups, the process also includes those aspects of cooperation that facilitate conflict management. Citing Osborn's

(1957) work on the process of brainstorming, DeVito (1986, p. 48) briefly summarizes the following general procedures for this process, aspects of which have been introduced earlier in the sections on descriptive communication and problem orientation.

Avoid Negative Criticism

Individuals involved in negotiation should treat equally and without prejudgment all the ideas each party generates. It is tempting to assume a position of "we" versus "they," which reflects a competitive win-lose orientation. An attitude of "we" versus "the problem," however, is likely to encourage the generation of ideas that may eventually be incorporated into the adopted solution.

The department head, for example, who strongly believes that achieving financial equilibrium can only be accomplished by personnel cuts must initially refrain from criticizing another department head's proposal to achieve a balanced budget by reducing space. To judge negatively another's ideas without allowing for the full expression of thought is apt to discourage communication. If individuals perceive that others do not judge them or their ideas fairly, they are likely to maintain staunchly their original positions.

Generate Viable Solutions

Participants in a conflict may initially regard solutions to a problem as an either/or situation. For example, one party may propose that either we reduce personnel or we cut back on space. Yet negotiation that encourages creative rather than inflexible approaches to managing differences is less likely to obstruct cooperative efforts to diminish or to resolve disagreements.

If, in the previous example, the two department heads do not feel that they will be criticized for proposing divergent ideas, they are likely to feel encouraged to seek additional ways to solve their financial problems. One department head may suggest restructuring the units to make the most efficient use of extant personnel and space. The other department head may recommend leasing rather than purchasing equipment. It is important to reiterate that the verbal communication employed to express these ideas needs to be as descriptive and nonevaluative as possible. Thus, one department head may meet resistance if she states, "As far as I'm concerned, there is only one way to solve our fiscal crisis and that is by cutting our staff." She would be far more likely to have her ideas considered if she were to propose, "One approach to solving our financial difficulties is to reduce staff."

Combine and Integrate Proposals

While entire proposals may not be acceptable to all parties, aspects of different ideas can often be incorporated into developing viable plans acceptable to both sides. In fact, Maier and Sashkin (1971) contend that integrating and combining the ideas of both sides to formulate creative solutions is a highly effective approach for managing conflict.

As with the other steps in the brainstorming process, assertions need to be descriptive and should reflect co-orientation among the participants. Moreover, Barnlund (1968) cautions that individuals who resist being open to new ideas and experiences are apt to remain prisoners of their own constructs and will be unlikely to maximize the potential for reaching sound decisions.

Extending the example of the department heads, one might state, "While I am opposed to the concept of staff reduction, if we explore your suggestion to re-organize some of the units, we might find that several individuals are performing the same functions. Perhaps we could re-allocate some of these individuals to other areas where we are currently understaffed, thereby saving on new office positions." This individual has asserted his beliefs (to not reduce staff), acknowledged the idea of the other party (to reorganize), and built upon this proposal (to reallocate staff) to achieve their mutual goals (financial stability).

Appraise Proposals

Once ideas have been articulated and expanded upon, a realistic appraisal (not a personal attack) is warranted. For example, one department head states: "While I am open to your suggestion to merge several units, we need to consider the costs involved with relocating staff. I don't believe we are in a position to support a major reorganization at this time." Here he specifies the area of disagreement (the cost of moving personnel) without attacking the other party directly.

Thus, individuals engaged in conflict need to match the ability to generate solutions with the ability to assess them. Both steps, however, are best achieved in a communication environment characterized by cooperation, mutuality, and trust.

EMPATHY

The term *empathy* derives from the German *einfülung*, which means, literally, "to feel with" another person's ideas, emotions, and volitions. In Gibb's analysis of supportive communication environments, he describes the ability to empathize as "particularly supportive and defense reductive" (1961, p. 146). To achieve empathy with another, individuals must willingly attempt first to understand the other party. Second, individuals must judiciously suspend their tendency to judge others.

Understanding the Other Party's Perspective

An important first step in achieving empathic bonds with another is to make an effort to understand the other individual. A mutual epistemological framework is essential to facilitate understanding, especially in a conflict situation.

For example, one party demands parity within an organizational hierarchy. The other individual will experience difficulty understanding fully his colleague's demand if he does not share a framework for the concept "parity within an organizational hierarchy." This illustration reflects a barrier to understanding that is typical of cross-cultural communication and international conflict (see Chapter 5).

The causes for misunderstanding, however, need not be so obvious. Gender, ethnicity, religion, geographical location, educational background, professional status—in sum, who we are and what we have experienced—affect our personal constructs and inform our ability and willingness to respond to others. Therefore, regardless of the numerous differences that exist between people, the ability to manage differences between conflicting parties depends in large measure on the willingness and efforts of both parties to understand one another.

Avoid Evaluating the Other Party

Fred and Johanna have taken their vacation at the same time for the past 10 years. When Johanna is promoted within her company, she learns that while she has not lost the amount of vacation time available to her, one of the two weeks' vacation coincides with the company's deadline for completing their budgetary projections. Johanna believes she cannot be away from the office during this week. She therefore proposes to her husband that they try to reschedule their vacation. If this is impossible, she would meet him for one of the weeks. When she expresses her ideas to her husband, Fred feels hurt that his wife would willingly forego their time together. He believes she values her position more than their relationship.

Ed and John are close friends who get together for dinner at least once a month. John confides that on two separate occasions during the past year he has been passed over for a promotion. Despite this, he continues to assume additional assignments with the hope of gaining the recognition and reward he feels he deserves. As Ed listens to John's account, he secretly believes that John is acting too passively. He feels his friend should fight for his promotion. That is what he would do if he were in John's position.

Both of these examples illustrate the tendency for individuals to evaluate others. Moreover, they reflect a response typical of individuals engaged in conflict. That is, we tend to project on the other party our own motivations, understanding, and interpretation of events. According to Triandis (1976), such responses serve as major obstacles to understanding fully the other party's position. Certainly, such responses impede our ability to feel with the other person.

Given the barriers to empathizing with those with whom we disagree, what steps can individuals take to assure that their ideas and feelings are listened to and understood? How can they assure that they will understand others? The process of providing and soliciting feedback is perhaps the most efficacious means for achieving empathy.

Hocker and Wilmot (1985, pp. 159–160) acknowledge the difficulty in managing conflicts that are either unarticulated or unrestrained. What they label as mid-range or moderated conflicts, however, are particularly suitable for effective management. Conflicting parties can deal with such conflicts if they are willing to attend to and understand the other party's messages.

Exchanging information, viewpoints, and responses in the communication process is called *feedback*. Many individuals are threatened by the implicit change implied by feedback. For example, they fear others will reject, criticize, evaluate, or misunderstand their messages. When managed properly in a supportive communication environment, however, feedback is a powerful mechanism for demonstrating empathic communication. Three basic verbal strategies to elicit or provide feedback include questioning, paraphrasing, and role reversal.

Verbal Constructs for Feedback

Questioning

The use of questions can lead to divergent reactions. For example, a hostile leading question that is accusatory in tone and content may serve to exacerbate rather than to ameliorate differences. To illustrate this kind of question consider the director who feels his colleague is being unreasonable. He asks him, "Do you really expect that your obvious attempts to avoid me are going to make me forget our differences?"An emotionally-charged question such as this is intentionally provoking. In turn, the recipient of a hostile question will likely feel defensive and may respond unfavorably.

Not all questions in a conflict need be hostile. Questions judiciously used, and the tone in which they are communicated can also facilitate communication and enable individuals with differences to gather important information and obtain feedback from each other. The three basic classifications of questions—(1) open or closed, (2) primary or secondary, and (3) neutral or leading—can be used appropriately during a communication exchange (Stewart and Cash, 1988). Moreover, the language employed, the tone in which the questions are articulated, the point at which questions are employed during the interaction, and the ability of the recipient of the questions to respond adequately will affect the quality of the encounter. Used appropriately, the questioning process will convey that each party's concerns and ideas are being fully listened to and understood (Wolvin and Coakly, 1982; 1985).

If establishing credibility, developing an environment of trust, and facilitating rather than impeding a shared understanding of the problem are the goals, then obtaining feedback by asking such questions as, "Do you feel there is only one way to resolve this dispute?" "What is your reaction?" "Are you avoiding me?" and "If I understand you correctly, you're upset with my tone of voice" will be far more productive than the hostile question presented at the beginning of this section.

Paraphrasing

DeVito defines the term *paraphrase* as "a sentence or phrase that conveys the same meaning but is presented in a different form from another sentence or phrase" (1986, p. 221). More than merely repeating another person's message, restating the sentence or phrase assures the other party that the content or intent of the message has been understood.

An employee may lash out at her colleague, "You never let me finish what I'm saying!" The colleague may reflect that she understands the message by asserting, "If I understand you correctly, you are upset because you feel I interrupt you too much" or by asking, "Do you feel that I interrupt you too often?"

Regardless of whether paraphrasing takes the form of a statement or a question the ability to paraphrase is an essential aspect of providing and receiving feedback to the other party. Moreover, this technique demonstrates a willingness to attend to and to acknowledge the concerns of all parties.

Role Reversal

In a conflict it is important for individuals to be able to express their own perceptions and ideas regarding the nature of their differences. Yet the inability to articulate the viewpoints of others impedes the ability to move toward an understanding of these differences.

One verbal strategy that enables individuals to state what Rogers (1951) calls the inner world of another individual is role reversal. Role reversal is a process in which an individual assumes the role of the other party and attempts to articulate the other individual's viewpoint using his or her communication style.

For example, a couple experiencing marital difficulty may be asked to assume each other's role and express in the role of the spouse why they feel they cannot communicate. Similarly, two members of a management team who staunchly disagree on how to reorganize their unit may be requested to enact their differences in the role of the other.

In cases where individuals are willing to cooperate, role reversal is particularly effective because both parties are mutually responsible for assuring that accurate and constructive communication occurs. Furthermore, because role reversal enables individuals to see clearly each other's ideas, views, and feelings, in cases where misunderstandings or false expectations are the source of disagreements, role reversal provides an expeditious process for clarifying these differences. Clarification of differences in turn contributes to decreasing conflict (Watson and Johnson, 1972).

Regardless of the verbal techniques used to provide or receive feedback, clearly the ability to understand fully or to feel with the other party is possible only when individuals are willing to assure that they understand, and are understood by, each other.

EQUALITY

The previous section on empathy explored how feedback can enable individuals engaged in conflict to feel with the other party. Communication is likely to remain both unbalanced and unproductive, however, if individuals do not have equal access to the communication exchange and if they endeavor to manipulate the interaction either through avoidance or control.

Hocker and Wilmot (1985) note that most conflicts belie efforts to balance the power between parties. Moreover, without a relative power balance, it becomes increasingly difficult to manage conflicts productively. Therefore, if one participant in a conflict is denied a voice in the conflict-management process, the belief that his or her own concerns have been ignored will negatively affect his or her willingness to accept the other side's position.

For example, a manager is likely to discourage feedback about a problem if she states: "I've been with this company for five years. I know this is the only way to settle the matter." Similarly, a husband may silence his partner momentarily by asserting: "Listen, I'm the one who brings home the money. I'll decide how we're going to spend it." It is highly improbable, however, that his wife's silence means that she is satisfied with his self-aggrandizing tactics.

Both examples reflect attempts to maintain superiority or control in the relationship and contradict a basic assumption about effective conflict management, that is, that all members should be encouraged to interact freely (Blake and Mouton, 1962). Moreover, this interaction should occur in an atmosphere characterized by trust.

Barnlund has observed that "human understanding is facilitated where there is a willingness to become involved with the other person" (1968, p. 20). Several verbal strategies exist to accomplish such involvement. Each strategy aims to empower conflict participants with the ability to articulate their concerns in the supportive communication environment described by Gibb (1961).

Encourage Participation in the Communication Process

One way to ensure equal participation in a communication exchange is to request it, even when participants represent different positions of status within the organization or within the relationship. A director, for example, may say to her assistant: "I realize we have different views about how best to accomplish this project. However, I would like to hear your viewpoint as well as your objections to my proposal." Despite the status differential, the assistant will be more likely to present her views if she feels they will be attended to.

Status differences, however, need not be the only barrier to equal participation in the conflict-management process. Parties who share equal status in a relationship may feel reluctant to articulate their ideas if they believe the other party really does not want their input. Thus, if two professors knowingly oppose each other about which courses in the program should become requirements, one colleague may initiate a dialogue about their differences by stating: "I realize we disagree about which courses should form part of the core. I'd like to hear your rationale for including courses other than the ones I have proposed." In so doing, this individual has made clear his intentions and willingness to listen openly to his colleague's ideas.

Respect the Other Party's Ideas and Experiences

If experiences shape perspectives, it is important to remember that each individual's experiences are unique. Therefore, her or his outlook will not always coincide with another individual's point of view.

A woman who is accustomed to spending every Christmas with her family may become defensive when her husband suggests that this year they go away for the holidays. If she remains unwilling to respect his desire to take a vacation, he in turn might be reluctant to respect her desire to adhere to familial traditions.

To defuse the conflict that is likely to erupt if both the wife and husband fail to understand one another, a cooperative attitude and willingness to attend fully to the other person's concerns becomes essential. Only by engaging in an open and equal exchange will the couple be able to generate potential solutions to their disagreement.

In this example, several solutions are possible. The husband may be willing to go away during another time period. The wife may be willing to celebrate the Christmas holiday with her family a week or two ahead of time. The couple may determine to alternate years: One year they will spend Christmas with her family; one year they will travel. Or they may decide to spend Christmas day with the wife's family and leave the following day for vacation. As the possible solutions suggest, the ability to manage and resolve differences is limited only by the willingness of both parties to acknowledge and respect each other's perspective.

Confirm the Other Party's Assertions

A supervisor disagrees with his manager over the allocation of staff to his unit. He feels he is severely understaffed to meet the company's production deadlines. The manager staunchly disagrees. He feels he has already assigned an adequate number of personnel. Further, he believes they are not performing to their fullest potential.

The manager, in an effort to placate his complaining supervisor, calls regular meetings ostensibly so that the supervisor may air his differences openly. Rather than leaving these meetings with the feeling that he has been heard, because nothing ever happens in these sessions the supervisor feels these meetings are a waste of time. Instead of feeling encouraged, respected, and positive, he becomes increasingly discouraged, frustrated, and negative.

Basically, the supervisor in the above example has had a disconfirming experience. He believes the manager has been unresponsive to his concerns. Several writers address disconfirming responses (Borisoff and Merrill, 1985; Cahn, 1987; DeVito, 1986; Hocker and Wilmot, 1985; Sieburg and Larson, 1971). Presented below are seven examples of disconfirming responses. Included in these examples are brief exchanges that illustrate verbal strategies for turning disconfirming experiences into productive exchanges.

Denial or Excuse Making

A basic tactic to avoid dealing with a conflict, individuals often deny or offer excuses for a problem.

PERSONNEL DIRECTOR: It's not my fault that so many staff members have been sick.
VICE-PRESIDENT: Admittedly, you cannot prevent illness. However, you can take steps to assure that offices are covered. For example, you can establish an internal procedure for sharing staff in emergency situations.

By acknowledging the director's assertion that she is unable to control attendance and by providing concrete examples about how to deal with staff problems, the vice-president forces the director to address and to manage the problem.

Underresponsiveness

The failure to address adequately another's concern represents a frequent criticism by those who feel ignored or dismissed. When individuals believe that others do not give adequate or appropriate attention to their ideas or problems, they need to enlighten the other party to the seriousness of the problem as the example below illustrates:

DIRECTOR OF STAFF DEVELOPMENT: Many of the employees feel they are not being considered for the promotions they believe they deserve. Some are considering leaving the firm.
DIRECTOR OF BUDGET: This kind of griping is common around evaluation time. Don't worry about it.
DIRECTOR OF STAFF DEVELOPMENT: I am convinced that the staff is serious. I would like us to review our promotion policy.

By not allowing her colleague to dismiss her concerns, the director of staff development will be able to explore further her ideas for retaining and promoting qualified staff.

Trivialization of the Problem through Joking or Sarcasm

Superficially, jokes or sarcastic remarks can be defended (for example, by the statement "I was only kidding"). Their use, however, may well serve to create or to exacerbate problems as demonstrated by the following exchange:

HUSBAND: Ever since you've gone back to work, the house hasn't been as clean as I'd like it to be.
WIFE: You've got two hands and two legs. If you want a clean house, why don't you use them to push a broom or carry out the garbage!

Admittedly, a great deal of control and a willingness to cooperate are essential for individuals to rebut cutting remarks. In this example, we can see how little it would take to escalate this exchange into a full-blown conflict. If individuals can view sarcastic or joking remarks as attempts by others to get their own way or defend themselves, however, this attitude makes it easier to avoid responding with similarly hostile comments.

If a clean house, and not the derision of his wife, is the husband's ultimate aim, he can avoid further exacerbating differences by responding with a comment such as, "I'm sorry I criticized your work. Let's discuss what we can do to get the house cleaned."

Silencing

An effective way to avoid dealing with another individual's concerns is to silence her or him, thereby also avoiding possible conflict. Four basic strategies to silence another individual include interrupting behavior, changing the topic, avoiding the topic, and blaming external procedures. Below are examples of these four strategies as well as ways to prevent being silenced.

Interrupting behavior

MARIA: I want to discuss our monetary situation . . .
KURT (interrupting):   I am so overwhelmed with cases right now, I can't even think about money. All I want is a nice, quiet evening at home.
MARIA: I realize you have been extremely busy. However, I am concerned that we stop postponing making decisions regarding the house and starting a family because you are always busy with work. When would be a good time to talk about this?

Changing the topic

CHAIRPERSON: We've already spent enough time on this issue. Let's move on to the next agenda item.
COMMITTEE MEMBER: I realize that we have an agenda to follow. However, I feel that this issue is so important that we should include it on our agenda and address it now.

Avoiding the topic before it can become an issue

PERSONNEL MANAGER: We've all had a long day. Let's not get into raises right now.
SUPERVISOR: I realize we've had a difficult day. However, if we don't address salaries, I'm afraid we're going to have a strike on our hands.

Ascribing blame to external procedures

DIRECTOR: Look, we have a week to complete this report. We can't consider equipment now.
ASSISTANT: I am convinced that including equipment needs will only strengthen our report because. . . .

The above examples reveal many ways to avoid dealing with issues. The four illustrations demonstrate, however, that individuals do not have to remain silenced because the other party wants to avoid certain issues or topics. In each of the above instances, the individuals who want to discuss the topic that the other party is avoiding may not in fact finish addressing the issue at this particular moment. Still, each has acknowledged why the other individual may not want to discuss the issue at present. Each has also articulated why it is important not to ignore the issue. In effect, each individual has asserted his or her equality in the conversation.

Generalizations and Stereotypes

This type of response aims to refocus the issue or problem. It is often employed to justify not having to deal with an area of concern. The following exchange illustrates the use of ascription to justify avoiding a problem:

CASE WORKER: We desperately need these funds to institute a viable program to prevent drug abuse in our community.
SUPERVISOR: Drug abuse is just one of many problems these people have. No one program can begin to meet their needs.

In such an example it is important for the individual wishing to discuss an area of disagreement to address specifically his or her concerns. Thus, the case worker might follow up with a statement such as, "Studies have shown that the program we are proposing has been highly successful. If you will agree to consider. . . ."

Definitional Side Tracking

Definitional side tracking occurs when parties engaged in conflict attempt to focus on a specific word or example, thereby avoiding the larger (or real) area of contention. The following exchange between boyfriend and girlfriend illustrates such side-tracking strategies:

DAN: You never have time for me anymore.
JOYCE: That's not true. Last night we had dinner together.

By responding with an example of a time when they were together, the woman avoids addressing the real issue: her boyfriend's perception that they do not spend enough time together. To make her respond to his feelings, the boyfriend may react with a statement such as, "I want to spend more time with you" and specify ways to accomplish this.

Incongruity

Frequently, individuals try to avoid a conflict by asserting that there is no problem. Their nonverbal communication, however, contradicts their verbal assertions. Typical of this kind of reaction is the manager who says,

"It's good to see you" but whose lack of eye contact and rapid tone of voice indicate that she is extremely busy and does not wish to be disturbed. The recipient of contradictory messages needs to determine whether to acknowledge the verbal assertions or the more accurate nonverbal message. For example, he could say, "I realize you are busy now. However we do need to discuss the project."

Individuals who feel that others dismiss or ignore their concerns by using any of the aforementioned tactics are likely to experience frustration and annoyance at having to suppress their ideas, feelings, or beliefs. Managing differences is an important function of communication. For individuals to feel that they can voice their concerns, they must be able to participate equally in the communication exchange. They must not allow others to disconfirm their concerns, ideas, and opinions.

Communicate Fairly

Not only do disconfirming strategies impede equal communication but controlling tactics, characteristic of competitive behavior, also inhibit equality (Argyle and Furnham, 1983; Ting-Toomey, 1983). If individuals are able to identify the basic controlling strategies that are conflict productive, they can counter these types of confrontative behaviors with responses that are conflict reductive.

The following examples of competitive behavior reflect in part the work of Filley (1975, 1977), Hocker and Wilmot (1985), Thomas and Pondy (1977), and Triandis (1976). Incorporated in the examples are brief situations that demonstrate how participants in a conflict can counter destructive communication and thereby re-establish a more equitable balance in the relationship.

Ascribing Blame

Accusing the other party of certain actions or beliefs is a common strategy that deflects attention from the speaker and forces the listener into a defensive posture.

A manager, for example, makes the following accusatory statement to his assistant: "I told you the forms had to be processed by today! Now it's your fault we've lost the account!" Such an accusation is likely to provoke a defensive reaction. If the accusation is true, the assistant may respond with what Thomas and Pondy (1977) call a repairing statement. For example, the assistant may say, "I'm very sorry for this error. . . ." She might go on to indicate how she will avoid future errors. On the other hand, if she feels falsely accused, she may counter her boss's accusation by asserting: "I admit I was late with the forms. However, because you were out of the office for the past three days, I was unable to finalize the proposal."

Although accusations generally flow vertically in a hierarchical structure (Brief, Schuler, and Van Sell, 1981), individuals in positions of less power need to assert themselves when confronted with what they regard as an unfair or unjustified accusation.

Denial of Responsibility

Individuals who adamantly refuse to admit any responsibility for a problem may engage in defensive rather than participatory tactics. This is evidenced in the following exchange:

DIRECTOR: Did the shipment come in?
ASSISTANT: It won't be in until tomorrow.
DIRECTOR: I told you we needed the materials by today at the latest!
ASSISTANT (raising his voice):   You never mentioned any shipment to me!

At this point, it is likely that a conflict about responsibility is starting and will escalate into an issue about who knew what unless the director or the assistant attempts to focus on the issue rather than on the other party. For example, the director might defuse the situation by responding, "That may be. However, I need your help now to track down the items."

Judging Others by Asserting One's Own Values

It is normal in a conflict situation to believe in and to want to defend one's position. Differences between individuals may be exacerbated, however, when one party asserts that his or her claims are correct and thereby diminishes or devalues the other party's views. The following exchange illustrates the debilitating effect of making such judgments:

WIFE: I've been thinking about taking a leave when the baby is born.
HUSBAND: Being a full-time parent is just an excuse for being lazy and not wanting to work. There's no reason you can't maintain your job and be a good mother.

The husband's response indicates his own assumptions about parenting (that it does not require a great deal of effort; full-time parents are lazy), and his belief that his wife should be able to handle parenthood as well as her career.

Individuals faced with evaluative remarks from those about whose opinion they care need to determine the basis for the remark. For example, in the exchange described above, the wife may wish to determine whether the husband's mother resented giving up a career to be a full-time parent. In addition, the wife should consider the context in which the husband issued the remark (financial difficulties, etc.) and the consistency of the assertion (the degree to which the husband usually supports his wife's decisions and actions). Finally, the wife must consider the appropriateness of the husband's comments; although the husband may have legitimate concerns about his wife's career, how he chooses to articulate these concerns is provocative and inappropriate. Only by assessing the nature of the remark in the context of the relationship can an individual determine how to respond.

Personal Attacks

One dictionary definition of the word attack is "to set upon forcefully" (Webster's Dictionary, 1981, p. 71). In an arena where all-out competition and winning are the goal, this meaning of attack would not be regarded negatively. The dictionary provides other definitions of this word, however, which include, "to assail with unfriendly or bitter words" and "to begin to affect or to act on injuriously." All too often, in an attempt to change the behavior or to gain compliance of another, individuals resort to strategies designed to injure the other party.

Two examples of personal attacks include beltlining and gunnysacking. DeVito (1986) defines beltlining as using privileged information inappropriately or unfairly (from the cliché "hitting below the belt"). The employer who uses his employee's confidences against her or the wife who uses her husband's weaknesses to influence his actions are examples of using personal attacks to influence behavior.

Gunnysacking, or storing up and unleashing grievances upon the other party, is another devisive strategy (DeVito, 1986). To illustrate this tactic, consider the teenager who arrives home one hour beyond curfew. Instead of addressing the issue of breaking curfew, his irate parents instead assail him with a barrage of complaints about his behavior in general. They complain about how he dresses, his grades, his messy room—issues they have been harboring against him but have left previously unarticulated.

All their concerns may stem from their belief that their son's behavior reflects irresponsibility and inconsideration for others. Yet, by raising criticisms without addressing the fundamental issue of responsibility, the parents are likely to provoke defensiveness and to escalate rather than resolve differences with their child.

Deutsch (1971a) has observed that a competitive orientation often results in communication that is destructive rather than productive. To the extent that personal attacks are likely to provoke suspicion and to foster an environment of mistrust, those who employ such communication strategies as beltlining and gunnysacking are not likely to obtain long-term behavioral compliance from the other party. In fact, such destructive strategies are apt to distance others and to increase alienation and hurt feelings.

Sarcastic Remarks

As with personal attacks, sarcasm and hostile jokes are likely to exacerbate differences and contribute to a defensive climate (Gibb, 1961; Kramarae, 1981; Pearson, 1985). Consider the following remarks: "*I* don't have to worry about making the meeting. You're never on time, anyway"; "How can *you* claim to want nice furniture. This place is like a pigsty"; and "You want a window office? Why? You're *never* here to look out the window." The initiators of the above statements can claim they were only teasing. The recipients of such statements, however, are not likely to misinterpret the intentions of the comments.

When individuals are the object of sarcastic remarks, they must determine the most effective and appropriate way to stay the continuation of the implicit criticisms. If the relationship is a valued or necessary one, it will further be required to correct the other party's perceptions without engaging in similarly offensive tactics. For example, a roommate may counter the statement regarding the cleanliness of the apartment with a suggestion such as: "I realize the apartment isn't as clean as we would like. Perhaps we should consider using a professional cleaning service." This statement focuses on the problem, not on the other roommate. Consequently it is a far more productive response than resorting to a similarly sarcastic retort as, for example, "This place is a pigsty because you refuse to lift a finger to help clean up!"

Reprisals

The threat of sanctions to control or to manipulate the behavior of others belies a struggle for power in the relationship and conveys a win-lose orientation. Basic familial differences and professional struggles, for example, are often conveyed in statements meant to assert authority, control, and power over the other party. Examples of such attempts to control another include the parent's warning to his child ("If you don't finish your homework, you won't be allowed to watch television") or the supervisor's admonition to her staff member ("If you are not at the meeting on Friday, don't bother showing up for work on Monday!").

Individuals may feel threats are justified when initial attempts to gain cooperation or compliance have failed. Indeed, the staff member may be motivated to show up for the Friday meeting and the child may work harder to complete her assignment. That the quality of the relationship will be improved or strengthened, however, is, according to Watson and Johnson (1972), doubtful when negative sanctions are employed to change or to motivate behavioral compliance.

Attribution of Belief

In an attempt to justify their own anger or discomfort with another person, individuals often will accuse others of holding certain views, even when these accusations are not necessarily justified. For example, an employee is passed over for a promotion by her boss. Rather than determine whether she was qualified for the position, she is quick to accuse her boss of being sexist and of not wanting to promote women to management positions in the organization. Such action may provoke defensive communication because the recipients of accusations will endeavor to defend themselves if they believe they have been falsely accused.

Certainly examples of sex stratification in the workplace abound (Bernard, 1981; DeWine, 1987; Stockard and Johnson, 1980). When individuals generalize behavior and apply pejorative labels or intentions to others, however, alienation and anger are likely to result. Rather than attempt to ameliorate differences, the parties focus on how best to defend themselves.

Barnlund (1968), Deutsch (1973a and b) and Gibb (1961) have found that it is relatively easy to create a defensive communication climate. Furthermore, they maintain that productive communication and conflict management become increasingly difficult in an atmosphere where either or both parties perceive in the other an unwillingness to cooperate.

The ability to assure equal communication between conflicting parties seems at first glance to be a logical and easily achieved condition. The ability to empower the participants and to assure equal communication is, however, impeded when perceived differences exist and emotions are fraught. To assure that participants in a conflict are able to voice their concerns and ideas, individuals need to encourage, respect, and confirm the other party as well as to communicate fairly.

PROVISIONALISM

The final verbal strategy for assuring the supportive communication climate proposed by Gibb (1961) is to adopt a provisional attitude toward reviewing decisions that have emerged from the conflict management process.

If individuals are willing to expend the effort required to integrate and to reflect the concerns of all parties, they will likely want to maintain this same sense of openness in reviewing the effectiveness of these decisions after they have been implemented. Maier (1963) encourages conflict participants to consider solutions from both objective and subjective standpoints.

The following statements reflect a willingness to remain open to the concerns of both sides:

"We'll try out this new procedure and review its effectiveness in six months."

"Let's see how the new plan will affect morale."
"Let's meet periodically so that we can adjust the plan if needed."

These examples of provisional statements reflect what Putnam (1987) terms *problem-solving communication*. All three examples allow for further interaction and communication, for leaving the door open for future review allows individuals the opportunity to live with and assess decisions simultaneously.

SUMMARY

Effective communication even under normal conditions is difficult because individuals tend to view events from their own perspective and want to articulate their feelings. They often therefore fail to attend fully to the concerns and ideas of others. Differences that result from conflict further exacerbate barriers to productive interaction.

These tendencies toward self-absorption belie traits that characterize what Gibb (1961) calls a defensive communication climate. He singles out aspects of communication that are impervious to productive communication. However, if individuals are willing to engage in communication strategies characteristic of Gibb's supportive climate—that is, communication that is descriptive, problem oriented, spontaneous, empathic, equal, and provisional—the ability to manage differences and to achieve productive communication is enhanced considerably. If participants in a communication exchange are able to achieve the co-orientation and mutuality that reflect a willingness to engage, then they have the opportunity to share in a process of productive communication.

SUGGESTED ACTIVITIES

The following exercises focus on strategies for using verbal communication to assess, understand, and manage conflict.

A. Focus on connotative meaning of words

Each student should write down approximately ten words that for them provoke strong negative responses. The group should share the words they have chosen.

Discussion may address the following issues:

1. What type of words were selected?
2. Are there similarities with the words chosen?
3. What events or experiences led to the pejorative meaning of the words?
4. Assuming that several of the group's words coincide, what assumptions can we make about the word choices we make when we communicate with others?

B. Focus on the expression of divergent viewpoints

Consider the following statements:

1. "Marijuana is not as harmful as other drugs. Therefore, it should be legalized."
2. "All people arrested for drunk driving should be treated like criminals."
3. "Instead of putting so much money into defense, we should be pouring these funds into education."
4. "In spite of what the Women's Movement has done for women, in fact men are still expected to provide for the family. Thus, higher paid positions should be given first to men."

The group should be encouraged to contribute additional statements that are likely to produce diverse reactions. Each statement should then be read to the group. On a scale of 1 to 5 (1 being "strongly disagree" and 5 "strongly agree") each participant should record his or her response to the statements.

Individuals read aloud the numbers they have ascribed to each statement. The class should then be paired off, with each pair representing opposing sides to one of the statements.

In turn, each pair should be asked to begin a dialogue discussing the reasons why they agree or disagree with the statement.

The rest of the group should observe each pair's discussion, keeping in mind the following:

a. Where are the areas of agreement; of disagreement;
b. Did both participants share equally in the exchange;
c. Assessment of the verbal tactics used (that is, direct statements, generalizations, sarcasm, and stereotyping, among others);
d. Assessment of communication style (that is, tone of voice, volume, rate of speaking, and so on);
e. Assessment of word choice and grammatical structures employed; and
f. Assessment of the overall effectiveness of the interaction.

C. Focus on supportive communicative environments

Students describe a recent conflict they have experienced (either as a participant or witness). Using the following criteria from Gibb's (1961) supportive communication climate, indicate how effectively each participant in the conflict engaged in the following:

1. Descriptive communication;
2. Problem orientation;
3. Spontaneity;
4. Empathy;
5. Equality; and
6. Provisionalism

What was the outcome of the conflict? If the participants engaged in defensive communication, how, specifically, would you alter their communication to achieve a supportive climate?

D. Focus on feedback

Students or group members should be divided into pairs. One partner chooses to be the speaker; the other becomes the listener. Each listener is instructed to look at the speaker but to refrain from providing any discernible verbal or nonverbal feedback. The speaker selects a topic—preferably one about his or her own experiences—and begins to speak. After a few minutes, the pair switch roles: The speaker becomes the listener; the listener takes his or her turn speaking.

Following the exchange, discussion should focus on the role of feedback in interaction:

1. How did the speaker feel when her or his statements were not responded to?
2. Was it difficult for the listener to refrain from responding? Why?
3. Can the group think of relationships they have with others where they feel they are not listened to? Specifically, what kinds of behaviors do these individuals demonstrate?
4. What are the functions of feedback in a communication exchange?

E. Focus on paraphrasing

The class should be divided into small groups of approximately five members each. Each group selects an issue that is likely to generate debate (that is, a political, moral, or ethical topic). The group is instructed to discuss the topic. After each speaker makes a statement, however, another member of the group must paraphrase it. The initial speaker either confirms or clarifies the paraphrased statement before discussion continues.

After 5 to 10 minutes of discussion time, the entire group should consider the following:

1. How accurately were group members able to paraphrase the statement?
2. Did the individuals experience difficulty paraphrasing others' statements? Why or why not?
3. Did the act of paraphrasing help clarify others' ideas?
4. Do you feel paraphrasing can facilitate interaction? Why or why not?

F. Focus on adaptation of conflict handling behavior

Consider the following situations.

1. Judy, Alec, and Curtis are three colleagues who have agreed to undertake a consulting project that represents a significant amount of money. They are scheduled to make a presentation on the fifteenth of the month and have agreed to review their portions of the presentation on the first.

   At the meeting on the first, Curtis indicates that while he has done preliminary work for the presentation, due to family problems, he will not be ready by the fifteenth. Aware that their deadline cannot be extended, Judy and Alec conclude that they will now have to do Curtis's work under extreme pressure.

The presentation goes well. Judy and Alec, however, feel that Curtis should turn over his portion of the fee for services to them because they have, in fact, done his work. Curtis does not agree. He feels that without his contribution to the project, Judy and Alec would not have been able to complete his work. He should not be penalized for circumstances beyond his control.

2. Charlotte and Anne have lived together amicably for 1½ years. They have agreed on most issues. Anne, however, meets Randy and starts to date him regularly. At first, Randy visits on occasion. After a while, Charlotte feels as if there is a third roommate living in their apartment.

   Charlotte's attempt to voice concern about Randy's presence is met by resistance, especially because Anne feels that the apartment is half hers. She can do what she wants with her half. Charlotte feels strongly that she wanted one, not two, roommates.

3. Kathy and Jim have been married for 4 years. Kathy is an account executive for a large firm. Jim is an actor. Kathy earns about two-and-a-half times what Jim makes. When they were first married, they both earned approximately the same and routinely shared costs.

   Recently, Jim has observed that Kathy has begun to make significant purchases without discussing them with him. This is a departure from past practice. One day, she appears with a $250 pair of gold earrings. Another time, she shows up with a $600 ring. On another occasion, she brings Jim a leather jacket that cost $400.

   Jim is upset by the fact that Kathy is making all of these purchases and is not discussing priorities with him.

   Kathy responds: "Look, I work hard for this money. And I buy nice things for you too. I don't think you should have an equal say in how I spend my money unless you contribute an equal amount." How does Jim respond?

● ● ●

The group should be divided into pairs or groups representing the above situations. Turns should be taken enacting these situations using the following conflict managing styles:

1. The situation with the three colleagues (Curtis, Alec, and Judy):
   a. Curtis, Judy, and Alec are competing.
   b. Curtis and Judy are competing; Alec wants to compromise.
   c. Curtis is competitive; Alec and Judy are accommodating.
   d. Curtis is competitive; Judy and Alec assume a collaborative approach.
2. The situation with the two roommates (Anne and Charlotte):
   a. Charlotte is competing; Anne is avoiding.
   b. Charlotte and Anne are competing. After a few minutes of enacting the situation, Anne and Charlotte should reverse roles.
   c. Charlotte and Anne are willing to collaborate.
3. The situation between the couple (Kathy and Jim)
   a. Jim and Kathy are competing.
   b. Kathy is avoiding; Jim is compromising.

c. Jim tries to collaborate; Kathy is competitive. After several minutes, Jim and Kathy should reverse roles.

d. Jim and Kathy are willing to collaborate.

G. Focus on descriptive versus evaluative language

The class should collect magazine or newspaper articles or advertisements that represent opposing viewpoints about the same issue. Discussion may focus on the following:

1. What words in particular evoke the article's or picture's tone?
2. What do the words actually mean? What are they supposed to connote?
3. Is the intended message conveyed effectively? Why or why not?
4. Distinguish between the explicit and implicit messages of the material. Which words reflect these messages?

THREE
THE LANGUAGES
OF CONFLICT
MANAGEMENT
Nonverbal Strategies
for a Supportive
Communication Environment

To this point, we have discussed communication only as it regards verbal or spoken messages. Much of what we communicate, however, is conveyed without words. Indeed, according to Ray Birdwhistell (1970), the receiver of a message derives as much as 65% of the meaning of that message from the sender's nonverbal communication.

In any given exchange therefore the receiver of a message who is unaware of the nonverbal elements in that message risks missing more than half of what is conveyed. This, in turn, leaves a great potential for misunderstanding that leads to conflict. For instance, a favorite ploy in spy films is to have the spy point to a hidden microphone and with a significant wink tell a visitor a piece of information both know is incorrect. Pointing out the microphone and the knowing wink nonverbally communicate to the visitor that the spy is deliberately telling a falsehood to mislead the counterspies listening to their conversation. Were the visitor to contradict the falsehood and provide the correct information, the spy would justifiably believe that the visitor belonged to the opposing espionage group. It is unlikely that the spy would consider that the visitor merely did not understand the significance of the pointing and the wink.

The nonverbal signals used by the spies in the movies, however, are more consciously sent and often considerably more blatant than the average nonverbal communication sent between communicators. A bitten thumbnail can—in the proper context—express a wide range of things from nothing more than a bothersome hangnail to extreme nervousness. The nailbiter can in turn be very aware that he or she bites the nail or almost unconscious of having done so at all. Yet how the person observing the bitten nail interprets this act can seriously affect whatever else the two communicate. To reduce the likelihood of such conflict the sender must, as described below, take steps consciously to control his or her nonverbal signals to convey the intended message.

In turn, the sender of a message may be unaware that the person to whom he or she communicates is interpreting not only the words used but also the nonverbal elements in the message. For example, a manager who is exasperated with the long-winded explanation of a subordinate may verbally tell him, if asked, to continue. Nonetheless, she may give what are to her very clear nonverbal signals to him to end his speech. She may roll her eyes, drum her fingers on the desk, and sigh audibly. The enthusiastic subordinate, however, if he is caught up in his idea, may be totally oblivious to these nonverbal messages. The result may be an abrupt verbal message from the superior telling the subordinate to stop talking and leave. The subordinate, unaware of the signals his boss had expected him to understand, would likely feel greatly surprised and probably hurt. A conflict situation resulting from these differences in perception would likely follow. In such cases the disparity between the words the sender uses and the way in which the receiver interprets the nonverbal messages accompanying that message may convey an entirely different meaning to the message's receiver than that which the sender intended. If the receiver interprets the nonverbal message in a way that contradicts or undermines the message of the words, a defensive climate and a sense of anger or distrust are likely to occur, leading to a very real conflict.

Conflict may result simply from misunderstanding the nonverbal messages one party sends to another. Even when the source of conflict is real rather than perceived, nonverbal signals can influence markedly the degree of conflict by adding elements of bias into the information being sent and received. Nonverbal messages can distort information by appearing to emphasize, understate, or contradict the intended meanings.

Thus, to minimize the likelihood of unwanted conflict situations, it is useful for communicators to be aware of the role nonverbal messages play in communication. To do so communicators must remain cognizant of both the nonverbal signals they send and of the way in which others understand their nonverbal messages.

WHAT IS NONVERBAL COMMUNICATION?

While the importance of communication sent and received through media other than words is increasingly beyond debate, much disagreement exists over what precisely is meant by nonverbal communication. Since this debate, although important, does not necessarily concern us here, we may agree to accept nonverbal communication expert Randall Harrison's definition for our purposes in this book.

Harrison (1974) defines nonverbal communication as "the exchange of information through nonlinguistic signs" (p. 25). In this definition, Harrison defines *signs* as "a stimulus which, for some communicator, stands for something else"; *nonlinguistic* as "nonword signs"; and *exchange* as "more than one communicator linked in some way so that at least one of them can respond to the signs produced by the other" (1974, p. 25).

Part of the debate alluded to above stems from the fact that in many instances, the verbal messages simultaneously communicated with the nonverbal messages are meshed together so that the verbal element is for all intents inseparable from the nonverbal one. Such elements as voice production, vocal expressiveness, and the various nonword noises (such as grunts, giggles, and ums) that accompany verbal messages fall into this category. While some question exists as to whether these are *truly* nonverbal signs, they still fit within Harrison's definition of "the exchange of information through nonlinguistic signs." To distinguish these from the more direct nonverbal signs, however, we will call these elements *paralanguage*.

Nonverbal communication, however, is by no means limited to paralanguage. The way we move, our use of eye contact, touching behavior, how we position ourselves relative to others, and our outward appearance and dress all communicate nonverbally but without the use of sound. Perhaps the most important discussion of these elements is a book written by Albert Mehrabian entitled *Silent Messages* (1981). Yet the title of even this classic description of the importance and pervasiveness of these aspects of nonverbal communication is misleading. Not all nonparalinguistic, nonverbal communication is silent. Snapping fingers, hand clapping, table pounding, burping, and expelling gas are all forms of auditory nonverbal communication that still belong in this category. Moreover, not all nonauditory communication is nonverbal, most notably, sign language for the deaf. We shall refer to these types of nonverbal behavior as *direct nonverbal communication*.

TYPES OF DIRECT NONVERBAL COMMUNICATION

As discussed above, direct nonverbal communication takes many forms. The five most important of these are appearance, body movement or kinesics, eye contact or oculesics, touching or haptics, and the use of personal space or proxemics. All five of these direct nonverbal communication forms can significantly influence the way in which a message's receivers interpret information. Consequently, all five types of direct nonverbal communication can affect the nature and level of conflict.

Appearance

People judge others by appearance, particularly in establishing first impressions. Moreover, some experts assert that these first impressions are often quite accurate (Burgoon and Saine, 1978). Appearance helps us determine key impressions about those with whom we speak regarding gender, age, profession, relative economic position, and race or culture.

Essentially appearance falls into two categories: artifacts and physical traits. Artifacts are those items of personal appearance over which one has control. The clothing and jewelry one wears are artifacts. Other artifacts include items associated with one's status or trade. An expensive automobile is often an artifact of a wealthy person. A collection of lenses and cameras dangling around one's neck and shoulders are artifacts of a photographer. Physical traits, by contrast, are characteristics that on the whole cannot be easily changed but by which people are nonetheless judged. Indeed, in his seminal works on the subject of physical appearance and behavior, William Sheldon (1940, 1942) categorized people into three physical types (endo or heavy, meso or muscular, and ecto or thin) that to some extent affected how people could be predicted to behave. Finally, certain physical traits can be altered or added to—such as false fingernails or dyed hair—combining both the artifact and physical trait categories.

The key thing to keep in mind is that mere physical appearance communicates a message. For example, a client walks into a U.S. law firm office and sees a 45-year-old graying man dressed in a three-piece dark suit and a 27-year-old man with jet black hair wearing a cardigan, an open-neck shirt, and contrasting slacks. The client, on the basis of her impressions of how attorneys should look, may begin to address the older man in the suit as the partner in charge based on nothing more than the clothing he wears (U.S. corporate attorneys traditionally wear dark three-piece suits) and his physical traits (partners in major law firms are more likely than not to be older and thus graying). While the client and the attorneys have not exchanged as much as a single word, communication has taken place indicating which of the two men the client faces is likely to be the person in charge.

Conflict occurs when what the person observes communicates a different message than actually exists. In the example above, for instance, it is possible that the younger, more casually dressed man could have been the partner and the older, more formally dressed man his assistant or even a paralegal or other lower-ranked position. The younger man may feel sensitive about having been mistaken for the lower-ranked position. The client, in turn, may feel uncomfortable working with an attorney who does not fit her impression of how an attorney ought to look. This alone lays the foundation for a possible conflict.

The chances of this increase, however, when such misjudgments based on appearance play into external elements to which one or the other party is particularly sensitive. For example, as discussed in Chapter 4, conflicts based on gender differences are at times linked to appearance. To illustrate this, let us imagine in the situation described above that the client had entered the law office and seen—instead of an older man and a younger man—a man and a woman of equal age. Based on appearances and (based on a history of strong sex discrimination) the relative lack of female law partners in major U.S. law firms, the client would be justified in assuming solely on the basis of appearance that the person in charge was the man. If in fact the partner in charge were the woman and the man were merely a paralegal or other lower-ranked assistant, the client might play into the partner's sensitivity at being so mistaken, particularly considering that the reason for the client's assumption reflects a sexist bias in the profession to which the partner is arguably an exception. The irritation that the partner feels is likely at least initially to produce a counterproductive environment in which conflict is relatively likely.

Kinesics

How we move—or "body language," to use Julius Fast's popularized term (1970)—is called *kinesics* by social scientists. Great differences in kinesics occur from one culture to another and—at least within most of these cultures—between the sexes. These are discussed at greater length in Chapters 4 and 5. Regardless of culture or gender, however, the purposes motivating nonverbal communication fall into identifiably discrete categories. When the body movements are misinterpreted or uncontrolled, conflict may follow. These purposes and possible conflict situations associated with kinesics are discussed here.

Paul Ekman and Wallace Friesen in a series of seminal works (1969, 1972, 1974) have established five basic purposes served by nonverbal communication and particularly applicable to kinesics: emblems, illustrators, affects, regulators, and adaptors. Each of these five purposes, in turn, risks misinterpretation by those who observe them. Indeed, because nonverbal communication is often indirect, the possibility for misunderstanding and subsequent unintended conflict is greater than that of written or spoken communication. Examples of such conflict are described in this section with each of the five Ekman-Friesen types of nonverbal communication laid out below.

Emblems

Emblems are nonverbal messages that a receiver can translate directly into words. For example, a common emblem is one in which the sender's hand is raised with the palm facing away from the sender and with the forefinger and the thumb touching to form a circle, while the other three fingers are extended. Often the emblem is accompanied by a short jerk of the hand followed by a momentary holding in place before the sender releases.

This gesture, known to researchers as the ring, is universally held within the United States to mean O.K. or good. When people from the United States see this O.K. emblem, they understand that the person showing the ring sign means O.K. The receiver can translate the emblem into the word *O.K.* directly, and the sign is understood unambiguously.

Emblems like the O.K. sign are the least likely of nonverbal communication forms to cause unintended disagreement or unexpected conflict. This is precisely because emblems are so unambiguous. They act like words and—in the case of sign language for the deaf—may be viewed as being verbal rather than nonverbal communication.

Despite their seeming commonality, however, a very serious flaw occurs in the use of emblems. For the most part, emblems are directly linked to the culture of the message sender. Later in this book, we will discuss that nonverbal behavior of all types is culture bound. This is nowhere more evident than in the use of emblems, since identical emblems very frequently have diametrically opposed meanings.

For example, the ring emblem, which we have just indicated means good or O.K. in the United States, has in Europe and North Africa alone four distinct meanings (Morris et al., 1979). In much of Britain, Ireland, Scandinavia, and Yugoslavia, the ring means O.K. or good—as it does in the United States. In Tunisia, by contrast, the O.K. meaning of the identical emblem is entirely absent. Instead, Tunisians interpret the emblem, depending on the context in which it is used, to mean either "zero" or as a threat (deriving from the implication that the person to whom it is shown is nothing but a "big zero"). Similarly, while the O.K. meaning of the emblem is not absent in France and Belgium, the ring emblem is more commonly interpreted to mean zero. Even though they share with the Tunisians the zero interpretation of the emblem, however, neither the French nor the Belgians share with the Tunisians the threat interpretation. In Greece, Sardinia, Turkey, and Malta both the threat and zero interpretations of the emblem are almost entirely absent, and the O.K. meaning is relatively rare. The ring emblem is very frequent in those countries, however, as an insulting obscene gesture representing an orifice, a symbol dating back to ancient times where the gesture appears on ancient Greek vases with this meaning. Even among those who use the emblem as an insult differ according to their culture as to which orifice and which gender they refer when using the emblem.

The impact of such cross-cultural differences is strong, since the users of emblems often feel that such emblems are at once universal and unambiguous direct translation of words into nonverbal symbols. Thus, a U.S.

tourist in Greece might indicate to the waiter pouring his wine that the exact amount was in the glass. Limited in the Greek he spoke, the tourist might not even think twice before using what he would take to be a universal sign for O.K. In turn, the Greek waiter—particularly if he were from a region not often frequented by foreigners—might likewise not think twice before deciding to pour the remainder of the bottle in the tourist's lap.

Illustrators

Illustrators are the next category that Ekman and Friesen describe. Illustrators are movements that complement verbal communication by describing, accenting, or reinforcing what the speaker says. Among other things, illustrators can describe what size an object is, emphasize the key word in a phrase, or sketch a picture in the air of the object a speaker describes. Illustrators tend to be cross-culturally more universal than emblems, although, as discussed in Chapter 5, the frequency with which people use illustrators varies greatly.

Within a single culture one might expect the frequency of illustrators to increase either when the speaker is excited or when the speaker senses a lack of understanding. Illustrators therefore both clarify what is said and act as indicators that the speaker is enthusiastic or trying hard to communicate. The presence or absence of illustrators is in itself unlikely to create conflict; however, the listener's perceived sense of the speaker's committed effort to communicate that accompanies the use of illustrators may establish a more collaborative atmosphere when difficult subjects or conflict situations are discussed.

Affect Displays

Affect displays are nonverbal messages of the body and face that carry an emotional meaning or that display affective states. Emotional or inner states—hate, disdain, fear, love, and anger—may all be communicated nonverbally in a variety of ways.

For example, in the United States, a bouncing gait generally implies a happy state of mind, whereas a slumped posture and shuffling, slack walking style usually indicate depression. Similarly, bursting into a big smile is an affect display of pleasure; frowning suddenly is an affect display of displeasure.

Because such affect displays are often done spontaneously in response to a strong emotion, they may lead to conflict, particularly in sensitive situations. For instance, a physician may wish to appear sympathetic and compassionate to his patients. The physician, however, on first seeing a dramatically disfigured patient, may be unable to prevent an affective display of revulsion. Even though the physician may have said nothing to give the impression that he or she is disturbed or disgusted by the patient's disfigurement, the patient is aware of the doctor's reaction due to the affect display. The patient consequently may distrust the physician's subsequent assurances that the disfigurement is not so severe. Indeed, the patient may no longer wish to deal with the physician based solely on the one displayed affect, resulting in a complete rupture of their relationship.

Regulators

Regulators are nonverbal messages that accompany speech to con-trol—or regulate—what the speaker says. Regulators are directly within awareness, but the communicators sending and receiving them are less directly aware of their use than they would be of emblems, illustrators, or affect displays.

Thus, when two people hold a conversation, the person listening may nod his head periodically. He does so to show that he is listening, although he remains less aware of the nod than he would be, for example, of a ring emblem to communicate that what was said was O.K. with him. Conversely, the speaker also is aware of the nodding but again at a lower level than a signalled emblem or illustrator.

Significantly, regulators appear to have more universality across cultures than do emblems. Even here, however, culture may play a part. For example, nodding is relatively common in most cultures as a way to communicate that one is listening in face-to-face discussions. Nevertheless, in some cultures it is common to face the speaker directly while nodding and making eye contact. In other cultures it is common to lower one's eyes (at least within certain relationships based on rank or gender) but still to nod. Still, elsewhere it is proper to nod while turning one's ear toward the speaker, since the ear is the listening organ.

The use of regulators increases when communication becomes more difficult. Thus in conflict situations we would expect participants to use more regulators than in nonconflict situations. Indeed, it is here where the less conscious perception of regulators (as compared to emblems, for example) becomes more evident. Neither party in a conflict situation (at least in most cases) would consciously indicate that the other party is being more or less cooperative or collaborative in resolving a difficult matter on the basis of the number of regulators being employed. No rough count of the number of head nods, for example, is tallied by either party to indicate that the other party is listening carefully to a given proposal.

Nonetheless, the absence of positive regulators or the use of negative regulators (such as drooping eyes) on the part of one party is very likely to give the other party the feeling that his or her position is not being well received. The lack of regulators therefore communicates a lack of interest and may impede delicate negotiations. The use of such neutral negative regulators as an impassive face or drooping eyes in itself causes significant misunderstanding. Thus, if party A suggests a way to resolve a conflict with party B, but party B sits motionless throughout the period in which party A makes the suggestion, party A may feel in an intangible way that party B does not favor the idea or has failed to hear out party A's suggestion in an unbiased manner. This may not be the case. Party B may have listened to party A's position very openly, but the fact that party A perceives that party B did not do so on the basis of party B's absence of regulators may lead to a hardening of party A's position. This, in turn, contributes to making conflict management more difficult.

Adaptors

The final category of nonverbal behavior that Ekman and Friesen have isolated is adaptors. These occur on a very low level of awareness and represent perhaps the hardest of the categories to define. Adaptors are in general terms those movements used to fulfill some personal need. These can take several forms. Scratching or holding oneself are examples of adaptors that one performs on oneself. Other adaptors are more outward, affecting objects within the person's reach such as chewing on a pencil or twisting paper clips while concentrating. Finally, some adaptors affect neither objects nor the body directly but represent movement without a direct outcome, as shaking or swinging one's legs.

Since people performing adaptors are fairly unaware of the adaptors they use, those with whom the adaptor-user interacts are often more aware of the adaptors than the people using the adaptors. Adaptors may therefore act unintentionally as clues to how a person feels. In particular, adaptors stem back to behavior learned early in life. As Mark Knapp observes, "Adaptors are not intended for use in communication, but they may be triggered by verbal behavior in a given situation associated with conditions occurring when the adaptive habit was first learned" (1980, p. 9).

Significantly, adaptors increase with an increased level of anxiety. Thus, a person who feels uncomfortable may scratch more than a person who feels at ease. As a result, attentive listeners can assess to some extent how much anxiety the person speaking to them feels based on the adaptors that person uses.

Since the use of adaptors is associated frequently with an increased state of anxiety or nervousness, verbal assurances of calmness or control may be undermined by the adaptors that accompany them. This, in turn, can lead to a conflict.

For example, an advertising executive may nervously shift in her seat and scratch the back of her neck in an initial meeting with a new and very large potential client. Because she wants the huge account very much, she may unintentionally demonstrate her concerns through her use of these adaptors. The potential client may not trust the advertising executive fully but may not be sure why, as he, too, is likely to be only partially aware of the adaptors he observes. To satisfy his lack of trust the potential client may ask the advertising executive how much experience she has had with accounts of his size. She may assure him verbally in a calm voice that she has much experience along these lines, even reciting past successes. As she knows that the potential client's cross-examination is a bad sign, however, her level of anxiety—high already—will increase even more. Now she may perform even more adaptors as a release for her uneasiness. She may bite at her cuticle and shake her leg under the desk. The potential client, now firmly aware that the advertising executive is for some reason nervous, may say that he has decided to look around a bit more before committing. The reason he gives is a nebulous lack of trust. The advertising executive, unaware to a large extent of the adaptors she has sent, may argue that the lack of trust is unfounded. The potential client is likely to agree with her that everything she has said to him should only build his trust. Since the potential client is unlikely to say that he has decided to look elsewhere on the basis of a bitten nail or a shaking leg, both parties focus on their verbal communication. In this case the client has little to support his lack of trust. The result is a conflict that remains at the unspoken level precisely because it is never fully realized. Often categorized as a personality conflict, the source of such conflict may never fully surface, as it is possible that neither party ever becomes totally aware of the adaptors that signalled it.

Oculesics

Oculesics, or eye contact, has long been recognized as a means of communicating without speaking. Poets and novelists for centuries have been fascinated with the power of eyes to communicate. "Drink to me only with thine eyes,/And I will pledge with mine" (lines 1-2), wrote the poet Ben Jonson in his poem "To Celia" and Miguel de Cervantes in *Don Quixote* defined "the eyes those silent tongues of Love" (pt. I, bk. II, ch. 3). Yet communication experts have examined the field of oculesics only comparatively recently.

How one uses his or her eyes can convey a number of meanings. As with other nonverbal communication, oculesics vary markedly from one culture to the other (as discussed in Chapter 5). When dealing with situations in which all parties are from the same culture, however, the eyes can communicate in a number of recognizable ways.

Oculesics have been identified, at least within English-speaking North American culture, to serve four main functions: (1) cognitive, (2) monitoring, (3) regulatory, and (4) expressive (Argyle et al., 1973, Kendon, 1967).

Cognitive Oculesics

Cognitive oculesics are those eye movements associated with thinking. In general, people communicate that they are thinking by looking away from those to whom they speak. To look away indicates that the communicator is not open to receiving further information. Conversely, we tend to make eye contact when we are open to receiving more information. A person who looks away from another indicates to some extent that the speaker should slow down the flow of information while the listener processes it. In turn, those who do make eye contact indicate that the communication they have just received has been understood.

Conflict may result from inappropriate cognitive oculesics. For example, in a labor negotiation session a union representative may find that her management counterparts are not looking at her when she makes her demands. When this occurs, she is likely to interpret the management representatives' lack of eye contact as indicating that they have not listened to her position attentively or that they do not take her demands seriously. The labor representative's conclusion, however, may be erroneous. The management representatives—although appearing inattentive due to inappropriate cognitive oculesics—may well have closely listened to the labor representative's demands. No verbal message was ever given to indicate otherwise. Conflict, therefore, could easily be introduced when the labor representative verbally reacts in a hostile way to the negative messages she wrongly believes she has received. In response, the management representatives would quite naturally respond verbally to the labor representative's hostile position, and the conflict would escalate.

Monitoring Oculesics

Monitoring oculesics are those eye movements associated with the receiving of responses to what the speaker has just said. For example, one would expect a listener who understands a speaker to look more steadily at the speaker than a listener who has trouble understanding the speaker (based on the nature of cognitive oculesics just described). To assess the extent to which a listener understands what has been said, the speaker would monitor the degree of eye contact provided by the listener. Monitoring oculesics are tied not only to observing the listener's eye movements, however, but also involve the entire range of the direct nonverbal communication behavior discussed in this chapter.

Conflict deriving from monitoring oculesics might occur when speakers misread the eye movements of their audience. For example, college professors often interpret the fixed gaze of their students as indicating that the students understand the course lectures. Conflict takes place when a large portion of the class later indicates through assignments or class discussion that it has not understood the lectures. Only then do these professors find that they have misinterpreted the class members' monitoring oculesics.

Similarly, conflict may occur when speakers mistakenly interpret the gaze of a listener who does not look steadily at them as lack of understanding. For example, a salesperson may oversimplify her sales pitch or unnecessarily rephrase points she has already made if she interprets a knowledgeable potential buyer's eye contact as indicating a lack of knowledge. The buyer, in turn, may feel affronted by this *verbal* response to his unintended nonverbal cues.

Finally, conflict based on even an *accurate* reading of a listener's monitoring oculesics is possible. The listener may, for example, be unaware that he or she so clearly shows a lack of understanding. Believing the lack of understanding to be hidden, the listener may resent even the speaker's *correct* interpretation of the listener's *nonverbal* cues if the speaker treats these cues as if they had been *admitted* verbally rather than *detected* nonverbally.

Regulatory Oculesics

Regulatory oculesics are those eye movements associated with the willingness or unwillingness on the part of a communicator to respond to what has been said. Relatedly, the speaker may regulate the flow of communication by making eye contact to indicate that the listener should respond or by failing to make eye contact to indicate the desire to keep speaking. As with cognitive oculesics, the major indicator of regulatory eye movement is the absence or presence of direct eye contact. Thus, listeners who do not wish to respond to what they have heard avert their gaze. Listeners who meet the gaze of the speaker indicate either that they are willing to respond at that point or that they have understood what has been said and that the speaker can continue.

Conflict based on regulatory oculesics also derives from misread cues. If, for example, a subordinate looks away from his boss when the boss asks him a question, the boss is likely to understand this eye movement to be a sign that the subordinate does not wish to respond. If in fact the reason the subordinate looked away was unrelated to the boss's question, the boss and the subordinate will base their commuunication on two different assumptions. The boss will respond to the subordinate's averted gaze in a manner that would suggest that the subordinate could not or would not answer the question. The subordinate, if unaware of this, will feel that the boss's behavior is unjustified and respond accordingly. This exchange of responses will in turn escalate the misunderstanding and may well lead to actual conflict.

Expressive Oculesics

Expressive oculesics are those eye movements associated with the emotional response of the communicator. Paul Ekman and Wallace Friesen (1975) have identified oculesic disgust, anger, happiness, and sadness. They have based these indicators on the position of eyebrows, eyelids, tautness of skin around the eyes, and the amount of white shown in the eye.

By reading the emotions expressed through the eyes, communicators gain an insight into how their messages are received and the extent to which they have interested, excited, or in some other way emotionally involved the person with whom they communicate.

Conflict based on expressive oculesics may arise when communicators misread the messages written in the eyes of those with whom they communicate. In particular, as discussed in Chapter 4, marked differences exist between the expressive oculesics of men and women. Similarly, as discussed in Chapter 5, cultures vary greatly regarding how their members interpret standard oculesic expressions. As a result, conflict due to distorted readings of expressive oculesics are very possible in communication between genders or across cultures.

Haptics

Making or failing to make body contact is another form of nonverbal communication. Such communication through touching behavior is called haptics.

When a father hugs his crying daughter, he reassures her and communicates that things will be better or that he loves her. No word has to pass between the two for this message to be exchanged.

As with the father and daughter in the example above, haptics often communicates intimacy. The more affectionate people are, the more freely they will touch each other. Haptics are not limited to love or intimacy, however. Haptics—excluding openly hostile touching behavior (such as slapping)—can be categorized into five major types: (1) functional/professional, (2) social/polite, (3) friendship/warmth, (4) love/intimacy, and (5) sexual/arousal (Heslin, 1974). Each of these categories represents progressive stages, each leading to the next, so that one moves from professionally acceptable touching behavior to socially acceptable haptics, and so on. Each of these categories is duly proscribed by the social norms of the culture in which an individual lives, although the differences between cultures is marked (see Chapter 5).

In most cases, when the boundaries of what is permissible within a haptic category are exceeded, the person doing the touching does so to communicate a message regarding the interpersonal relationship between the person touching and the person being touched. What is communicated to the person being touched is that the person doing the touching either believes the relationship is closer or more intimate than the previously appropriate category would imply or that he or she *wishes* it to be so. Conflict can occur when the one touching and the one being touched do not agree on the appropriate haptic category. When one person touches another in a way that is too intimate, the resulting tension caused by the touch can cause conflict.

Nancy Henley (1975) has indicated that a relationship exists between haptics and dominance. She asserts that those in power are more likely to touch their subordinates than they are to be touched by their subordinates. Thus, it is more likely than vice versa for doctors to touch their patients; police, their detainees; teachers, their students; and advisors, those they advise.

Consequently, when a person touches another, it may not be a message of increasing intimacy but instead of dominance. If the two parties do not agree on the relative dominance such touching implies, conflict is possible. It should be noted that Henley pointed out in particular that in status situations, men tended to touch women more often than vice versa. The gender-linked status differences in this touching behavior are discussed in Chapter 4.

Proxemics

The way in which people use space communicates a message. How people use space in this way is called proxemics.

The use of space has a powerful effect on communication. As Edward Hall has observed, "Spatial changes give a tone to communication, accent it, and at times even override the spoken word" (1959, p. 160). If a person moves to a point that we believe is too close, we back up. Conversely, we tend to move closer to a person we believe to be too distant. How close is too close and how far is too far, however, are carefully proscribed. While the actual distance involved varies from culture to culture, the categorization of personal space according to appropriate and inappropriate distances when speaking is universal. Hall, in a later work on the subject (1966), observes four categories of personal space: intimate, casual-personal, social-consultative, and public.

Intimate personal space is, as its name implies, that space nearest the body reserved for those with whom one is intimate. In the United States, this area is a bubble extending approximately 1½ feet around the body.

The casual-personal area is acceptable only for the interaction of friends. In the United States, this usually covers an area from 1½ feet to 4 feet.

Social-consultative personal space is the space employed in conducting most day-to-day affairs. It is the space in which business is conducted and is impersonal enough for use with strangers. In the United States the acceptable area for social-constructive personal space is between 4 and 12 feet.

Finally, public space is the zone outside social-consultative space. Reserved for public speaking situations, it is too distant for most other activities.

Since how close or far we choose to stand communicates a strong message, a possibility for conflict deriving from miscommunication or disagreement exists. For example, if a husband makes a sincerely intimate statement to his wife, she would expect him to do so from the intimate zone described above. If instead he does so from the social-consultative zone, his proxemics undermine his spoken message.

In response, the wife may feel affronted by this nonverbal incongruity. She may therefore return the husband's intimate statement more coolly than he expects based on his verbal statement alone. The husband, in turn, is likely to feel affronted by his wife's response. These exchanges can rapidly build on one another, resulting in conflict.

PARALANGUAGE

As defined earlier in this chapter, paralanguage is the group of vocal elements that accompanies verbal messages. These elements include the qualities of voice production and expressiveness as well as the various non-word noises that people use in speech.

The various qualities of a speaker's voice provide information about the speaker. Studies show that people make assumptions about intelligence, friendliness, rank, general attitudes, and honesty based on paralanguage or *how* a speaker sounds (Addington, 1968; Davitz, 1964; Kramer, 1963; Williams, 1970).

Unskilled listeners are readily able to interpret accurately paralinguistic cues regarding the speaker. The average listener, however, is unaware of exactly from what he or she has obtained this information when it is conveyed paralinguistically. In short, the listener processes paralinguistic messages as unnamed feelings or intuitive hunches about the speaker without being fully cognizant of their source. As J. A. Starkweather explains: "Voice alone can carry information about the speaker. . . . Judgments appear to depend on significant changes in pitch, rate, volume and other physical characteristics of the voice, but untrained judges cannot describe these qualities accurately" (1961, p. 69).

The paralinguistic messages that Starkweather's untrained judges accurately assess but cannot describe *can* be identified. What is important for our discussion is that when communicators unintentionally convey messages through the paralanguage they employ or when the message they attempt to convey is not the same as the message the audience receives, misunderstanding and attendant conflict may follow.

Pauses

A subset of paralanguage meriting individual attention as a source of communication-based conflict is the pause. Pauses are powerful tools in speech, often conveying strong messages. These messages, though, are frequently imprecise and in their imprecision rests the possibility of misinterpretation leading to unintended conflict.

Two types of pauses occur in speech: unfilled and filled. Unfilled or silent pauses and the use of silence, although nonvocalized nonverbal communication, are included here because their use depends on placement within speech, and they are used as a form of vocalized nonverbal message, that is, as the absence of vocalized messages. Unfilled pauses in speech are differentiated from silence as a matter of degree. A short silence is an unfilled pause; a long pause, an intended silence.

Unfilled pauses act as a verbal cue to listeners depending on their frequency. Hesitations and pauses—both filled or vocalized and unfilled or silent—are expected in spontaneous speech at spots other than those determined by grammatical closure. Indeed, one way to differentiate between a read speech and a spontaneously delivered speech rests in the relatively high consistency of grammatical pauses and absence of nongrammatical pauses in the read speech as against the spontaneously delivered speech. Knapp (1980) indicates that in spontaneous speeches "only 55 percent of the pauses occur at grammatical junctures, whereas oral readers of prepared texts are highly consistent in pausing at clause and sentence junctures." (p .222) Thus, one vocal cue listeners determine from the use of unfilled pauses is the degree to which the speaker's words seem to be spontaneous. Misevaluating these pauses therefore can skew the listener's perception of a speaker and his or her message, which in turn may lead to conflict based on misunderstanding.

Other studies have shown unfilled pauses to act as vocal cues in other ways. Unfilled pauses have been linked to listeners' perceptions of the speaker's conciseness and a decrease in predictability (Goldman-Eisler, 1961). Excessive use of unfilled pauses, however, appears to lead listeners to perceive the speaker as contemptuous, angry or anxious (Lalljee, 1971). Conflict may result when the listener's emotions are colored in this way by the speaker's pauses, unbeknownst to the speaker.

Silences are intentionally used unfilled pauses of long duration. Silence can be a very powerful nonverbal communication tool. One amusing example, although probably apocryphal, of the use of silence to communicate a message forcefully involves the address of Nikita Khrushchev to the Politburo soon after he succeeded Josef Stalin as head of the Soviet Union. Khrushchev was attacking Stalin for various atrocities and abuses in a vitriolic speech when an anonymous voice shouted from the back of the large room. "If Stalin was such a monster, Comrade Khrushchev," the voice asked, "then why did no one—including you—stand up to him? Why did no one speak out? The members of the Politburo gasped almost as one, and a hush fell over the room as Khrushchev set down his speech and looked over the faces of the men and women in the room. "Who said that?" he demanded and glared at his audience. Khrushchev allowed a long silence to follow his question. No one spoke. The huge room was so quiet that each Politburo member could hear the breathing of the member next to him. After over a minute of this nearly palpable silence, Khrushchev smiled. "That, Comrade," Khrushchev said, referring to the sense of dread the silence just passed had communicated, "that is the reason why no one spoke out."

J. Vernon Jensen (1973) suggests that a wide range of meanings are attributable to silence. He suggests that silence indicates

a. Mental activity such as reflection or thoughtfulness;
b. Evaluation and passing judgment;
c. Revelation, for example, hiding or making known a fact by answering an inquiry with silence;
d. Emotional expression, generally of strong emotions such as love or disgust; and
e. An accent or underscoring of a point, as in the Khruschev example given above.

Due to this variety of possible interpretation, listeners may relatively easily misinterpret a speaker's use of silence. While misinterpretation in itself may not necessarily create conflict, the perceptual gap between the received and sent message can strongly affect reactions to information exchanged in a conflict situation by contributing an element of bias that may be unfounded.

The other type of pause, the filled pause, is much more akin to other paralanguage. Filled pauses are hesitations and pauses which the speaker fills with various nonword vocalizations. In English these commonly include such sounds as "um," "eh," "er," and "ah." Filled pauses also include word repetition or false starts, stuttering, and verbal expressions acting as fillers (such as "OK" or "you know" when used out of context). On the whole, filled pauses are less well received than unfilled pauses. Filled pauses have been associated with long-windedness and the predictability of what the speaker is attempting to express (Goldman-Eisler, 1961). As discussed in Chapter 2, filled pauses have been shown to lead listeners to perceive the speaker as bored or anxious (Lalljee, 1971; Mehrabian, 1972). When these perceptions do not reflect the reality of a situation, each party may behave in what seems to be an incongruous manner to the other party. For example, if an attorney uses numerous filled pauses, her client may grow irritated with the attorney after a very short period, since he anticipates a long-winded speech. He therefore feels justified in interrupting the attorney after only a few minutes. He may even tell her to get to the point. However, she is likely to be surprised at her client's abruptness, since she has only spoken for a few minutes. It would be unlikely that she would be aware that her client is reacting to her filled pauses. Consequently, she would respond to her client's interruption as an unmotivated rudeness. The client would, in turn, react to her reaction and so forth until the initially harmless misinterpretation of a nonverbal cue escalates into a very real basis for conflict.

NONVERBAL COMMUNICATION STRATEGIES FOR CONFLICT MANAGEMENT

We have discussed in this chapter the ways in which nonverbal communication can affect the environment in which the whole communication process takes place. Messages conveyed nonverbally both while speaking and while listening help to establish what we have termed in Chapter 2 a *collaborative climate for interpersonal communication.*

Nonverbal behavior, as we have noted, is often overlooked by those who send the message. Thus, a speaker may be unaware of what her body motions or facial expressions convey while she speaks. Those who watch the speaker, however, are unlikely to remain equally incognizant of these nonverbal signals. Thus, the first step in maintaining a supportive climate likely to avoid interpersonal conflict is self-awareness of our own nonverbal behavior.

The insights that an observer may draw from watching another's nonverbal behavior are varied and rich, although often imprecise. Consequently, the second step for maintaining a supportive communication climate is to resist too rapid a judgment of nonverbal messages. Instead, the observer should balance any individual nonverbal message against other such messages as well as against the verbally conveyed messages of the person observed. In short, because of such messages' imprecision, the observer must take care to place his or her observations in context.

By no means, however, should the communicator disregard nonverbal messages because of their imprecision. While imprecise, nonverbal messages as we have discussed can be most expressive in sending messages. Relatedly, nonverbal messages are equally revealing when observed, in part because the sender of the message is often less aware of his or her nonverbal communication than of other outlets of communication such as the words used.

One means of assessing nonverbal behavior in a manner that would reduce tension and defensiveness is to employ the principles of Gibb's supportive climate characteristics (1961) described in greater detail in Chapter 2. As we have explained, Gibb's approach regarding verbal strategies for establishing a supportive communication climate, the discussion here will only briefly discuss how to modify these strategies to the nonverbal arena. Gibb suggests six categories for establishing a supportive verbal communication environment: description, problem orientation, spontaneity, empathy, equality, and provisionalism. We will discuss the first five as equally applicable to nonverbal communication as well. Gibb's last category, provisionalism, is not discussed in this section, however, as it is primarily manifested verbally and so does not apply to our subject.

Description, for Gibb, is the opposite of evaluation. He suggests that when people believe they are being evaluated or judged according to how they communicate, they become defensive. Applying this to nonverbal behavior, the communicator should attempt to avoid expressing judgment being passed on the nonverbal behavior of the person observed. The information obtained should be used for the observer but not necessarily shared with the sender, whom, Gibb indicates, would likely become insecure or defensive. Indeed, this is particularly important for nonverbal messages, since, as we noted earlier, the sender of the message is not always wholly aware of the message he or she sends. Consequently, an openly judgmental reception of such messages might very easily make the person observed self-conscious once made aware of this nonverbal behavior. The resultant tension could readily lead to counterproductive conflict.

Gibb writes that problem orientation rather than attempts at control helps to establish a collaborative environment for verbal interaction. To a lesser extent, this holds true in nonverbal exchanges as well. Gibb asserts that in the verbal arena "a bombardment of persuasive 'messages' . . . has bred cynical and paranoidal responses in listeners" (1961, p. 204). Attempts to manipulate and persuade using nonverbal messages may, however, in fact be more effective than their verbal counterparts precisely because people *are* less aware of their presence and so have less of an opportunity to become as jaded by them. Still, Gibb's principle that the attempt to control is in its very nature more likely to provoke conflict than an attempt to solve a problem collaboratively holds true for any communication, including nonverbal.

As discussed in Chapter 2, Gibb explains the difference between strategy and spontaneity as the difference between deliberate manipulation (through feigned guilelessness and other forms of pretense) and genuine responsiveness and openness to a communication exchange. Although Gibb refers to verbal situations, this distinction parallels precisely the difference between interactive listeners and pretending listeners described earlier in this chapter.

Nonverbal behavior is particularly well suited to maintaining the next characteristic in Gibb's supportive communication climate, empathy. Since nonverbal behavior, as we have discussed, is particularly effective in communicating emotions, it is useful in conveying to others that its user feels empathy with them. Empathic listening in particular is useful in encouraging a speaker to continue and in expressing to him or her without interrupting that the listener understands and cares about what is said.

SUMMARY

In this chapter we have discussed various nonverbal communication messages. We have described how appearance, oculesics, proxemics, touching behavior, and body motion communicate messages. We also examined how paralanguage, and pauses convey messages.

We noted that while nonverbal behavior communicates messages in every culture, what is actually communicated is culturally determined. Therefore, the nonverbal communication discussed in this chapter is limited to the United States. The use of nonverbal communication in other cultures is discussed in more detail in Chapter 5.

Finally, we have shown how nonverbal messages can lead to conflict through unintended disclosure or through misinterpretation. To lessen the chance for undesirable, counterproductive conflict, we have indicated methods for using nonverbal behavior as a supportive communication tool.

SUGGESTED ACTIVITIES

A. Focus on appearance

Take two photographs of a friend or person whom you know well. For the first photograph have the friend dress in very formal business attire (a dark suit, for example). For the second photograph have the same friend dress very casually (jeans and a t-shirt, for example).

Next show the first photograph to five people who do not know the friend. Ask them to tell you what they think the person in the photograph is like. Ask them to indicate what they think he or she does for a living, what relative economic status he or she has, how intelligent the friend is, what level of education he or she has attained, what his or her goals seem to be, and so forth. Record their answers.

Then take the second photograph and show it to five different people who also do not know the friend. Ask them the same questions that you asked of people regarding the first photograph. Record their answers.

Compare the responses. How similar or dissimilar are the responses of those people who viewed the same photograph? How similar or dissimilar are the responses of those who viewed different photographs? To what extent did the appearance and dress affect these people's responses?

Now compare the responses of these people to what you actually know about your friend. How accurate or inaccurate were their first impressions based on appearance? Was one group of viewers more accurate in your estimation than the other? Were attributes you believe to be true about your friend noticed by one group and not by the other? Be prepared to discuss your findings and observations in class.

B. Focus on kinesics

For this exercise a short videotape of two people speaking will be played in class. The volume will be turned off. If this exercise is done at home, a VCR can be used as long as the viewers watch a film with which they are unfamiliar.

Each student will take out five pieces of paper. Each student will write out the categories of the Ekman-Friesen types of nonverbal communication so that the top of one page will read EMBLEMS, another ADAPTORS, the next ILLUSTRATORS, the next AFFECT DISPLAYS, and the last REGULATORS.

Next the students should draw a line down the center of each page, forming two columns. The first column should be marked SPEAKER ONE; the second SPEAKER TWO.

As the students watch the film, they should quickly record the number of body motions they observe on the sheets according to the appropriate categories and for the appropriate speakers.

At the end of the film, the students should discuss how frequently the various types of kinesics were used. They should also discuss which speaker used more or less of each type and what significance, if any, they believe this had.

They should consider as well what, based on kinesic behavior alone, they believe the conversation of the two people in the videotape was about. Was this a conflict situation? Did one speaker appear more dominant than the other? What nonverbal messages were sent between the two communicators? How receptive to these signals did each seem to be?

C. Focus on oculesics

Hold a conversation with a friend. Make very direct and unbroken eye contact throughout the conversation, staring very intensely without stop as you speak and as you listen. Observe what your friend's reaction is. What is your *own* reaction?

Now hold a conversation in which you make as little eye contact as possible. When the person with whom you speak is talking, look away. Again record the reactions you observe.

Next enter an elevator and make strong eye contact with a stranger in the elevator. How did that person seem to react? How did *you* feel?

For each situation be prepared to discuss whether your behavior causes any tension. If so, could there have been enough tension to have caused a conflict situation? How were the reactions in each situation alike or different?

D. Focus on haptics

Shake hands with a friend. Use a very firm grip and, pumping vigorously, extend the handshake much longer than you normally would.

Next shake hands with the friend again. This time use a very limp handshake and cut the clasp off quickly.

Ask the friend to evaluate the two handshakes. What message did each communicate?

E. Focus on proxemics

Obtain three male and three female volunteers.

Ask two of the male volunteers to come to the front of the room. Have the third male volunteer and the three female volunteers stand outside the room with the door closed so that they are unaware of what is happening in the room.

Have one student stand at the center of the room and the other at the opposite side of the room against the wall. Have the student at the center of the room stand still and ask the other student to approach until he feels he has reached a comfortable conversational distance. Mark the spot inobtrusively. Have him return to his seat.

Ask the remaining male volunteer to enter the room. Have him approach the student in the middle of the room in the same manner and to stop when he has reached a comfortable conversational distance.

Did he select the same approximate spot?

Now ask one of the female volunteers to enter the room. Ask her to approach the male student in the center of the room in the same manner and to stop when she has reached a comfortable conversational distance.

Did she select the same approximate spot?

Have the female volunteer replace the male volunteer in the middle of the room. Ask the remaining female volunteer outside the room to come in and repeat the exercise.

Did she select the same approximate spot?

Inform the volunteers of where they stopped relative to one another. Is there a universal proxemics for comfortable conversation? Does this distance shift by gender? By any other factor? Discuss what the differences and similarities of their proxemics signify.

FOUR
GENDER DIFFERENCES
The Impact of Communication Style on Conflict Management

In Chapters 2 and 3 we presented the kinds of effective verbal and nonverbal communication skills required to facilitate both communication and problem solving in conflict management. Without developing such skills, satisfactory conflict management may be highly unlikely because true transactional communication will not be realized.

But simply developing, strengthening, and using what we call effective communication strategies is problematic, for according to psychologist Lillian Breslow Rubin, men and women acquire different languages with which to communicate: "They are products of a process that trains them to relate to only one side of themselves—she, to the passive, tender, intuitive, verbal, emotional side; he, to the active, tough, logical, nonverbal, unemotional one" (1976, p. 116). Rubin's observation and an entire body of research by sociologists, linguists, psychologists, and speech communication specialists indicate that men and women learn to communicate differently; further, they often possess divergent attitudes toward these communication differences.

In recent years the need to address how gender affects the ability of women and men to manage conflict has emerged as an issue for serious consideration. As women and men continue to pursue careers that reflect collegial interactions (as opposed to subordinate-superior interactions) and as both sexes struggle to reconceptualize and redefine their social relationships (Blumstein and Schwartz, 1983), the communicative acts of women and men and moreover, society's attitudes toward these acts have been undergoing considerable scrutiny. Such an analysis may result in the ability of women and men to understand more fully their own communication behavior as well as the behavior of members of the opposite sex. Such understanding can inform the ability of both sexes to manage conflict productively and will hopefully begin to dispel the misunderstandings between women and men that experts like Rubin observed more than a decade ago.

As we review our model for the process of conflict management—assessment, acknowledgment, attitude, action, and analysis—we will see that the process of recognizing and changing society's views toward the roles and behaviors of women and men in U.S. culture is a slow and painful, albeit necessary, process.

ASSESSMENT

Before engaging in a confrontation, it is important for individuals to: (1) assess their individual traits to understand who they are and their relationship with the other party, (2) assess the nature of the conflict, (3) clarify their own goals, (4) examine the climate in which both parties function, and (5) make a preliminary determination of the appropriate conflict style.

Individual Traits

In Chapter 1 consideration was given to understanding individuals' traits and the relationship between individuals in conflict. It was demonstrated that the nature of the relationship between people can cause conflict, especially when there are perceived differences in individual's traits. Further, one must contend with the traits we as individuals perceive in ourselves versus the traits society as a whole has imbued us with solely as a condition of gender. Discrepancies in self-perception—as opposed to those traits attributed to us by others—seem to be resolved in favor of societal determinations regardless of individual assertions. A woman who is a manager, for example, might feel compelled to work harder than her male colleagues to demonstrate her competence to her coworkers who believe that women are too emotional to be effective managers. A father who takes care of the home and children while his wife works may feel similarly driven to convince others that his role as house-husband does not imply that he is weak or a failure. Both the woman and the father in these examples feel pressured to prove to others that they do not fit into the stereotyped role that society has defined for them.

Traits assigned to men or women on the basis of gender are referred to as *sex-trait stereotypes*. Williams and Best (1982, p. 16) define sex-trait stereotypes as those "psychological characteristics or behavioral traits that are believed to characterize men with much greater (or lesser) frequency than they characterize women." As part of their extensive pan-cultural study of sex-stereotyping in 29 countries, these psychologists found that in all participating nations, the adjectives "adventurous," "dominant," "forceful," "independent," "masculine," and "strong-willed" were applied to men, while the terms "emotional," "sentimental," "submissive," and "superstitious" were used consistently to describe women.

Without exploring here the positive and negative connotations that accompany such stereotypes (described later in the attitude section of this chapter), it is important for both men and women to assess accurately attributes or labels applied to them on the basis of gender. This is especially important when these labels support or contrast with their own perceived behavior.

For example, a corporate executive acknowledges that in her personal relationships with men she is both emotional and submissive, preferring to avoid those situations that she believes could threaten the relationship. In her professional work with women and men, however, she regards herself as extremely independent and assertive. Her ability to assess and subsequently confront a problem will therefore be affected by her assessment of the situation, of her relationship with the other party, of her perceived conflict-handling behavior, and moreover, by how others expect her to respond because of the sex-trait stereotypes that are an integral part of culture.

Similarly, men who fail to conform to the behavioral norms our society has ascribed to them are confronted with reconciling their individual conflict-handling style with the expected standard of behavior. Failure to meet these expectations might result in their being labelled weak and incompetent.

As explained in Chapter 1, Thomas and Kilmann (1974) devised a conflict mode inventory designed to enable managers to assess their own conflict handling style. (This instrument is one of several that assess conflict management in organizations [Putnam, 1988].) Although this instrument is based on behavior in professional contexts, the more than 100 students to whom we have administered this instrument over the past 5 years found that their resultant conflict style strongly coincided with their own estimation of how they manage conflict. Through role-playing and case study analysis, we were able to work toward developing flexible conflict management behavior in these students so that they were able to employ conflict-handling behavior appropriately.

Assess the Nature of the Conflict

Cora is a well-known physician and researcher who has pursued a field of medicine with relatively few women. Although she is very aware of the existence of an old boys network in her hospital and in her area of expertise, she has tried to avoid direct conflict with her male colleagues who joke about her feminine appearance. At a staff meeting one morning, her department head casually turns to Cora and asks her to order coffee for the group. Cora loses her temper over the request and storms out of the meeting.

Larry is manager of the research and development division in a major company. Although he faces many deadlines and pressures, Larry's style of management is open; his problem-solving behavior varies from compromising to collaborating. Larry's supervisor is Michael, vice-president for research and development. Michael, who considers himself a "man's man," is highly competitive in all areas of his life. He has high expectations for Larry and is concerned that Larry does not demonstrate the same drive, energy, and competitive spirit that in Michael's estimation he will need to move ahead. At his annual evaluation Michael admonishes Larry for the apparent lack of drive that is keeping him from advancing in the company. Disgusted with Michael's unfair demands, Larry silently vows to leave the company.

In both these examples Cora and Larry allowed their feelings to mount to the point that they felt compelled to abandon their work environment rather than confront the issues that bothered them. Both failed to assess accurately the conflicts they experienced with their colleagues and superiors. Cora thought she could withstand her colleagues' comments. She failed to recognize that she was tacitly engaging in a conflict of attitude. Intellectually, she tried to brush off the comments as immature or unimportant. Emotionally, however, she was greatly disturbed by remarks that she felt both demeaned her and trivialized her professional accomplishments.

Similarly, Larry felt threatened and unfairly treated by an individual who assumed that his competitive style was the only correct behavior for the company. Clearly, Larry and Michael shared the same goals of increasing production and profits. How best to achieve these goals, however, was a matter of contention.

To prevent irreconcilable differences individuals must assess early on potential conflicts and initiate intervention strategies to stay the exacerbation of these differences. These techniques are addressed in the next section.

Goal Clarification

In both examples the conflicts that occurred may be attributed to gender-related expectations. Cora's case is quite clear. She felt her professional expectations were continually thwarted by references to those feminine aspects of her behavior that had little to do with her role as a physician. Her goal was to be treated as a professional, hopefully as a colleague. Yet rather than articulate these goals, she allowed herself to be treated as a victim. Further, her male colleagues may have regarded their teasing behavior as typical, and they intended no harm. From Cora's perspective the teasing was an insult. Perhaps from her colleagues' point of view, their comments represented camaraderie. Yet the use of humor is largely based on ingroup/outgroup relationships and often, according to Barnlund (1973, p. 18), "serves defensive and destructive ends." In their writing on gender differences and communication, Kramarae (1981) and Pearson (1985), for example, discuss at length how telling jokes or teasing behavior can be an aggressive act, especially when a minority or ostensibly less powerful group (that is, women) is the target. If Cora fails to clarify her sentiments, then her resultant frustration and anger can be anticipated.

In the case of Larry and Michael, although the responsibility for the conflict may lie with Michael's attitude toward individuals who are not totally competitive, Larry is also responsible for failing to indicate that his management style of openness, compromise, and collaboration is highly productive. Because Larry failed to demonstrate to Michael that styles other than overt competition are valuable, successful, and rewarding and that these styles do not negate one's masculinity or effectiveness, his withdrawal served instead to support Michael's erroneous assumptions.

Once Cora and Larry could assess and clarify their professional goals, they would be able to resolve their conflicts. Cora realized her primary goal was to do research and hopefully find cures to many diseases. While she wanted to get along with her colleagues, she felt she no longer had to risk her feelings to do so. Consequently, the next time her colleagues passed some remarks about her femininity, she simply stated that this type of comment in fact had nothing to do with her competence and that she did not appreciate them. Her colleagues had not intended to offend her. Once Cora made her feelings known, the others stopped teasing her.

Larry's situation required considerable self assessment. He had been with his company for 8 years, following 7 years with another major firm that was far more low-keyed than his present environment. Further, he had relocated across the country to assume his current position. When he first came to the firm, he tried to emulate Michael who was an obvious success within the organization. But Larry was unable to be as competitive, extroverted, and aggressive as his boss. Yet his own management style enabled him to perform his responsibilities admirably. Once Larry realized that his goal was not to be like Michael, indeed, that he did not want to be like him, he was able to respect his own accomplishments. He finally confronted Michael, telling him that while he admired Michael's management style, he realized he could never be Michael, and that he hoped Michael would recognize his achievements and accept him as he was. As a result of their discussion, Michael did in fact stop trying to pressure Larry into becoming something he was not.

Ironically, Cora and Larry experienced similar problems that stemmed from their gender. Because Cora was a woman working in a predominantly male environment, her colleagues singled out these differences making her the object of their jokes. Because Larry was a man in a predominantly male and highly competitive organization, his boss criticized his different management style for not being sufficiently masculine. Once these individuals were able to clarify their goals—to themselves and to their colleagues—further conflict was avoided.

Examination of Climate

Most students who enroll in our speech communication and business communication courses feel they know exactly what they want to do upon graduation and, more specifically, where they want to work. Unfortunately, these students often pay little attention to understanding themselves, understanding the environment in which they hope to work, and reconciling these two very important criteria with their professional aspirations. We frequently hear from students who several years out of college lament the choices they have made, realizing that their hopes and expectations about a particular company were unmet.

We have noted in Chapter 1 that conflicts do not exist in the abstract; rather, they arise between people. In Chapters 2 and 3, we explored the kinds of verbal and nonverbal communication required to facilitate conflict management. Understanding basic concepts about conflict management and about those communication skills that facilitate such management, however, is of little help if one has not attempted to assess the climate in which one will interact.

In general for either women or men to integrate successfully within an organization, making the following initial evaluation will help prevent conflicts and will facilitate effective management of those conflicts that do arise. These questions enable individuals to anticipate stress factors in organizations (Brief, Schuler, and Van Sell, 1981), increase awareness of one's role in society (Goffman, 1959; 1963), and understand conflict in organizational settings (Cross, Names, and Beck, 1979):

1. What will be my role/function in the organization?
2. Does this role coincide or contrast with my personality traits?
3. With whom will I be required to interact? (subordinates, colleagues, superordinates)
4. What kind of interaction/communication will be required? (one-to-one, group, public; oral and/or written)
5. Is open communication within the organization encouraged or discouraged?
6. Where do I expect to be in the next 5 years?
7. Does this organization have a position for me in the future?

At best, understanding a communication environment and one's role in this environment is difficult. Yet the prototype for most organizations is based on the hiring, job performance, evaluation, and promotion of men (Bernard, 1981; Deaux, 1983; Stockard and Johnson, 1980). When one adds gender as a factor, additional considerations, especially for women, emerge (although many of these concerns are applicable to any minority group):

1. What is the highest position in the organization occupied by a woman?
2. How many women hold executive/management positions and at what levels?
3. What has been the promotion/retention history for women?
4. Are there equivalent salaries for women and men holding comparable positions within the organization?
5. Are facilities for women and men comparable?
6. Do benefits include maternity and/or child care policies?
7. Is an adequate leave of absence for child care permitted by the organization?
8. Where can women in line positions expect to find themselves within 5 years?

Sociologist Jessie Bernard (1981) explains that most women are encouraged to pursue pink collar, or service, and often low-paying employment. Because strong societal sanctions motivate women in this direction, assessing the practical policies of management-level opportunities is especially important for those women who wish to exceed society's expectations. Anticipating problem areas and examining a professional environment thus become critical steps to preventing conflict over professional expectations, practices, and goals.

Preliminary Determination of Appropriate Conflict Style

Regardless of the anticipatory steps an individual takes before entering an organization, conflicts will undoubtedly occur. Even under ideal circumstances where everyone knows the players in a conflict situation, managing conflict is not easy. The problems are exacerbated when the players are of the opposite sex because, as Deaux (1983, p. 47) notes: "Males and females differ in their perceptions of and approaches to the management of organizational conflicts. These differences are likely to affect the way men and women respond to contradictory messages."

Thus, a woman in an all-female organization may willingly accept the responsibility of taking notes at a particular meeting knowing that at subsequent meetings this task will be assigned to another committee member. This same woman may react negatively to the same request if she is the only woman in the group.

In the first situation she anticipates a spirit of cooperation among the women and views taking notes as contributing to this unified spirit. In the second situation she regards being asked to take notes as a sex-stereotyped assumption and male bias that women are typically better at secretarial tasks and will willingly undertake these duties. Her negative response to the men's request therefore belies her interpretation of the implicit connotation of a female colleague being asked to perform those duties normally expected of a secretary (usually a woman's job).

We can see clearly that the same task (note taking) may result in two different styles of behavior: accommodating in the first case; competing in the second example. The reason for this discrepancy of response is due to the woman's understanding and interpretation of the same request, which vary based upon who makes the request and on the assumptive behavior of the individual who initiates the request.

Because women and men come to situations with their own backgrounds, experiences, and expectations, it is important for both men and women to assess carefully how their own actions may be construed or interpreted in ways different from their intentions. An obvious parallel exists here with cross-cultural understanding. This issue will be addressed more fully in Chapter 5.

According to Barry (1970) women and men learn to perceive acts differently. If it is, as conflict theorists tell us, the perception of a problem that matters in a conflict situation, then the likelihood for conflict increases if two parties come to an encounter with different ways of perceiving a particular event or situation.

Until we reach a point of shared understanding among women and men, we advise both sexes to carefully scrutinize conflicts that emerge between them to determine if any part of the difficulty can be attributed to a misunderstanding or misinterpretation based on their divergent backgrounds. As Borisoff and Merrill (1987) have noted, once the conflicting parties are able to understand the nature and connotation of the problem, they are able to adopt the conflict-handling style appropriate to the situation, and the possibility of satisfactorily managing the conflict becomes likely.

If we return to the example of the woman who when asked to take notes at a meeting by her male colleagues staunchly refuses, we might suggest a compromising approach. She might say, for example, "I'll agree to take minutes at this meeting. However, I don't want the secretarial duties to be my permanent assignment. I assume someone else will take minutes at our next session." By demonstrating a willingness to cooperate (by agreeing to take minutes), yet asserting her feelings about the task (I don't expect to do this regularly), she has prevented a conflict from erupting without compromising her own beliefs or feelings.

ACKNOWLEDGMENT

In Ellen Rothman's book *Hands and Heart: The History of Courtship in America* (1984), the correspondences of women and men consistently reflect that during the eighteenth and nineteenth centuries in America, women had greater difficulty adjusting to marriage than their husbands.

> The contract (marriage) is so much more important in its consequences to females than to males, for besides leaving everything else to unite themselves to one man they subject themselves to his authority—they depend more upon their husband than he does upon his wife for society and for the happiness and enjoyment in their lives—he is their all—their only relative—their only hope.

While a man's life remained essentially intact, a woman had to leave her home, friends, and family to accompany her husband to the place where he would be able to work. If she had developed a career, admittedly uncommon during this period, she would need to relinquish these professional aspirations to tend to the hearth. An additional major adjustment occurred when a woman assumed the role and responsibilities of motherhood, a duty she was required to perform largely on her own.

This description of life of the early nineteenth-century American woman has not changed that considerably. Even if one were to argue that the number of women in today's work force has increased tremendously among married couples, one career—usually the husband's because his earnings are greater—still takes priority, and women remain the primary caretakers of the home and of the family (Bernard, 1981; Blumstein and Schwartz, 1983; Stockard and Johnson, 1980).

In the previous section we indicated that women and men come to events with different perspectives based on their own backgrounds, experiences, and attitudes. Many conflicts between men and women are in fact due to misunderstandings that result from divergent perspectives and interpretations of the same event because the event means something different to each party. It is unlikely that these differences can be managed or resolved effectively without both parties being able to view the situation from the perspective of the other party. To extend the viewpoints of both men and women, it is necessary to acknowledge the differences in the backgrounds of women and men that have served to shape their present outlooks.

From the time the question "Is it a boy or a girl?" is asked, the answer to this question will greatly influence how the child will be raised, what kind of behavior will be expected and tolerated, and what kind of personal and professional achievements will be encouraged.

The most direct way of presenting the extent to which gender differences shape what we mean by male and female is to examine culture and to explore what anthropologist Edward Hall (1961) calls the "formal" and "informal" cultural dimensions of the United States, for herein reside those elements and outlooks in our backgrounds that have caused us to grow up male or female.

Acculturated Sex Differences in the Family: Formal or Explicit Cultural Transmission

How is culture transmitted? How do boys and girls acquire appropriate behavior and gender-linked attitudes? What kinds of gender-linked behaviors are encouraged in children? Hall (1961) provides a valuable anthropological model for how culturally linked behavior is transmitted. Although Hall presents the formal, informal, and technical transmission of culture as his model, we will address the formal and informal modes of transmission, for it is at these two levels that young children learn what behavior is accessible and expected of them as males and females in U.S. culture.

While many parents do not consciously set out to sex type their children, studies reveal that middle-class fathers in the United States are especially concerned about sex typing. These parents overtly reinforce sex-typed behavior with greater frequency than mothers (Macoby and Jacklin, 1974). Through play, dress, household tasks, socialization, and education, girls learn to be polite, expressive, nurturant, compliant, dependent, and pretty. In contrast, boys are encouraged to display aggressiveness, emotional control, independence, competitiveness, and physical strength (Bernard, 1981; Gilligan, 1979; Stockard and Johnson, 1980). (It should be noted that most of the data emerges from studies of white, middle-class families, and therefore generalizations should not be applied to all members of U.S. culture.)

At an early age children learn what types of toys and activities are acceptable. In Fagot's (1978) study of 2-year-olds, for example, she found that her subjects demonstrated marked toy preferences. Girls preferred dolls and soft toys; boys were attracted to blocks and other objects they could manipulate. This preference, however, was not biologically motivated, for the parents of these children reinforced this behavior by giving positive responses when the children played with the aforementioned objects and negative feedback when their children selected what were regarded as inappropriate toys. In fact, when boys played with girl's toys, their fathers reacted strenuously to discourage such preference.

In "Growing Up Female," Graebner (1982) articulates the overt pressures placed upon young children who attempt to deviate from society's expectations. In his description of a young woman's development, Nancy's predilection as a teenager for playing football with the boys and climbing trees is discouraged: "Several times she overheard her mother and grandmother discussing her exploits, worrying that she was becoming a tomboy. And gradually she learned that a lady could never be a tomboy" (1982, p. 157). As a result, Nancy "tried to be a little more restrained and to act like a lady" (1982, p. 157). To be a good girl, that is, to conform to societal stereotypes of female behavior, becomes a potent admonishment to follow, and receiving approval for being good emerges as a strong motivation behind the behavior of women.

In contrast to women's motivation to be personally pleasing and accepted, Douvan and Adelson (1966) found that competitive achievement is a major factor contributing to the self-esteem of teenage boys. If women are encouraged to seek approval and acceptance and boys to seek action and accomplishment, then psychologist Rita Freedman's observation that "males seek mastery mainly for its own sake, whereas females often regard mastery as a way of developing relations and gaining approval" belies a fundamental and powerful divergence in the motivating impetus behind the behavior of women and men (1986, p. 103).

Acculturated Sex Differences in the Family: Informal or Implicit Cultural Transmission

While formal cultural learning is more direct and is transmitted through instruction and direct modeling, informal cultural learning is acquired essentially out of awareness. The implicit or tacit level of transmission, as Graebner calls it, is accomplished in such a subtle and pervasive way "that neither teachers nor learners are aware of it, but instead do not look on the definitions of male and female as culture at all, but as part of human nature" (1982, p. 156).

Children learn through formal transmission that they are either boys or girls. But learning how to act as either sex, learning appropriate conventional modes of communication, and learning what society expects from women and men is presumably imparted on subtle or informal levels. These lessons and their evidence are not so subtle, however, when one is expressly examining or questioning cultural values on a microanalytic level.

Through imitative behavior at first, children help their parents around the house. If parents roles are prescribed spatially, young girls and boys learn to become more competent and comfortable in these roles. According to Hall (1966), space talks: The kitchen and laundry room communicate in feminine terms; the garage and den exude a masculine tone. Through initially helpful gestures girls and boys acquire different competencies and perspectives toward what is expected and begin to establish patterns of behavior that will follow them into adulthood. Thus, the husband who asserts, "I am the breadwinner, she is the homemaker. . . . I don't mind her working as long as dinner is ready on time and the house is neat and clean" (Blumstein and Schwartz, 1983, p. 117) or the woman who believes she needs a man to take care of her needs are merely reflecting their ties to these early patterns.

The sex-role expectations initiated in the home are reinforced in school. In their recent study of how fourth, sixth, and eighth graders receive instruction in mathematics, science, language arts, and English, Myra Sadker and David Sadker report that sexism persists in the classroom. These researchers found that despite the articulated advances in education to reduce sexism, "at all grade levels, in all communities and in all subject areas, boys dominated classroom communication. They participated in more interactions than girls did and their participation became greater as the year went on" (1985, p. 56).

This is not simply a matter of initiative. Upon reviewing the classroom tapes, it was learned that teachers treat boys and girls differently. While boys were allowed to call out answers and were given consistent, precise, and positive praise and criticism, girls were expected to behave politely (that is, they were reprimanded when they called out answers without raising their hands), and their responses did not receive the same level of positive reinforcement as boys'. The results of the Sadkers study are significant, for they help to perpetuate many stereotypical assumptions about how women and men are expected to behave.

We have indicated in Table 4-1 several of society's expectations for women and men. Many of these descriptions have come from our students; others have appeared in the works of Bem (1974), Heilbrun (1976), Rubin (1976), and Wheeless and Dierks-Stewart (1981).

The characteristics listed in Table 4-1 are not a function of biological sex differences. Rather, they result from a legacy of expectations and adaptations to meet culturally prescribed behavior. To the extent that the need to conform to society's expectations is compelling, women and men have learned to choose styles of language and nonverbal modes of behavior that reflect cultural norms. Many of these so-called traits are, in fact, inappropriate, exaggerated, or true for both sexes. How these characteristics have been used to shape our attitudes toward men and women and toward their abilities to manage conflict will form the core of the section on attitude.

TABLE 4-1 Gender-Linked Attributes

MASCULINE TRAITS	FEMININE TRAITS
Active	Accessible
Aggressive	Accommodating
Analytical	Appreciative
Assertive	Approachable
Atheltic	Compassionate
Blunt	Compliant
Bold	Considerate
Brash	Coopertive
Candid	Correct
Competitive	Cute
Confident	Dainty
Dark	Demure
Decisive	Dependent
Direct	Emotional
Dominant	Enduring
Egocentric	Fearful
Forceful	Feminine
Handsome	Fickle
Harsh	Flowery
Independent	Forgiving
Individualistic	Friendly
Industrious	Frivolous
Intelligent	Gentle
Logical	Gossipy
Loud	Graceful
Macho	Helpful
Masculine	Indecisive
Outspoken	Intuitive
Physical	Loving
Powerful	Manipulative
Practical	Motherly
Rational	Nurturing
Rude	Open
Self-confident	Perfumed
Sexy	Pleasant
Short-tempered	Poised
Shrewd	Polite
Stern	Pretty
Strong	Quiet
Tall	Refined
Tough	Reserved
Unemotional	Sensitive
Virile	Sentimental
	Sexual
	Sincere
	Submissive
	Sympathetic
	Talkative
	Tender
	Timid
	Understanding
	Warm

ATTITUDE

At the start of our courses that include units on conflict, we ask students to provide their own adjectives or terms to describe what conflict means to them. Responses we obtain continually include "misunderstanding," "disagreement," "hostile", "problem", "aggression," "tension," "confusion," "dispute," "turmoil," "inflexible," and "opposition." The character traits students at first believe are required to deal effectively with conflict include "aggression," "assertiveness," "power," "strength," "intellect," and "understanding."

Initially, many individuals regard conflict as a contest. The traits they deem most appropriate for managing conflict are reflected in their own perceptions of masculine characteristics (see Table 4-1). Although these perceptions are not necessarily accurate, the natural assumption emerges that men are better equipped to deal with the problems that conflicts present because men presumably possess those qualities required for effective conflict management.

As explained in Chapter 1 attitudes, once formed, particularly when these attitudes apply to an entire segment of a population (women or men), can be used to explain behavior, to justify actions, and to limit the activity of others. When this type of ascription occurs, we call it a *stereotype*, a dangerous assumption defined in Webster's dictionary as a "standardized mental picture that is held in common by members of a group and that represents an oversimplified opinion, affective attitude, or uncritical judgment."

Sex-Role Stereotyping

Because gender (like ethnicity) is an immutable trait, stereotyping remarks that target gender or race are particularly pernicious. Consider the following example: "Most corporate executives are men. Executive tasks should be performed by men. Men are analytical, aggressive and competitive. Thus, women should not assume executive positions in corporations."

This example, sadly, is typical of the kind of stereotyping that exists in U.S. culture. It is modeled on Williams and Best's syllogism for sex stereotyping. If we examine the example, we see that "sex roles" ("most corporate executives are men"), "are often 'explained' by reference to sex-role stereotypes" ("executive tasks should be performed by men"), "which in turn are 'explained' by reference to sex-trait stereotypes" ("men are analytical, aggressive, and competitive") (1982, p. 16). The conclusion one is expected to draw from the example is that because the traits required to perform executive responsibilities are those that supposedly belong to men, men make better executives than women.

Although the syllogism presented is fallacious, the belief or attribution of qualities to one group of people often provides sufficient justification to attempt to exclude qualified individuals from attaining positions of authority in many companies. More than denying individuals access to positions or roles, ascribing attributes to individuals solely on the basis of gender serves to perpetuate pervasive gender-linked socialization that subtly leads women and men in disparate and often limiting directions.

To dispel stereotypes it is important first to acknowledge their existence and our attitudes toward them. Second, it is important to understand why stereotyping occurs. Only after identifying and explaining stereotyped behaviors are we able to examine their veracity.

Gender-Linked Stereotypes as Barriers to Effective Conflict Management

Communication skills required for effective conflict management include openness, clarity, assertiveness, empathy, credibility, flexibility, and the ability to listen. Many of the assumptions about how women and men communicate, however, conflict directly with the above-mentioned skills and cast doubt on the effectiveness of both sexes to engage in productive conflict management. Some of the following limiting assumptions about women's and men's behavior have been commented upon by Borisoff and Merrill (1985), Eakins and Eakins (1978), Hall (1984), Henley (1977), Kramarae (1981), Lakoff (1975), Pearson (1985), and Zimmerman and West (1975).

Women are compliant and tentative in their assertions.
Men make generalizations and sweeping claims.
Women's speech lacks power and is hyperpolite.
Men's speech is forceful, often offensive.
Women's voices belie weakness and emotion.
Men are inexpressive.
Women are unable to assert their concerns—they are often silenced.
Men dominate conversations and interrupt others.
Women and men listen differently: she listens too much; he, not enough.
Women's smiling behavior often masks their true feelings.
Men are unable to express their true feelings and emotions.
Women can better read the nonverbal behavior of others because they are less powerful than men.

Several studies have disproved many of the above claims (i.e., men listen more than assumed, women do not end declarative sentences with a questioning tone, the more successful and liberated woman is a better nonverbal decoder than women in subordinate positions). Despite these findings, however, more often than not, stereotypes rather than actual data govern our assumptions about the communicative behavior of women and men (Edelsky, 1979; Williams and Best, 1982).

McClelland has argued that "sex role turns out to be one of the most important determinants of human behavior" (1975, p. 81). Unfortunately, determining differences in behavior has been accompanied with assigning pejorative connotations to this behavior. Since male behavior has traditionally been regarded as the norm, female behavior is often regarded as a deviation from that norm. McClelland also adds that this deviation is considered less valuable.

Women and men are limited by society's assumptions and prescriptions for their behavior. We can evaluate and hopefully alter many of these expectations and attitudes once we understand the process of stereotyping.

Processes of Stereotyping and Cultural Acquisition

In their work on cross-cultural communication barriers Borisoff and Victor (1987) propose that how we acquire, use, and interpret cultural variations provides a useful basis for addressing how and why individuals develop their own belief and behavior systems. In this process we find that the cultural expectations and stereotyping of women are consistent with pan-cultural evaluations.

Social psychological research provides several factors that contribute to stereotyping behavior. Williams and Best (1982) consider stereotyping behavior. They point to implicit personality theory to explain sex stereotyping and gender.

Implicit Personality Theory

Cross-cultural theorist Triandis (1976) postulates that because culture is created by humans, different subjective cultures exist that reflect diverse nationalities, religions, social classes, occupations, languages, geographical environments and sex. During interaction with others we bring our own expectations and assumptions about how these individuals should act. These assumptions are based on our own self-concepts and experiences.

Williams and Best maintain that these assumptions or stereotypes "create expectancies about the behavior of other persons and may allow us to anticipate their behavior as well as the consequences of our own behavior. Once a person's sex has been identified, our implicit personality theories regarding women and men are engaged and lead to assumptions about the personal attributes possessed by the target person" (1982, p. 276). Thus, if we expect that men are more assertive and are able to deal with conflict more effectively than women, we are likely to interact with them according to our own preconceived notions of how we expect them to act, regardless of whether our beliefs are justified. Two important factors that influence the processes of stereotyping are the need for cognitive consistency and motivational factors.

A recent study on negotiating tactics of women and men in fact contradicts many pervasive stereotypes about women's purported weakness in negotiating situations (Womack, 1987). While it is likely that many of the communication behaviors of women studied in the 1970's still persist, many strategies that belied powerlessness have been replaced by more assertive behavior, which reflects the professional and personal progress women have made in the last decade.

Cognitive consistency Hall's (1961) contention that our intimate knowledge of the informal aspects of a particular culture allows us to function predictably and thus successfully has been widely accepted. Indeed, our society would be chaotic and unmanageable if we had no prior knowledge or justified ability to predict the behavior of others.

Whereas the implicit personality theory explains how we regard another's behavior in relation to our own, the theory on cognitive consistency purports that once our belief systems have been found, we seek experiences and interactions that will tend to confirm and strengthen these beliefs. Consequently, if we have come to expect that women should be nurturing, polite, and self-effacing, we may be at a loss to deal with those women who in contrast evidence independent, assertive, and competitive behavior, for we lack in our cultural repertoire the responses to deal with these ostensibly defiant actions. We may similarly be at a loss to deal with men who prefer to avoid rather than confront a problem because the behaviors displayed by these men and women are not *consistent* with the expectation we have formed for both sexes.

Such expectations inform our proclivity for clinging tenaciously to assumptions about men and women—assumptions, as mentioned earlier, that span at least the 29 nations surveyed by Williams and Best (1982).

It is important to note that our attitudes about men (dominant, independent, forceful, adventurous, strong-willed, and masculine) and about women (submissive, sentimental, superstitious, dependent, emotional) are rooted in role assignments. If women, because of their biological ability to bear children, came naturally into their role as nurturer to their offspring, we can see why this attribute for women persists (regardless of men's capability to be nurturing). If men, because of their physical strength and size, came naturally into their role as protector, we can see why this attribute for men persists (regardless of women's capability to be strong and forceful).

It matters little what quality one ascribes to women and men. What matters greatly, however, is the connotation (often pejorative for women) that accompanies the label (Borisoff and Merrill, 1985; Henley, 1977; Kramarae, 1981; Lakoff, 1975; Pearson, 1985). Because cultural expectations are so resistant to change, it would appear that more than legislative acts are required to reshape men's and women's attitudes.

Motivational factors for stereotyping   Another important factor in the stereotyping process is how men and women, boys and girls, are socialized. To cite Williams and Best, "As one learns that certain characteristics are considered appropriate for one's own gender, and other characteristics for the other gender, these belief systems become intimately involved in personality identity" (1982, p. 278).

We learn what is culturally appropriate and acceptable. We learn the common bonds that set us apart from others different from ourselves. Little boys learn that competitiveness, independence, strength, and intelligence are desirable and appropriate qualities. For men, to pursue feminine endeavors, interests, and traits is to risk negative sanctions from society. Little girls learn that cooperation, dependence, compliance, and beauty are desirable and appropriate traits. For women, to succeed in a male-dominated context is often to jeopardize their femininity and to risk prejorative labels (Putnam, 1983).

The double bind becomes apparent. To succeed as a male boys must learn to reject what is feminine (Stockard and Johnson, 1980). To succeed as a female girls must learn that in many situations to pursue a male model of communication is unacceptable and to act in a feminine way is equally criticized. Despite evidence to the contrary McClelland's (1975) observation that along with being different, women's behavior persists in being regarded as worse or deviant from the norm (male behavior).

Thus attitudes toward behavior with others are shaped by these motivational factors. In the area of conflict management these differences are important. In their study on gender differences in negotiation strategies, Gilkey and Greenhalgh (1984) found that men tend to view bargaining situations as short-term and episodic in nature, while women tend to view transactions with others as part of a long-term relationship. Consequently, that the women studied adopted more flexible bargaining stances than their male counterparts can be explained by this attitude toward the length of relationships. But this difference in negotiating behavior can also be explained by what Gilligan (1979) describes as women's concern for the quality of interpersonal relationships.

It is significant that the factors that impel the behavior of women and men are distinct. It is significant that in conflict situations, as Hocker and Wilmot (1985) point out, what constitutes a reward for one sex may be of relatively little value to the other. The differences between women and men, like those between nations, are rife with misunderstandings, and potential stereotyping. This type of destructive labelling serves primarily to perpetuate the barriers that have been created between the sexes—barriers that can only be eliminated through mutual understanding. (The parallels here to cross-cultural relationships are strong and will be addressed in Chapter 5.

At this point, we can return to the sex-typed syllogism presented at the beginning of this section. If a business executive has spent a lifetime developing what for him represents manly success and to achieve this he has had to set himself apart from what are considered feminine roles and traits, he may be hard-pressed to accept a woman as embodying those very qualities that have contributed to his own self-image as a man. The fallacy in the above conclusion is that to possess what are regarded as positive qualities as a man is not mutually exclusive from the values of being a woman. Each gender has values, ideas, and understandings, some shared, some apart. It is the willingness to expand one's own notion of accept-ability, of success, of positive attributes that we advocate. It is the ability not only to learn our own culture on the "informal" level but also to practice cultural acceptance of women and men equally so that we can begin to break down the barriers that persist in preventing true understanding among human beings.

ACTION

In her work on the psychology of power Hilary Lips (1981) contends that agonic power derives from physical strength, education, money, status—sources that have traditionally been more accessible to men. Because women have typically been denied access to the same opportunities as men, they have been forced to resort to indirect or hedonic modes of influence, such as using their appearance and adopting communication strategies that are neither nonthreatening nor construed as too assertive. Power imbalance in the communication styles of men and women is the focus of works by Borisoff and Merrill (1985), Eakins and Eakins (1978), Hall (1984), Henley (1977), Lakoff (1975), Kramarae (1981), and Pearson (1985).

If we turn to examples of direct and indirect modes of male and female communicative behavior, we will see that many of the conventions of both sexes may serve as either barriers to, or facilitators of, effective conflict management. We will also address many stereotypical behaviors presented in the section on attitude to determine the veracity of these behaviors and their impact on managing conflict.

Gender-Linked Verbal Differences and Their Effect on Conflict Management

Vocabulary

Many criteria exist by which we evaluate the effectiveness, credibility, and power of a speaker. How we voice our ideas and concerns affects the way we are listened to and judged. But the words we choose to articulate our ideas equally reflects not only how we regard ourselves but also how others will respond to us.

In each speech act, according to Cora Kaplan (1976), the self and the culture are reflected simultaneously. Because men and women have access to and are expected to employ distinct lexical choices, the linguistic culture differs for both sexes. More than reflecting diversity, though, the words that men and women choose to reflect their ideas, concerns, or values have divergent connotations: Men's word choices reflect power and assertiveness; women's vocabulary connotes weakness and passiveness.

Adverbs of intensity, (i.e., carefully, such, terribly, so), and the adjectives adorable, cute, divine, heavenly, and lovely, for example, are found more in women's speech. Clearly, until recently, Lakoff's (1975) contention that strong language was the domain of men and polite language the norm for women was fully accepted.

A study by Staley (1978) revealed that women and men have more lexical ground in common than previously thought. Although her research demonstrated that women and men are equally cognizant of expletives and their usage, her work also showed that the perception persists that women use such words less frequently. The notion that women are more polite than men in and of itself is not a problem unless politeness is equated with weakness, hesitancy, and incompetence.

Clarity and confidence are two important traits for effective conflict management. A statement such as "I'm awfully upset with your actions" or "We have such terribly little time left to go to contract" have far less impact than the more direct assertion "I'm upset with your actions" or "We have little time left to go to contract." Individuals who employ words that are regarded as weak or precious need to assess how assertive they wish to sound and adjust their vocabulary to reflect accurately the image they wish to convey.

Qualifiers

Qualifiers (such as somewhat, in my opinion, maybe, perhaps, and sort of), have typically been more indicative of women's speech. These phrases, when interjected into a direct statement, reflect the speaker's uncertainty or tentativeness and serve to weaken the statement.

There are inappropriate and appropriate uses of qualifiers. In a conflict situation where it is important to articulate clearly one's goals, ideas, and feelings, the use of qualifiers can seriously damage the strength and credibility of one's assertions. "I'm sort of disappointed that I wasn't promoted." "Maybe I deserve a raise" and "Perhaps we need to meet this deadline" have far less effect than the more direct "I'm disappointed I wasn't promoted," "I deserve a raise," or "We need to meet this deadline."

Because qualifiers soften the impact of assertions, however, when situations arise where the channels of communication between conflicting parties have been closed or severely damaged, the use of qualifiers may also indicate a willingness to communicate about a problem. For example, the statements "Perhaps we should discuss this over lunch," or "Maybe we should think about the situation for a few days," allow the other party to participate in the decision-making process regarding how to address the problem.

It is important for individuals to determine the appropriate use of qualifiers. In cases where qualifiers are employed to soften statements that are intended as assertions, it is especially useful for individuals to understand the message they want to convey and to communicate that message as clearly as possible without qualification.

Disclaimers

A major intention of communicative acts is to share feelings, ideas, and information with others. The use of disclaimers creates a barrier to communication because this type of hedging serves instead to separate the speaker from the listener and to reflect in part an apology for asserting one's ideas or feelings.

Disclaimers are words or phrases that diminish the speaker's statement or request. "I'm probably wrong but . . ." and "I'm no authority, however . . ." when preceding statements for which the speaker does not wish to claim full responsibility are examples of disclaimers. In both examples the listener is given the option or power to accept the speaker's claim ("That's correct, you are wrong because . . .") or to reject it ("You are as much of an authority as I . . .")

Cases exist where disclaimers can have positive or negative consequences in a conflict situation. In Chapter 1, one of the steps listed to ensure effective conflict management included keeping the channels of communication open in an atmosphere that supports interaction. When these channels have been closed, the use of disclaimers to distance oneself from one's assertions may facilitate interaction. Such statements as "I may have misinterpreted your report" or "Perhaps I misunderstood your intentions, however . . ." are intended to engage the other party in a discussion about the report and the intentions.

In conflict or potential conflict situations where it is important for both parties to retain their power until the conflict can be successfully managed or resolved, however, we would discourage the use of disclaimers that abrogate responsibility for assertions. To the extent that women are thought to include disclaimers in their discourse with greater frequency than men, they should be cognizant of how their authority can be greatly diminished when they choose to disassociate themselves from, or to apologize for, their assertions.

Fillers

In dyadic communication such fillers as "I see," "go on," and "un huh" serve to encourage the speaker to continue. Zimmerman and West (1975) and West and Zimmerman (1983) in their studies of men and women in naturalistic and laboratory settings and Fishman's (1977, 1978) findings from her observations of three middle-class families confirm that in mixed-sex dyads women employ more fillers than men. Conversely, women who attempt to speak often receive minimal responses from men that serve instead to discourage or to disconfirm their attempts to communicate.

Women and men need to be aware that these gender-linked behaviors can present enormous difficulties when attempting to manage conflict. In a conflict situation it is important for both parties to be able to articulate fully their concerns in an atmosphere that is supportive and conducive to communication.

Individuals who employ fillers to encourage another's communication are likely to obtain a great deal of information necessary to resolve or to manage a problem. Those, however, who employ fillers to disconfirm or discontinue communication are likely to discourage the disclosure necessary to satisfactorily resolve or manage the conflict.

Syntactical and Structural Differences and Verbal Contexts

Tag Questions

Like disclaimers that often reveal hesitancy in speech, the addition of such tags as "isn't that so?" or "don't you think?" to declarative statements may also serve to weaken the impact of the statement and to discredit the speaker who appears unable or unwilling to assert him- or herself.

Pearson (1985, p. 189) summarizes five appropriate uses of tag questions. They can be used legitimately to (1) clarify information ("He's taking this new job, isn't he?"), (2) elicit information ("This is a round-trip ticket, isn't it?"), (3) obtain an answer to a question ("The fireworks display was spectacular, wasn't it?"), and (5) persuade another person to share your viewpoint ("It would be fun to go camping this summer, don't you think?").

When tag questions are used as a means to avoid asserting one's beliefs or ideas, however, ("The administration is being pretty unfair with its budget, don't you think?" or "My report seems good, doesn't it?"), the speaker is allowing the listener the power to agree or disagree and in a sense make a judgment through his or her response.

Zimmerman and West (1975) confirm that women employ tag questions more frequently than do men. Moreover, women use tag questions in ways that diminish the impact of their statements (Lakoff, 1975). More recently, however, it was further determined that even when men use tag questions, they are regarded as more intelligent and knowledgeable than women who employ similar devices (Bradley, 1980).

In a conflict situation where it is necessary to appear credible, intelligent, articulate, and clear, it is especially important for women not to use tag questions to avoid asserting their opinions and ideas in a forceful and legitimate way. "I'm being unfair to you" is far more effective than "I'm not really being unfair to you, am I?" when trying to explain or to defend one's actions.

Compound Requests

A manager tells her subordinate, "If it wouldn't be too much trouble, I would like you to try to complete the report by Friday morning." When the report is not on her desk, the manager becomes enraged and accuses her assistant of being totally irresponsible. The assistant defends himself by arguing that he had assumed his boss was asking him to try to finish the report "if it wouldn't be too much trouble." Because he had other pressing deadlines, he thought he could postpone this assignment.

This conflict of understanding occurred because the manager employed a compound request rather than making a direct request such as "I need the completed report by Friday morning," or "Please give me the completed report on Friday morning."

Compound requests soften statements and make the speaker appear more polite and less assertive. Research indicates that women employ this linguistic form more frequently than men (Zimmerman and West, 1975). If women are described as employing compound, as opposed to direct, requests too often, men, in contrast, are frequently accused of being overly direct and terse in their requests. "I need the report immediately" may be intended as a request but may be understood as a command. The potential for dissatisfaction and conflict with the listener is likely to increase if the intended and received messages are not reconciled.

While we do not advocate either form of questioning—for in many instances direct and indirect strategies are appropriate—we would encourage women and men to consider how they communicate their requests. We would further suggest they reflect upon how others respond to them and the extent to which their requests are satisfactorily met.

Control of Topic

The ability to introduce and maintain a topic of conversation is ostensibly a simple act of assertion. On closer inspection, however, we find that most relationships are contextually hierarchical (i.e., employer and employee, parent and child, doctor and patient, teacher and student, etc.). In addition, the situational propriety, according to sociologist Erving Goffman (1963), allows power to reside with the individual who in a particular situation or environment holds power.

For example, a doctor may wield tremendous influence in his or her office, but this power currency is diminished significantly when he or she is off duty. We would assume, however, that in the environments reflected by the aforementioned hierarchies, the individual in a greater position of authority will control the topics and regulate the flow of conversation.

While a power imbalance in topic and conversational control is understandable in an overt hierarchical structure such as in a corporation, university, hospital, or school, even in situations where no overt power imbalance exists, a discrepancy still remains in topic control and length of speaking when the communicating parties are women and men. Fishman's (1977, 1978) findings in familial relationships (presumably of equal status) and Eakins and Eakins's (1978) evaluation of college professors (presumably colleagues of equal status) reveal that even in the absence of an overt hierarchical system, there is an implicit hierarchy based on gender. In both the social and professional contexts, men introduce more topics and speak with greater frequency and for longer intervals than women.

Effective conflict management depends on shared communication. While individuals who normally dominate interaction need to monitor their own patterns of communication, those who allow their ideas to be ignored or suppressed must be equally responsible for asserting themselves. For example, if there is disagreement at a department meeting about how to implement a project, a manager who states, "I have three questions regarding the process that I would like to address before we continue with the next agenda item" will be more likely to assure that her concerns will be addressed than if she were to remain silent.

Interruptions and Overlaps

When individuals are engaged in conversation, certain rules of etiquette are expected (that is, allow each participant a voice, indicate active listening through appropriate verbal and nonverbal cues, provide feedback, etc.). While we would expect all parties to have equal access to and participation in a conversation, studies indicate the contrary.

As part of the research by Eakins and Eakins (1978), Fishman (1977, 1978), West and Zimmerman (1983), and Zimmerman and West (1975), it was demonstrated that in mixed-sex dyads, men control conversations. Two ways that this regulation is demonstrated is through interruptions and overlaps (cases when individuals speak simultaneously).

The use of interruptions and overlaps can be explained by the following rationales: (1) one individual is unable to contain his or her enthusiasm and interrupts or overlaps; (2) one individual believes that what he or she has to say "can't wait" because it is more important than the speaker's message, and/or (3) one individual believes that he or she is personally more important than the speaker.

Pearson's (1985) second and third explanations for interrupting behavior are sobering indeed. When one sex explicitly evidences this type of behavior, the other sex is likely to receive clearly the implicit message that what he or she has to say is less important and further that it is acceptable for his or her own assertions to be regulated by others.

The use or avoidance of interruptions and overlaps in conflict situations can be defended depending upon the nature and desired outcome of the conflict. In an adversarial context interruptions or overlaps can be a useful strategy to confuse or to stop an opponent. For example, on numerous occasions during Lieutenant Colonel Oliver North's testimony at the congressional Iran-Contra hearings, North's attorney, Brendan Sullivan, employed interruptions forcefully and effectively to control lines of questioning that could be detrimental to his client.

In a conflict situation where compromise or collaboration is indicated, it is important for both sides to be able to articulate their cases confident that their assertions will proceed uninterrupted. Women who are socially conditioned to be polite and not interrupt may experience difficulty interrupting others. Their tendency to allow and encourage full communication in others can, however, be an asset when attempting to manage or mediate a conflict.

It is important for both women and men to understand when interrupting is called for and to avoid inappropriate interrupting behavior or not allow themselves to be interrupted unnecessarily. When interruptions belie dominance, we encourage individuals to develop intervention strategies, such as asserting themselves directly. For example, they could say, "Please let me finish," "I haven't finished speaking," or "You are interrupting me. Let me finish," which are intended to discourage interruptions.

Impact of Gender-Linked Nonverbal Communication on Conflict Behavior

Verbal conventions that differ according to sex are matched by differences in nonverbal gender-linked behavior. While Kramarae (1981) contends that women's indirect speech patterns (such as tag questions, compound requests, and disclaimers) developed because, as a muted group, women needed to create strategies to allow their voices to be heard, psychologist Judith Hall (1984) posits a similar justification for sex differences in nonverbal communication. Gender-linked behavior in the areas of proxemics, kinesics, oculesics, haptics, paralanguage, and artifactual communication are indicative, according to Hall and other researchers, of women's subordinate position in our culture (Hall calls this "oppression hypothesis,"p. xi).

Regardless of the explanation as to why differences in nonverbal communication of women and men developed, we will see that the nonverbal behavior of both sexes imposes certain limitations on, and provides, positive values to effective conflict management.

Space

Territorial space in U.S. culture represents a strong determinant of power (that is the size of an office, the physical size of an individual—

especially height, location, and size of residence, and so on). Comfortable interpersonal spatial distance, however, varies according to sex; moreover, it is affected by the relationship between individuals. Thus, spatial distance as a sign of power or dominance is more problematic and cannot be so easily ascribed to one sex.

Studies on boys and girls ages 8 to 15, and on college students, for example, reveal that spatial distance is determined by the knowledge of and attitude toward the other person. Whereas girls maintain greater distances between themselves and strangers and/or individuals whom they either fear or dislike, boys maintain a greater distance from those they like or from friends (Knowles, 1980; Meisels and Guardo, 1969). Thus, interpersonal spatial distance appears to be a function of the willingness to affiliate with others.

Although several naturalistic studies have demonstrated that men approach women at closer distances than women approach men, these results may be more a function of context rather than an attribution of power. In other words, if the opposite-sex individuals who approached one another were friends, it is possible that opposite results might have been obtained. A further explanation why men in these studies approach women more closely may also be a function of women's orientation toward acts of affiliation, which Hall (1984) maintains encourages rather than discourages physical proximity.

If men more willingly approach strangers and enemies, adversarial conflict or competition with unknown others may be more easily handled by those who have been acculturated to demonstrate aggressive or confrontative behavior. If women more willingly allow spatial proximity with friends or liked others because closeness belies attempts at affiliation, proximity under such circumstances could enhance disclosure, empathy, and openness, which facilitate conflict-handling behavior.

Kinesics and Oculesics

Kinesics or body language (gestures, facial expression, posture, bodily movements) and oculesics, or eye contact, also reflect cultural variation in women and men. The way we deport ourselves, the way we act or react toward others nonverbally speaks volumes about how we feel and may, in fact, be a more accurate indication of how we feel than what we say (Birdwhistell, 1970; Knapp, 1980; Mehrabian, 1972).

Barriers to effective transactional communication and to effective conflict management emerge when our nonverbal behavior is incongruous with verbal assertions, is inappropriate, or is confusing.

Two directors who have had a major disagreement about a subordinate encounter one another after work. The first director states: "I realize I came down hard on Ms. Jones today. No hard feelings, I hope." The second director responds, "No. None," and walks away. Although he is ostensibly acquiescing verbally, if the second director's facial expression conveys anger, then the first director is likely to assume that although his colleague's verbal and nonverbal behavior are incongruous, the nonverbal expression of distress reflects his true feelings despite his verbal assertions to the contrary.

A worker is dissatisfied because her attempts to discuss work-related problems with her supervisor are continually thwarted. He presumably maintains an open-door policy. Yet every time she tries to approach him with a problem, his nonverbal behavior discourages her. Although he invites her into his office to talk to him, the way he looks at the ceiling, taps his desk, increases his rate of speaking, and tightens his lips conveys his unwillingness to engage in productive dialogue.

A husband and wife continually battle over how they express their anger. The husband becomes particularly enraged whenever his wife smiles in response to his raised voice. His ire is exacerbated further by the fact that he is fully aware that his spouse is extremely upset.

The three examples reflect instances where individuals receive conflicting and therefore confusing messages because the nonverbal communication clearly gives a message opposite to what is articulated. In the case of the two directors the first director is likely to be annoyed with his colleague's mixed message, especially since in his estimation he has offered an apology that has been refused nonverbally. In the second example the employee will eventually mistrust her boss's empty words because his nonverbal behavior during their meetings eloquently communicates that he does not want these meetings to occur. In the third instance the husband's frustration with his wife's behavior is likely to remain unresolved until she is able to communicate her feelings honestly and consistently.

Although a male model of kinesic and oculesic behavior (i.e., expansive gestures and body movements, sustained and controlled eye contact, and facial expressions that are not too revealing) seems initially to be a model for effective conflict management, we would caution that such a model would appear to be effective only in instances where aggression and competition are warranted. Women caught in a conflict that requires such strategies must monitor their own behavior so that their own assertions can be articulated. When women mask their true feelings with false smiles or avert their gaze in cases where sustained eye contact would signal equality in an interaction, such behavior may be construed as an indication that women are more submissive or weaker than men (Henley, 1977). Such assumptions, true or false, can be debilitating in conflict situations where accurate communication and assertiveness are required.

Despite the aforementioned apparent limitations of women's behavior, women's nonverbal behavior can also be an asset in a conflict situation. Women are socialized to be more polite and self-disclosing. Further, they are able to decode and encode vocal and facial cues more accurately than men (Henley, 1974; Rosenthal and DePaulo, 1979a; 1979b).

Borisoff and Merrill contend that the ability of women to demonstrate their own and to interpret accurately the nonverbal behavior of others reflects two important traits of a negotiator:

> First, accurate responses to another's feelings reflects sensitivity to the other party. Second, without empathic bonds between the parties in conflict, the likelihood for reaching a satisfactory solution is diminished. When women connect with the feelings and concerns of others—even if they are not in agreement—they are demonstrating empathy, which is essential for bargaining and negotiating to be truly productive. (1987, p. 357)

Haptics

There is a strong perception that women receive more touch and are touched more by men because they are weaker and more vulnerable (Henley, 1977). Recent studies, however, reveal conflicting information on who receives more touch and further, that same-sex touch exceeds opposite-sex touch (Hall, 1984).

Touch has many meanings. On the one hand, it can convey warmth, affection, or interest in the other party. In contrast, it can reflect anger, or abuse and be used as a punitive measure. Whether touch is reciprocal (initiated by both parties) or unilateral (initiated by one party) depends upon several factors: (1) the relationship of the parties involved (that is, parent and child, husband and wife, employer and employee, doctor and nurse, colleague and colleague), (2) the age of the individuals, (3) the context of the relationship or encounter (that is, the home, an institution or professional office, a wedding, a sporting event, etc.), and (4) the culture's attitude toward touching behavior. Cross-cultural differences toward touching behavior are addressed in Chapter 5.

The act of touching another individual is open to diverse interpretations and can serve to defuse or incite conflict. While touch often belies attempts to affiliate, to encourage, or to empathize with the other party—acts that can be constructive in conflict management—touch can also reflect efforts to control or to impose one's will on another. A male supervisor lightly touches the arm of a female colleague and states that he would like to discuss their disagreement. The woman is likely to interpret his touch as an attempt at reconciliation and respond positively to such action. If an individual receives unwarranted touch despite efforts to discourage this action, however, the other party (male or female) may find him- or herself embroiled in a conflict when he or she is accused of sexual harrassment.

It is important for women and men to examine carefully both their motivations for touching and their responses when others touch them. Such scrutiny can do much to dispel the prevalent negative stereotypes about tactile behavior between women and men.

Paralanguage

Because the model for effective conflict behavior has been based primarily on male forms of expression, the paralinguistic modes ascribed to men have gone largely unquestioned (especially nonexpressiveness, louder volume, and lower pitch). In contrast, an often-cited rationale for keeping women from advancing toward, or being hired for, certain positions is that their voices do not sound sufficiently authoritative. They are described as sounding soft spoken and as speaking in a nonthreatening high pitched voice. When women employ rising inflections, this tendency may convey tentativeness. Finally, when women use standard speech norms, they are frequently viewed as sounding too proper.

Clearly, when one is dealing with conflict management the attributes ascribed to women's voices become debilitating labels. If credibility, self-confidence, and assertiveness are requisite communication skills for effective conflict management, then it is incumbent upon women to adopt those conventions which will reflect strength and assuredness.

The bind for women especially can be explained by Kramarae's strategy model (1981, p. 118). Because women and men have traditionally had different resources and different amounts of legitimate power, they are required to use different strategies to obtain their goals, "Because of the implicit and explicit power differentials, women and men will employ different strategies to shape events and influence others." Women's verbal conventions and structures (as discussed earlier in this chapter) and the way these are conveyed have done much to damage women's credibility, particularly in the workplace.

Basia Hellwig (1985) has indicated that many consulting firms maintain that women's ability to assume positions of authority is often challenged because women are considered too emotional and passive to deal with conflict. This perception is slowly changing. Many placement firms confirm that women in positions of authority employ collaborative conflict-handling behavior—a mode that Putnam and Wilson (1982) and Thomas and Kilmann (1977) defend as a highly productive conflict-management style.

Women and men are working together in similar professional situations and settings. Such proximity has resulted in a greater sharing of attitudes and behaviors. Women are learning to adopt and express many aspects of communicative behavior that reflect self-assuredness, strength, and power. Men, too, are encouraged to adopt strategies that reflect empathy, emotion, and accessibility. By encouraging flexibility in their communication strategies, by advocating that men learn how to identify and express more empathic responses and that women practice modes of more direct expression, individuals may well achieve the androgynous communication techniques that presume the best human communication traits.

ANALYSIS

Saul Bellow's protagonist in *More Die of Heartbreak* describes one way individuals can hope to better themselves:

> The way to change for the better is to begin by telling everybody about it. You make an announcement. You repeat your intentions until others begin to repeat them to you. When you hear them from others you can say, "Yes, that's what I think too." The more often your intention is repeated, the truer it becomes. The key is fluency. It's fluency of formulation that matters most. (1987, pp. 90-91)

Bellow's words belie a subtle process through which women and men can begin to effect changes in how they are perceived as communicators and, moreover, in how they can initiate changes in their own conflict-management styles. We do not advocate that one conflict-handling mode is superior. The situation, the rewards or goals at stake, the players in the conflict, and their relationship to one another will determine how they should address a conflict.

Until recently, a male mode of communication provided the standard against which women's communication styles were measured. Because of divergent acculturation processes and societal expectations, women learned a different communication style that has largely been regarded as weaker, less assertive, less effective—in effect, inferior. Jessie Bernard (1981, p. 384) concludes in her analysis of women's communication behavior that this style has greatly inhibited the accepted leadership skills required in many professional positions. Because of their inability to speak with precision and force, women have been at a disadvantage in serious discussions.

Much of women's ostensible inability to compete successfully with men or to articulate forcefully their concerns stemmed, according to Matina Horner (1972), from a perceived conflict between femininity and success (or "fear of success"). Gilligan (1979) has ascribed this fear of success in part to women's sensitivity to and concern for the needs of others.

Understanding the sources of divergence in the communicative behavior of women and men has led to a revaluation of the communication strategies of both sexes. No longer, Kramarae (1981) cautions, should society assume that successful women should behave like men. No longer are men criticized for being expressive and nurturant. In fact, they should be encouraged to be so.

The attributes of an effective negotiator include clarity, trust, empathy, openmindedness, confidence, flexibility, fairness, and the ability to listen and to present constructive suggestions. These traits are the purview neither of women nor of men but are skills more descriptive of an androgynous model of communication. To manage or to resolve disagreements and to prevent many unnecessary problems from developing, we recommend that while we continue to scrutinize the sex-role related patterns of behavior that have led to debilitating stereotypes for both sexes, we strengthen those traits which allow for effective human communication. Only by repeatedly asserting to others those qualities in ourselves which reflect effective communication are we able in Bellow's terms to be perceived and to thus perceive ourselves as having made progress.

SUMMARY

McClelland (1975) has observed that sex role is perhaps the most significant determinant of the behavior of women and men. That women's and men's roles may differ is not a problem. What is problematic, however, is the fact that one style of communication—a male style—has been traditionally considered the norm (Deaux, 1983). The behavior of women, in contrast, has been traditionally regarded as a deviation from that norm and has, in turn, been devalued (McClelland, 1975; Kramarae, 1981). Women and men find themselves increasingly in collegial positions at work. Additionally, both sexes are striving to redefine their personal relationships. Because of these revaluations of their relationships, women and men are forced to confront not only how effectively they communicate with one another but also the conflicts that arise when change is implied.

Using the five-step model for managing conflict, this chapter focuses on how the communicative behavior of men and women reflect in part the way individuals articulate their differences. Moreover, this chapter explores how the styles of communication of both sexes are interpreted.

During the first, or assessment step, women and men need to consider how gender may affect the nature of (1) the relationship, (2) the conflict, and (3) the communication climate to make a preliminary determination of the appropriate conflict-managing behavior. It is important to recall that what might constitute a reward for one sex may not be considered as significant for the other.

Second, men and women need to acknowledge the differences in their upbringing that reflect both explicit and implicit acculturation processes. How both sexes acquire and become a part of U.S. culture also informs their perspectives and behavior.

The impact of gender differences on attitude formation forms the third step in how both sexes can approach conflict management. The fact that women and men are raised differently and are encouraged to display distinct behavior contributes to the formation and sustenance of sex-trait stereotypes. All too often, sex-trait stereotypes are used as a basis for sex-role stereotyping. The literature on conflict management indicates that communication skills required for effective conflict-handling behavior include openness, clarity, empathy, credibility, flexibility, assertiveness, and the ability to listen (Deutsch, 1971, 1973a and b; Hocker and Wilmot, 1985; Wolvin and Coakley, 1985). Many assumptions about how women and men communicate, however, conflict directly with the above-mentioned skills and create skepticism about the ability of both sexes to engage in productive conflict management.

Until individuals are able to put aside the sex-trait stereotypes that serve to prescribe, define, and limit the roles and behavior of both sexes, the stereotypical attitudes about how individuals are able to address and manage conflict will continue to be a barrier to productive communication.

The effects of gender formation on the communication strategies for conflict management form the fourth, or action, step in our communication model. Effective conflict management depends on shared communication. Much has been written, however, to indicate that women and men do not share equally in their verbal and nonverbal communication. Each sex has different access to and has learned to manifest different overt communication behavior. Semantic choices, syntactic structure, and nonverbal communication have prescribed limits for each sex. Moreover, these choices are assigned a qualitative value.

Recently, women and men have been encouraged to alter and to expand their communication repertoire. Men have been encouraged to embrace modes of communication that allow for accessibility, emotion, and flexibility. Women, too, have been advised to develop communication strategies that reflect self-assuredness, power, and strength. In the final analysis stage, how adept individuals are in pursuing communication strategies that reflect human, rather than gender-linked traits, will have a significant effect on their abilities to productively manage conflict.

SUGGESTED ACTIVITIES

The following exercises focus on gender differences and conflict management.

A. Focus on female-male conflict styles

Participants are asked to view on television one situation comedy and one serious television series. Both shows should involve women and men as part of the regular cast. After watching these shows, discussion should focus on the following:

    a. Describe and define the types of conflicts that occurred between the protagonists

    b. What conflict style(s) did the men use; the women?

    c. Were the styles in question (b) stereotypical or accurate representations of women's and men's responses for the given situation(s)?

d. Specify your answer to (c) by indicating the verbal and nonverbal communication behavior of the actors.

B. Focus on self-evaluation of conflcit handling behavior

Each student or seminar participant should write down a conflict situation in which he or she participated.

Address the following:

a. How did you behave in the situation? (avoiding, accommodating, competing, compromising, collaborating) Describe specifically your behavior.

b. Were you satisfied with the way you dealt with the problem? If yes, defend your actions. If not, how would you act if the same situation were to again occur? What would you do differently?

c. Did your behavior conform or deviate from the sex role–related expectations for your gender?

C. Focus on gender differences and nonverbal cues

Either using the same television programs in example A or selecting different programs, have students or seminar participants watch a program with the sound turned off. Select one male and one female character. Using the following chart, fill in the kinds of actions that demonstrate that the characters are angry:

	Male character	Female character
Kinesics		
Oculesics (eye contact/gaze)		
Facial expression		
Gestures		
Posture		
Bodily movements		
Proxemics (Use of space)		
Haptics		
Kinds of touch		

D. Focus on gender differences and verbal cues in conflict management

Discuss each of the following situations and statements as effective or ineffective for conflict management, specifying why in each instance.

1. A director's recently hired secretary has been submitting a series of assignments to her boss with serious errors (that is, in a recent budget she typed $20,000 instead of $200,000). The director feels her own effectiveness will be severely compromised if the quality of her reports does not improve. She asks the secretary to meet with her. This is their first meeting. Below are a series of statements the director might make. Discuss the effectiveness of each for managing a problem such as the one described:

   a. "Jane, you're fired."

   b. "Jane, I don't understand. Is there anything wrong?"

    c. "Jane, I really need to talk to you about your work. It may sound like I'm nitpicking, but the quality of your work isn't really as good as it should be. I'm not pressuring you too much, am I?"

    d. "Well, Jane. What are you trying to do? Get me fired?"

    e. "Jane, I've made an appointment for you to discuss your performance with the Director of Personnel."

    f. "Jane, I'm concerned about the quality of the work you have been submitting to me. It is filled with errors and is seriously affecting my ability to function. I know that your skills are suitable for this position. I would like to discuss what might be causing you to make these errors so that we can rectify the situation right away."

2. The president of a firm has noticed in recent meetings with his vice-presidents that one of the female officers wears skirts or dresses that are too tight. Further, she sits with her legs slightly apart—enough to be a bit too revealing for a corporate setting. He doesn't want her appearance to affect her highly valuable contributions. What does he do or say to help her without offending her? Below is a series of steps the president might take or say. Discuss the effectiveness and appropriateness of each.

    a. The president does or says nothing. It's the vice-president's responsibility to know how to dress properly.

    b. The president asks another female vice-president to speak to her colleague about the situation.

    c. The president says, "Ms. James, if you must sit like that, I suggest you wear pants."

    d. The president says, "Ms. James, if you were a man, I'd tell you to close your zipper."

    e. The president says, "Ms. James, I don't know quite how to say this, but the way you sit is a bit distracting."

3. Consider the following situation. Esther has worked for the Tally Advertising agency for 7 years. While ostensibly doing well in her department (that is, receiving regular praise, raises, and bonuses), she has watched two men be hired for the position of vice president of her department. One man came from another firm—less well known than Tally and with less experience in the field than she. He did not last long. Upon his departure the president asked her coworker to step in as the new vice-president, and he was thus promoted. Esther is upset because she feels qualified and deserving of this new responsibility and yet was not even given the opportunity to apply for the position. Esther decides to meet with the president to discuss her concerns.

The president's opening remarks to Esther are: "Look Esther, I know that you're an excellent employee. But we all know that men are more competitive than women—and that's what we need to get accounts."

What can/should Esther say to her boss to convince him that she can effectively handle the responsibilities of vice-president?

E. Focus on power in dyadic gender-linked communication

Students or group participants are asked to role-play the following situations.

1. Sara has just been hired by a major public relations firm to work for Sam Fielder, the noted public relations whiz. Sara is flattered and attributes her success to her outstanding educational background.

   After a few short weeks of working for Sam (he wants her to call him "Sam"), it becomes apparent that Sara has been hired for reasons other than her grade-point average. Sam continually asks her to work late; he has taken her out to lunch a couple of times, ostensibly to discuss business. But yesterday he invited Sara to join him at a convention in another city. They would share a suite. The invitation, coupled with the way Sam has touched her, looked at her, and so on, has now made Sara uncomfortable.

   Sara's problem is that she is not interested in having an affair with the boss. Sam is married. Sara is engaged and is very much in love with her fiancé. But she also does not want to lose this position. It is prestigious. It also pays very well. Sara decides she must confront Sam. What does she say?

   After two participants have enacted the above situation, select two more individuals to assume the parts, only this time the situation is reversed: Sara becomes the boss who is ostensibly making sexual advances to Sam. Once the two scenarios have been represented, discuss the following issues:

   a. Were there any similarities in the verbal and nonverbal behavior of the men and women who played "the boss"; who played "the employee?" If yes, discuss what kinds of behavior were evidenced and if these behaviors belong stereotypically in the communication repertoire of men and women.

   b. Assess the strategies used by the individuals portraying the employee. Did they resolve the situation? Can the situation be resolved? Discuss other approaches to the situation.

2. Bill and Sue are both 26 years old. They graduated from top law schools last year. They have obtained positions in major corporate law firms and are working extremely hard. They enjoy their work but are finding it increasingly difficult to communicate effectively with each other. Problems are erupting, for example, about taking care of the house, buying food, making social plans, how to spend their leisure time, and so on. During one particularly volatile exchange, Bill exclaims, "I'm all for women's lib, but I also expected I'd have a wife." Sue retorts: "And just what do you mean by a wife? I expected to have your support." Before the exchange gets entirely out of control the couple decide to discuss their differences.

   a. Students or group participants should role-play the discussion between Bill and Sue. Each participant should focus on what it means to grow up female and male in their culture and how each of their expectations has evolved. (The remainder of the group should focus on the verbal and nonverbal strategies of Bill and Sue.)

   b. In the middle of the role-play the leader should instruct Sue and Bill to reverse roles: Sue "becomes" Bill; Bill "becomes" Sue. (They physically exchange positions and literally pick up the dialogue from the point they had left off.) The remainder of the group should note if and how the communication behavior of each participant changes once Bill and Sue switch roles.

c. Discussion should address the following issues:
How effectively the participants have articulated and defended their positions;
How satisfactorily (or unsatisfactorily) the conflict was managed;
What steps could be taken to improve conflict management (if any); and,
Whether the participants were able to empathize with the other's viewpoint once they reversed roles.

F. Focus on gender differences and flexibility of conflict handling behavior: dyadic communication

1. Consider the following situation: Jim is a 43 year old account executive for a major firm. He is married and has two children ages 7 and 11. His wife, Maggie, having returned to graduate school after the children were in school full-time, has received an MBA and has been working for the past few years at a major corporation earning a substantial salary. Jim learns that his company is relocating halfway across the country. To entice him to remain with the firm, he has been offered a promotion and a large raise. Jim wants to make this move, although it would mean uprooting his family. (Maggie is very ambitious in her position; the children have found their niche in school.) How can Jim discuss his concerns with Maggie?

Groups of student pairs or seminar participants should enact the above situation using the following conflict handling behaviors:

a. Jim is confrontative; Maggie is competitive;
b. Jim is competitive; Maggie wants to avoid the issue;
c. Jim and Maggie want to compromise;
d. Jim and Maggie want to accommodate each other's needs;
e. Jim and Maggie want to collaborate on the issue.

Discussion should focus on how the verbal and nonverbal communication strategies of the participants changed to reflect the different conflict-handling behavior and on the effectiveness of each mode.

G. Focus on gender differences and cross cultural conflict: intragroup

Students or seminar participants should be divided into small groups of five. Each group should discuss the following situation and take turns presenting their case and rationale for dealing with the situation to the entire group.

A woman is a top accountant in a major firm. One of the biggest clients is a Middle Eastern company. A team of accountants is being assembled to go abroad. The woman is a key figure on the team. At one of the planning meetings the woman's colleague raises the issue that this firm does not like to deal with women and recommends that she not participate in the visit. The woman is upset by this recommendation, especially since her firm has always had a positive attitude toward women in executive positions. The group becomes polarized. How do they approach/resolve this conflict?

FIVE
CROSS-CULTURAL AWARENESS IN CONFLICT MANAGEMENT

The most universal quality is diversity. (Montaigne, *Essays*, Book II, Ch. 37)

ASSESSMENT

In this chapter we are dealing with those conflicts rooted in cultural differences in the way people communicate. To the extent that all parties involved are fully aware of one another's cultural differences, these differences may themselves be the source of conflict which is unresolvable. As our attention in this book is directed toward that conflict for which one can effect change, the focus of this chapter is primarily on pseudoconflict, which Miller and Steinberg define as conflicts emerging from disagreements created by inaccurate communication (1975, p. 267).

In actual conflict, the concerns of two or more parties are incompatible to one or both parties. In pseudoconflict these concerns do not *actually* exist but instead are *perceived* as existing. In cross-cultural pseudoconflict the mistaken perception that a conflict situation exists derives from cultural differences in how people process information and communicate. While certainly not all conflict in a multicultural setting derives from misunderstanding culturally determined behavior among the parties, a great proportion of what passes for actual conflict in cross-cultural situations is tied to the pseudoconflict of such misunderstandings. This chapter discusses ways for understanding and reducing the causes of the cross-cultural pseudoconflict.

Before we can assess adequately the sources of pseudoconflict stemming from cross-cultural differences, it is necessary to define two broad areas. First, we should recognize the importance of intercultural communication. Second, to assess the nature of cross-cultural conflict we must be familiar with what is meant by culture. Only then is it possible to understand the climate in which communication-based cross-cultural conflict takes place, and relatedly, the means to manage conflict situations likely to occur in such an environment.

Need for Intercultural Communication

Before an individual can successfully eliminate pseudoconflict that arises from misunderstanding of cultural differences, it is necessary to understand the importance of intercultural interaction in the first place. The need for cross-cultural awareness and the skills needed to communicate effectively across cultures is not always a given for all people. Cross-cultural pseudoconflict, however, is difficult to eliminate unless we believe it is necessary. Therefore, the first step in the assessment of intercultural conflict management is the establishment of the *need* and value *of* such cross-cultural communication skills.

The importance of intercultural communication, particularly in the United States, has increased dramatically since the early 1960's. As Louise Fiber Luce and Elise Smith have noted, "Global interaction, whether political, economic, or educational, has intensified so dramatically that, as a nation, we have begun to understand the significance of cultural pluralism and its impact on national affairs and daily life" (1987, p. 3). To interact with others in this integrated global arena, the individual must be able to communicate across cultures and with other minority subcultures within his or her own culture. In short, to interact with others in a globally integrated environment, we must become adept at intercultural communication, "the sending and receiving of messages within a context of cultural differences producing differential effects" (Dodd, 1982, p. 9).

To illustrate the importance of intercultural communication, it might prove useful to consider a specific field of human interaction in a specific nation. For the sake of example, we will examine the increasing importance of intercultural communication in conducting business in the United States.

Since the 1960s the volume of world trade has grown enormously. As Donald Ball and Wendell McCulloch have observed:

> By 1980, the volume of international trade in goods and services measured in current dollars had surpassed by over 15 times the amount exported just 20 years earlier. Merchandise exports alone amounted to $2 trillion. . . . One can

appreciate its magnitude by noting that this figure is larger than the gross national product of every country in the world except the United States. (1985, p. 21)

At the same time the United States has seen its dominance of the world marketplace slip. "At the end of the war and in the early postwar years," as Lars Anell has written,

the United States accounted for almost half of the world's total industrial production and possessed three-quarters of the gold reserves and half the shipping tonnage. At present the American share of industrial production is well below one-fourth. The USA has the largest foreign debt in the world and can compete for maritime freights solely through enormous federal subsidies. (Garvin, 1985, p. 54)

The United States' role in this increasingly integrated world economy has grown even as its competitiveness in the global marketplace has shrunk. Thus, the need to communicate effectively with businesspeople from other cultures has grown as well. Business, however, is not conducted in an identical fashion from culture to culture. Business relations are enhanced when managerial, sales, and technical personnel are, at the least, trained to be aware of areas likely to create misunderstandings across cultures. Consequently, the need for U.S. businesspeople to be skilled in intercultural communication has become increasingly important. Of course, intercultural misunderstanding occurs in any number of fields, not just in business.

What Is Culture?

At this point it would be prudent to define what is meant by culture. First, it should be noted that although culture is often defined, few experts agree as to exactly what they mean by it. Over 30 years ago, Alfred Kroeber and Clyde Kluckhohn reviewed almost 300 definitions of culture in *Culture: A Critical Review Of Concepts and Definitions* without reaching a general consensus as to the term's meaning (1954). Since then, the term has only broadened. Still, we might agree to define culture in a broad sense as it affects communication. Kluckhohn's own definitions of culture are informative here: the "patterned ways of thinking, feeling and reacting" (1951, p. 86) and "the total life way of a people, the social legacy the individual acquires from his group" (1964, p. 24).

In the view of many experts, culture and communication cannot be separated (Porter and Samovar, 1982; Ronen, 1986; Ruben, 1977; Singer, 1987). As Condon and Yousef note, however, while "we cannot separate culture from communication . . . it is possible to distinguish between cultural patterns of communication and truly intercultural or cross-cultural communication" (1985, pp. 34–35). We can, in other words, identify specific dimensions of what Hofstede has called the "collective programming of the mind" (1984, p. 21). In the next two sections of this chapter—on acknowledgement and attitude—we present an overview of some of the most prominent of these dimensions in the context of conflict management.

ACKNOWLEDGMENT

After having assessed the general influence of culture underlying the communication process, we can next place in cultural perspective how conflict can stem from communication-based cultural differences. To do this we need to analyze why cross-cultural misunderstandings occur. This section examines the general causes of cross-cultural misunderstanding. The next section of this chapter—on attitude—then analyzes those specific aspects of cross-cultural communication variables most likely to create a perceived conflict.

Why Does Culturally Caused Misunderstanding Occur?

Misunderstanding, and from this counterproductive pseudoconflict, arises when members of one culture are unable to understand culturally determined differences in communication practices, traditions, and thought processing.

Jone Rymer Goldstein has objected to the view of many communication experts who hold that "language could serve as a window or direct conduit to an objective reality about which there could be perfect agreement by all who apprehended it rightly" (1984, p. 25). While the experts she cites believe that if the sender is careful enough in designing his or her message, the receiver will understand the message without interference, Rymer Goldstein herself argues that such a communication window is unlikely to allow a message to pass through unhindered. Her objection holds particularly true for cross-cultural communication. Indeed, in communicating across cultures, we might say that the message in the same situation is being transmitted through a stained glass window. To understand how people from another culture perceive the message sent to them, it is first necessary to understand to what extent their culture has tinted the window of communication.

Meaning, in intercultural communication, must not be seen as an objective constant. As G. A. Kelly has argued:

> Meaning is not extracted from Nature but projected by people upon it. People's behavior can be understood only in terms of their own constructs: that is, from their own internal frames of reference. Even people's most familiar

constructs are not objective observations of what is really there; they are instead inventions of personal and group culture. (Singer, 1987, p. 9)

While communication across cultures can in some cases proceed smoothly without any particular awareness of cultural differences, many authorities in fields as varied as business, communication, sociology, anthropology, foreign language instruction, and linguistics strongly argue that the likelihood of effective communication diminishes when that awareness is lacking (Bass and Burger, 1979; Dodd, 1982; Condon and Yousef, 1985; Hall, 1961; Hofstede, 1984; Miller and Kilpatrick, 1987; Nostrand, 1966; Seelye, 1984; and Terpstra and David, 1985).

Ethnocentrism

At the most fundamental level cross-cultural pseudoconflict may come about when one or more of the people involved clings to an ethnocentric view of the world. Ethnocentrism may be defined as the "unconscious tendency to interpret or to judge all other groups and situations according to the categories and values of our own culture" (Ruhly, 1976, p. 22). Ethnocentrism manifests itself in many ways in intercultural communication:

A U.S. executive, for instance who considers English to be the "best" or the "most logical" language will not apply himself to learn a foreign language which he considers "inferior" or "illogical." And if he considers his nonverbal system to be the most "civilized" system, he will tend to reject other systems as "primitive." In this sense, ethnocentrism . . . can lead not only to a complete communication breakdown but also to antagonism, or even hostility. (Almaney, 1974, p. 27)

In such situations, the ethnocentric party views culturally derived variations in communication as *wrong* rather than simply *different*.

Conflict due to misunderstanding in cross-cultural communication, however, may affect even enlightened communicators. "Being aware," as Ronen writes, "does not necessarily mean that one can eliminate one's own ethnocentrism" (1986, p. 104). Ethnocentrism is deceptive precisely because members of any culture perceive their own behavior as logical, since that behavior works for them. Thus, to see beyond the ethnocentric boundaries of our own culture is difficult even when we are aware that our own behavioral patterns may not be universal.

Indeed, some experts assert that much of that on which the communicator bases his or her assumptions derives from perceptions below the conscious level (Berelson and Steiner, 1964; Key, 1968; Singer, 1987). While the degree of importance of subliminal perception in communication is open to debate among these experts, the very possibility that the framework of values and perceptions on which the communicator's message rests is subconcious has great ramifications for the intercultural communicator. If the communicator's assumptions derive from subliminal perceptions, then, as Singer observes, "It becomes particularly difficult to get people to establish different perceptual frames, precisely because they do not know—consciously—what caused them to establish those frames in the first place" (1987, p. 77). To reduce communication-based conflict across cultures, we must strive to be conscious of our own culturally imbued ways of viewing the world. The effective communicator is one who understands *how* the perception of a given message changes depending on the culturally determined viewpoint of those communicating. To this end, the next section of this chapter—on attitude—provides a set of guidelines for communication between members of different cultures.

ATTITUDE

This section discusses ways in which to recognize how we can shape our attitudes toward individuals from other cultures and approach specific sources of cross-cultural pseudoconflict. Again, pseudoconflict is defined as conflict that arises out of misunderstandings based on perceived rather than actual opposing views or goals in which the misperception is rooted in cultural differences.

This chapter describes a four-point checklist designed to provide a more open attitude toward communication in a multicultural setting by helping communicators be aware of the most prominent factors causing pseudoconflict and misunderstanding in cross-cultural communication. By understanding those factors which are most likely to shift in the perception of people from other cultures, communicators can prepare themselves to lessen the likelihood of pseudoconflict related to intercultural differences in communication.

Factors Affecting Cross-Cultural Communication

The factors mentioned above are likely to appear in cross-cultural communication in four categories. These are factors of

1. Language
2. Place
3. Thought Processing
4. Nonverbal communication behavior

While all of these elements are to some extent interdependent, they are not examined here as a system in the sense that systems theory uses and inteprets the term. Instead, these guidelines are intended to be used as a checklist of major considerations in cross-cultural communication, offering specific suggestions for evaluating each variable.

Admittedly, these four variables alone do not provide a thorough knowledge of another culture. Moreover, these four dimensions are not intended to represent the *only* cause of intercultural pseudoconflict. These guidelines do, however, provide an underlying foundation on which the average communicator can construct a framework for understanding the culture in question. They also provide a way to maintain an open attitude toward those differences which may produce real anxiety in individuals whose own outlooks and beliefs may seem to be diametrically opposed.

By asking the right questions the communicator should be able to manage more effectively pseudoconflict that arises from the most significant cultural differences. In her classic study, *Patterns of Culture*, Ruth Benedict argues that the only way we can know the significance of a selected detail of behavior is against the background of the motives and emotions and values that are institutionalized in that culture (1934, p. 55). The four points of this checklist are intended as a guide for the person wishing to construe an overview of that background.

Factors of Language

As discussed in Chapter 2, even when all parties use the same language with equal familiarity, the very nature of language provides a source for misunderstanding any attendant conflict. Among the most often cited barrier to conflict-free cross-cultural communication is the use of different languages and dialects.

Accentual Differences

How one pronounces, enunciates, and articulates words falls under the general category of accent. Within nearly every language, standard and variant pronunciations exist for each word. A host of social and cultural factors influence how listeners react to these variations. Most variations are tied to geography and the social class of the speaker and therefore remain cultural factors affecting communication (see Chapter 5).

Such pronunciational and articulational differences are compounded by dialectical differences in actual word choice (the effect of which is discussed in more detail in Chapter 6 on writing). An entire field of study—sociolinguistics—is devoted to the study of the perceptions of these variations from standard dialects of each respective language. Briefly, though, listeners judge speakers on the nature of their enunciation. If the speech is strongly Northumberlandish in accent, the Northumberlandish listener may feel more comfortable but may also be aware that the speaker is less likely to be educated than one who uses standard British English—the dialect of the educated upper class, which varies very little despite its speakers' geographical differences. The relative social class of those from Northumberland as a whole vis-à-vis the rest of Britian is also assessed in such a case, often negatively so against the accents of the generally more wealthy populace of southern England.

Not all accents possible in a given language, are judged the same by all of that language's speakers, however. To stereotype speakers sociolinguistically, the listener must first be familiar with the culturally learned associations of the appropriate accents. Thus, in the United States, the distinctions described above may be entirely lost, as no familiarity with Northumberland exists. Consequently, the Northumberlandish accent is undistinguished from other accents from England and is usually judged according to U.S. stereotypes of those from England. This is not to imply that speakers of U.S. English do not divide themselves into dialect categories based on social class and geography, which they do; U.S. English speakers are usually unable to judge many non-U.S. English accents according to their place in a sociolinguistic continuum.

Foreign accents are also judged according to cultural stereotypes within each language group. These sociolinguistic prejudices often reflect the cultural biases of the host culture. Thus, in the United States listeners place a great deal of emphasis on speaking English without the accent of a foreign language. It has been shown, for example, that those born in the United States rate Europeans speaking English with the accent of their native language more negatively than other U.S.-born speakers using a recognizably U.S. accent (Mulde, Hanley, and Prigge, 1974). It is possible to argue that this prejudice derives from numerous cultural factors: U.S. global insularity and views of Europeans or the use of standard English as a sign of assimilation in a nation composed primarily of immigrants or immigrant stock. One might also argue that the use of a non-U.S. accent prevents the U.S.-accented English listener from accurately determining sociolinguistic cues about the speaker. Without the help of such cues, the listener cannot determine the speaker's social class and so attributes the lower social class until proven otherwise.

Linguistic Differences

It is difficult to underestimate the importance that an understanding of linguistic differences plays in intercultural communication. Indeed, the proponents of the so-called Sapir-Whorf hypothesis believe that language shapes the culture that uses it, affecting the way that its users think (Gumperz and Hymes, 1964; Hoijer, 1982; Hymes, 1972; Lander, 1966; Niyekawa-Howard, 1968; Pike, 1971; Romney and D'Andrade, 1964). To quote Edward Sapir:

> No two languages are ever sufficiently similar to be considered as representing the same social reality. The worlds in which different societies live are

distinct worlds, not merely the same world with different labels attached. (Mandelbaum, 1962, p. 162)

Similarly, for Benjamin Whorf: "the linguistic system . . . of each language is not merely a reproducing instrument for voicing ideas but rather is itself the shaper of ideas" (1952, p. 5). Thus, even if one can approximate the meaning of a message through translation, it is at best difficult to convey the ideas connected to the translator's choice of words in that language. This can be a source of pseudoconflict. Since language shapes thought, those speaking different languages understand the world around them—including the message they communicate—in a way which is essentially linked to the language used.[1] For anyone not using that language, the message received will, by nature, be only approximate.

Language itself reinforces cultural associations contained within the group which speaks it. Robbins Burling observes that "the terms of one language carry a burden of irrelevant connotations that interfere with our grasp of the terms of the other" (1970, p. 13).

As Jonathan Slater notes, "Lexicons may differ so radically between languages as to prohibit reaching equivalence" (1987, p. 37). Harvey Daniels has written that "each language allows its speakers to easily talk about whatever is important to discuss *in that society*" (1985, p. 31, emphasis added). Daniels is careful, however, to point out that "this does not mean that every given language will work 'perfectly' or be 'equal' to any other in a cross-cultural setting." The resulting inaccuracy in the message can lead to misunderstanding and, consequently, to perceived conflict.

To avoid pseudoconflict one must determine the degree of error probable in translating whatever communication is exchanged. To do so the communicator should remain sensitive to the degree to which the environment in which he or she operates is similar to that of the person into whose language any given message is communicated. As Mary Douglas has argued, where experiences in the culture of one linguistic group roughly matches, language is less an impediment to communication; however, "where there is no overlap, the attempt to translate fails" (1975, p. 277). For the cross-cultural communicator the main purpose of translation ought not to have as its main goal an exact equivalence but, to quote Douglas again, "to prevent any confrontation between alien thought systems" (1975, p. 277).

[1] The premises of linguistic relativity are ultimately unprovable and highly debated. Harry Hoijer, expressing the general argument against the Sapir-Whorf hypothesis, warns that it is "easy to exaggerate linguistic differences of this nature and the consequent barriers to intercultural understanding. No culture is wholly isolated, self-contained, and unique. There are important resemblances between all known cultures—resemblances that stem in part from diffusion . . . and in part from the fact that all cultures are built around biological, psychological, and social characteristics common to all mankind" (1982, pp. 211–12). Still, as Noam Chomsky argues: "The existence of deep-seated formal universals . . . implies that all languages are cut to the same pattern, but does not imply that there is any point by point correspondence between languages" (1968, pp. 29–30).

To this end, the other variables discussed in this chapter can help the communicator determine how "alien" the "thought systems" are between people of different cultures.

Translation Difficulties

Aside from the effect of language on actual thought processing discussed above, one might argue that difficulties with the translation of language fall basically into three categories: gross translation problems, the conveyance of subtle distinctions from language to language, and recognizing culturally based variations among speakers of the same language.

Gross translation errors, although frequent, may be less likely to cause conflict between parties than other language difficulties for two reasons. First, they are generally the easiest language difficulty to detect. Many gross translation errors are either ludicrous or make no sense at all. Thus, the General Motors standard slogan "body by Fisher" was embarrassing but readily caught when it was translated into Flemish in its Belgian campaign as "corpse by Fisher" (Ricks, Fu, and Arpan, 1974, p. 11). Only those translation errors which continue to be logical in both the original meaning and in the mistranslated version pose a serious concern. Thus, while "this is not available" and "this is now available" differ by only one letter in writing or one mispronounced word in speech, the meaning of each phrase is diametrically opposite, although both versions may be perfectly logical in any number of situations.

Nor do such mistranslations need to actually cross languages in cross-cultural situations. Dialectical differences within the same language often create gross errors. One frequently cited example of how variation within a single language can affect business occurred when a U.S. deodorant manufacturer sent a Spanish translation of its slogan to their Mexican operations. The slogan read, "If you use our deodorant, you won't be embarrassed." However, the translation, which the Mexican-based English-speaking employees saw no reason to avoid, used the term *embarazada* to mean *embarrassed*. This provided much amusement to the Mexican market, as *embarazada* means "pregnant" in Mexican Spanish (Ball and McCulloch, 1985, p. 199).

Even when easily detected, gross translation errors waste time and wear on the patience of the parties involved. Additionally, some such errors imply a form of disrespect for the party into whose language the message is translated because it may be construed that the individual who made the error did not consider the foreign language (or people) important enough to assure accuracy. These feelings and perceptions in turn can produce an unnecessary and easily avoidable conflict.

The subtle shadings which are often crucial to negotiations are also weakened when both parties do not share a similar control of the same language. In English, for example, the mild distinctions between the word *misinterpret* and *misunderstand* can prove significant in a sensitive situation. To a touchy negotiator, to say that he or she *misunderstands* may imply that he or she is not prepared or not fully competent to handle the negotiation. To say that the same negotiator *misinterprets* a concept, by contrast, allows the negotiator a way to save face, since all interpretations are arguable. He or she has reached an understandable, although inaccurate, interpretation of the matter. In such a situation the term applies more objectively to the matter at hand than to the specific negotiator. To a nonnative speaker with inadequate control of the language, however, such subtle distinctions might be lost. When other parties with full control over the language with whom the nonnative speaker communicates assume that knowledge of this distinction exists, it is likely that classic pseudoconflict, as defined at the beginning of this chapter, will derive from misunderstanding.

To reduce the risk of inaccurate translation, the communicator should take great care to find a qualified translator. The choice of translator should not rest on chance. A friend who has lived in Rotterdam for a year or two, for example, may have rudimentary knowledge of Dutch but hardly has the requisite skills to ensure that the sorts of translation errors described above are avoided. To some extent we may protect ourselves by employing translators who are certified or who work with a respected translating firm.

Nevertheless, it is important to stress that even when one eliminates linguistic barriers, he or she still faces numerous other obstacles to clear cross-cultural communication. As Lennie Copeland and Lewis Griggs note: "Learning the language is no substitute for learning the culture and appropriate behavior. People who are fluent in a language but not sensitive to the culture can make worse mistakes, perhaps because the locals expect more of them" (1985, p. 114). The remaining three factors in the checklist delineated below provide a foundation on which the communicator can build an understanding of the "culture and appropriate behavior" to which Copeland and Griggs refer.

Factors Of Place

Factors of place may be defined for our purposes as (a) the physical environment in which one lives and (b) existing technology, or the way in which one manipulates that environment. Both these factors of place profoundly affect the way one views the world. The differences in this world view in turn are prime sources for pseudoconflict.

To some extent the environment and technology of a culture are interrelated, forming a cultural system. The interrelationship of environment to technology may be defined as that "cultural system concerned with the relationships between humans and their natural environment" (Terpstra and David, 1985, p. 148).

The way in which people use the resources available to them often shifts notably from culture to culture. "The environment in which a communication occurs," Singer observes, "can be a major factor in determining how effective one can be in intercultural communication" (1987, p. 58). Culturally engrained biases regarding the natural and technological environment can create communication barriers. The communicator accustomed to ways of looking at the environment and the use of technology particular to his or her culture may find it difficult to adapt to those views. This, in turn, can create misunderstandings and pseudoconflict.

These place-related differences manifest themselves when communicating on a wide spectrum of subjects. Many of these differences are relatively easy to overcome as sources of pseudoconflict for the communicator. This is because many place-related differences are based primarily on lack of *knowledge* rather than on culturally intrinsic *values*. These can be eliminated or at least reduced by acquiring an understanding of differences in transportation and logistics, health care and sanitation, accident prevention and occupational safety, settlement and territiorial organization, and energy cost and availability (Seelye, 1984). Even the role of weather and the climate in general are subject to drastic change from one culture to another (Seeyle, 1984).

To illustrate how such knowledge-based differences may cause a communication-based pseudoconflict, we might consider how the standard means of transportation and logistics in one culture may seem patently absurd in another. The manager of a Canadian company doing business in South America might never think to ship goods from Chile to neighboring Argentina by the circuitous route of the Panama Canal. Because Canada is relatively flat and has an excellent network of railroads and highways, the Canadian manager might assume that the easiest way to transport goods for any short distance would be overland. Indeed, the Canadian might well specify this preference in any relevant communication. What the Canadian might not understand in such a situation is that the rugged physical environment of the Andean terrain and the related absence of cross-Andean railroads and freeways would make such an option unreasonably expensive or even impossible.

Not all place-related sources of pseudoconflict, however, are so easily resolved. Many place-related issues go beyond mere knowledge-based differences, embracing actual cultural values. For example, as we have seen in Chapter 3, the perception of living and working space—whether office space or the use of space in domestic housing and buildings in general—can carry distinct meaning within any one culture. The way one interprets the messages inherent in the use of space is, however, subject to great cross-cultural variation that is often imbued with deep-rooted cultural associations. Simply being aware of differences may not reflect these value-linked differences and therefore might affect how we communicate matters relating to the notion of space.

Thus some have argued that in Germany the use of space reinforces extended social distance (compared to the United States) through greater emphasis on such environmental features, among others, as soundproofing, physical barriers such as double doors and a preference for heavy curtains, and the use of shrubs and barriers to shield yards from neighbors (Condon and Yousef, 1985; Hall, 1966).

Pseudoconflict in turn may result when someone from a culture that places less emphasis on these qualities—such as a North American—interprets the German emphasis on privacy and use of space by standards other than those actually held in Germany. In such a situation the North American might view the German behavior as intentionally isolating, cold, or standoffish, creating a possible source of irritation, resistance, and consequent misunderstanding. Pseudoconflict can easily escalate into true conflict when the North American shows signs of irritation and the German has no idea of its source. The German would naturally assume the irritation arose elsewhere and respond accordingly, the misplaced response leading to more negative reactions from the North American until both parties become engaged in a full-scale conflict cycle.

In Japan, by contrast, people are accustomed to living and working in much closer and less private quarters. Indeed, a European Economic Community Report—which at least in part reflects a German frame of reference—claimed that the "Japanese lived in rabbit hutches" (Fields, 1983, p. 27). While such a claim in Europe (or the United States) would have represented a deep insult, the Japanese, as one marketing expert observed, took the comment as a reinforcement of their own cultural self-perception as "underprivileged self-achievers" (Fields, 1983, p. 27).

The difference (vis-à-vis Europe and the United States) of Japanese emphasis on space creates a similar difference in the way people interact with one another in a "rabbit hutch" environment. The physical environment of the standard business office, for example, varies drastically from that in the German example described above. Unlike the German manager, who places great emphasis on the physical separation of his or her office—emphasized by size, location, soundproofing, and the use of doors—the Japanese *bucho* or department chief generally has no separate office at all. Instead, the *bucho's* desk is simply one of many desks in a rectangular patterned arrangement in a large open area. The *bucho's* desk is usually farthest from the door, often near a window, and offers an easy view of the department. While workers within the box-shaped arrangement are often strictly postioned by rank as to where in the box they have their desks, the open environment is more conducive to greater visibility and to greater ease of access and communication. As Japanese business expert Boye DeMente has observed:

> Within each of these basic boxes, responsibility and activity is more or less a

team thing, with work assigned to the group as a whole. Members of each section are expected to cooperate and support each other. . . . The effectiveness of a particular section is strongly influenced by the total morale, ambition and talent of the whole team. (1981, p. 70)

While teamwork and ease of access for communication in the Japanese system are perhaps more emphasized than in the German situation described above, the German entering such an environment may well misinterpret such a system—from its physical appearence judged by German rather than Japanese standards—as egalitarian. The German reflecting this in his or her communication, however, would be making a serious error. The Japanese are strictly ranked by importance within this seemingly (by German standards) open seating and are very concerned not only by their placement in the seating box but also to which box they beloing (DeMente, 1981, pp. 69–70).

Another environmental and technological factor affecting communication that is likely to differ across cultures in a value-related manner and thus result in cross-cultural pseudoconflict is the *human* climate, that is, the nature of a culture's human resources. The literacy rate and the role of mass media, for example, may change greatly from one culture to the next. Thus, using written warnings to notify a largely illiterate population of a potential hazard with a product is unlikely to serve its purpose. In a well-known case of such conflict a Swiss corporation provided only written instructions for the safe use of its baby formula. To large numbers of the baby formula's illiterate users in the Third World, such a written warning proved useless and, when coupled with other factors, was ultimately fatal to the children to whom the formula was fed.

Finally, value-based misunderstanding and pseudoconflict may arise when people do not adapt their world view to the technological level of sophistication of a given group of people or work force. For example, among those from the more industrialized nations, a comon assumption is that the way people in less industrialized nations use their resources results not only from an inferior level of technology but also from an inherently inferior culture. Such a view is particularly dangerous when we consider the power available to cultures with a high level of technological sophistication to impose a cultural dominance over those to whom they introduce that technology (Ellul, 1964; Illich, 1977; Rybczynski, 1983). Technology may break down cultural barriers but may create enormous resentments if all its ramifications are not carefully considered. As one expert has observed:

If in one sense technology—particularly communications—no longer permits the "separate state," in another sense technology that confers these powers also makes possible—at any rate, for the favored few—a policy akin to autarchy. (Tucker, 1977, p. 99)

Not only pseudoconflict but also a very real conflict may derive from how technology is shared. In instances in which a nation depends on another country for the technology needed to sustain its economic viability and in which a nation is unable to maintain that technological capability on its own, communication dealing with that technology is likely to be charged with negative sentiments. Conflict arises because, as David Blake and Robert Walters have noted, "outright resentment toward foreign sources of technology are likely to arise" (1976, p. 145). Such an attitude is not limited to the so-called lesser industrialized world but, as Blake and Walters describe, are prevalent wherever such disparity exists: "Europeans, particularly the French, took note of the seemingly unassailable scientific and technological predominance of the United States" (1976, p. 145). Similarly, U.S. concerns and resentment about the growing strength of Japanese technology have been voiced by a growing number of experts (Brooks, 1985; Feigenbaum and McCorduck, 1983; Gregory, 1986; Hofheinz and Calder, 1982; Vogel, 1979).

A relatively low level of technological sophistication, however, may be a quite deliberate choice of a specific country. As Terpstra and David note, "Existing sets of priorities defining what is good, proper, desirable, or important in a society may set limits on the kinds of technology that can successfully be introduced in a society" (1985, p. 152). One extreme example of a nation reacting against the kinds of technology introduced into it from outside the culture is the revolution in Iran in the late 1970's. The shah, whom that revolution overthrew, had rapidly introduced many technologically based changes into Iranian society. The shah conceived of these changes as advances. He, however, remained unaware of the mass resentment these changes produced among his subjects, who believed such changes were tearing away the fabric of traditionally Iranian values.

A culture need not feel threatened, however, by high-level technological innovations to reject them in favor of a lower level of technology. A nation may use the lower technology available to them as they do because it makes good sense to use it in that fashion within the context of that culture. An example of weapons technology—the case of the halberd—may serve to demonstrate this. The halberd was developed in Switzerland in the Middle Ages. This weapon was, for its day, of a technologically low level. It consisted of a long spike with a hook and cleaver attached. Swiss farmers used the halberd as a means of defense against marauding German and French barons, who used the high-technology weapon system of horse and armor. The halberd, although a lower level of technology, was adopted by the Swiss because it made sense within their culture to use it. First, the halberd was cheap, as compared to horses and armor. Second, this simple weapon involved little training. Unlike equestrian combat equipment, the halberd consisted of farm implements (hook and hatchet) with which the Swiss farmers were familiar, and its use was elementary—the cental object being to hook the armor of the attacking knight and, using the cleaver, hack the grounded horseman immobilized by the weight of his armor. Yet despite its significantly lower scale of technology, the halberd was used extremely successfully by the Swiss, with at least one expert (Rybczynski, 1983) asserting that it helped bring an end to the era of the armored knight.

The halberd significantly did not develop among the German or French peasantry. This was not because they were free from attacks by knights; they were probably attacked more than their Swiss counterparts. Nor was this because the farm technology from which the halberd was born was unavailable in France or Germany, for the hook and cleaver were as common to the peasants there as to the farmers in Switzerland.

Instead, the halberd was not conceived of in France or Germany because it was a culturally inappropriate weapon for them. As serfs to the barons who raided their lands, the German and French peasants actually accomplished little in holding off the marauding nobles, as the land itself was already owned by the attackers. Thus, it made little sense to risk great bodily harm or even death in defending the land. As Rybczynski has noted:

> While the halberd did not require great skill, it demanded considerable bravery. . . . The halberd involved close combat, and until the halberdier, who wore no armor, was able to unseat or incapacitate the charging enemy, he was at great risk. (1983, p. 170)

For cultural reasons, however, the Swiss farmer had the needed bravery his French or German counterpart did not. In contrast to the French or German peasant, the Swiss farmer fought for his own land: "a free man fighting for home and family—neither a serf nor a slave—a necessary prerequisite for the bravery required to use this kind of weapon" (Rybcznski, 1983, p. 170). Thus, Swiss culture in the late Middle Ages used with highly favorable results the lower technology available to them because it was culturally better suited to their needs.

The attitudes that a particular society may hold toward technological innovations and its overall effect on the cultural values of that society are often at variance with those from other cultures. To the extent that the level of technology is determined according to preexisting cultural values, the attitudes toward its use will most likely be reflected in any communication regarding that technology. In the United States, for example, technological innovation is generally regarded as positive. One need only look at the U.S. investment in research and development (R&D) and the number of scientists and engineers to demonstrate this:

> National investment in R&D is frequently used in international comparisons as a proxy for innovative effort. By this measure the U.S. can still be regarded as a world leader, at least in the "free world". . . . The absolute level of U.S. R&D expenditures, when adjusted for purchasing parity, was 1.5 times that

of Japan, Germany, France and the United Kingdom combined in 1977. The United States had 1.3 times as many scientists and engineers employed in industrial R&D per 1,000 workers than in any one of these countries. (Brooks, 1985, p. 342)

Thus, for the entire industrialized world one may claim that the United States places the strongest value on technological innovation. U.S. communicators therefore would most likely reflect this outlook by seeing technology as generally good for its users. Indeed, the average individual from the United States might well be expected to believe that all those *without* an equally sophisticated level of technology would of necessity *want* to acquire it, with only lack of access or ability impeding such acquisition.

This view would fall far from the mark for many other cultures. Even in Japan, the country with next greatest emphasis on R&D, the U.S. penchant for technological innovation has been considered extreme. Naohiro Amaya, an influential senior official of the powerful Ministry of International Trade and Industry and among Japan's greatest planners, has been recorded as questioning the value and extent of U.S. emphasis on technological innovation: "The Americans seemed to him to have reached the outer limits of inventing devices of use to the average citizen. Machines that opened cans and machines that polished shoes were different from heavy domestic machines like washers and dryers, they were less basic, less necessary" (Halberstam, 1986, p. 39).

It is, however, not from the Japanese or other technologically sophisticated cultures that the United States and other technology-centered cultures diverge most notably. Rather, it is with those cultures where such technology—at times by choice—is not so prevalent that a difference in the view toward technology is most likely to affect communication and to create conflict. Thus, in prerevolutionary Iran highly sophisticated technology had been imported as a showpiece. The pervasive influence of much of that technology was viewed, however, as contributing to the undermining of traditional values. This led, at least to some extent, to that nation's revolution and stongly anti-Western stance. Thus, some governments find that acquiring state-of-the-art technology is inappropriate:

> They often find that their factor proportions of labor and capital and their consumer demand patterns are at variance with the product and process technology. . . . These host nations also look askance at . . . product technology, finding it inappropriate to local income levels and the basic needs of low-income levels and the basic needs of low-income earners. (Rugman, LeCraw, and Booth, 1985, p. 288)

To incorporate such technology would be disruptive to the society as a whole. Neil Chesanow relates a pertinent example:

> The Chinese usually are less interested in what's newest in a given field than what's best for China. For example, most of the country's billion-plus popula-

tion is composed of farmers, yet only 11 percent of the nation's land is arable. Thus, modern, efficient, labor-saving farm machinery is of little interest to China, where there is already a chronic shortage of jobs. Similarly, a technology like robotics that reduces factory workforces does not meet China's economic needs. The Chinese want more employment opportunities, not less. (1985, p. 230)

In such a case, the best level of technology is not necessarily, as in the U.S. view, a positive good.

For communicators, the danger of such a difference in the perception of technology is the industrialized world's deeply ingrained bias toward technological innovation as beneficial. Thus, even if a person from the United States were aware of this variant view, he or she might well hold such a view as a sign of an inferior culture, at least when communicating about technology. This, in turn, would contribute to a sense of arrogance and ethnocentrism that would not go unnoticed. Such a position would likely contribute not only to misunderstanding and pseudoconflict but also to real conflict if the variance between the two views were left unreconciled. The communicator must remain flexible to the choices a culture may make regarding the appropriate level of technology, keeping in mind that those choices may not reflect the usual technologcal presuppositions common in the communicator's own culture.

Thought Processing

The third conflict-causing factor in our cross-cultural communication checklist is thought processing. As used here, thought processing may be defined as the way in which people interpret the world around them. The entirety of thought processing goes much beyond what we will discuss here. We may, however, limit this term for the purposes of this discussion to the way in which four specific variables likely to shift across cultures affect how a person understands what is communicated. This is assuming that a common understanding exists of environmental and technological factors and of the verbal and nonverbal means of communication used.

The four variables are (1) social organization, (2) contexting, (3) authority conception, and (4) temporal conception.

Social Organization

Social organization, as it affects communication, is often culturally determined. Pseudoconflict is likely to occur when an individual assumes as universal his or her views on issues reflecting the social organization of his or her culture.

Social organization has been defined as the "set of social definitions of reality" (Terpstra and David, 1985, p. 176) and as the "roles played by individuals and groups in a society and the relationships between these individuals and groups" (Terpstra, 1982, p. 36). A society defines reality through the relationships it imposes on the members of its cultures. Those relationships most likely to affect communication in a cross-cultural situation are "familiar, religious, economic-occupational, political and judicial, educational, intellectual-aesthetic, recreational, the mass media, stratification and mobility, social properties . . . status by age group and sex, ethnic/religious and other minorities" (Seelye, 1984, p. 41).

Social organization shapes the most fundamental beliefs of members of a culture. Indeed, such beliefs are likely to be taken by members of a culture as a given. John Condon, specifically speaking of U.S.-Japanese business communication, warns that those differences which are most notable are often of less importance than the more subtle differences that reflect "some unseen or unstated meaning which is usually not pointed out but that everybody is supposed to know" (1984, p. 6).

Arvind Phatak observes that "social institutions—whether they be of a business, political, or family or social class nature—influence the behavior of individuals" (1983, p. 30). The influence of a culture's social organization on that behavior translates directly into the field of communication in many areas. For instance, the nature of praise and personal or employee motivation are socially determined (Adler, 1986; Haire, Gheselli, and Porter, 1963; Hofstede, 1984; O'Reilly and Roberts, 1973; Reitz, 1975). The communicator must be aware that what may be motivating, convincing, or persuasive in one culture may not be so in another.

For example, many East Asian cultures' deeply ingrained feelings toward face-saving, seniority, and the maintenance of harmony in the workplace would be likely to affect what motivates workers differently than in northern European and North American cultures where those feelings are less marked. Thus, in Japan praise is likely to be as disruptive to employees as blame would be in such countries as the United States or Canada. Thus, the promotion of a single member of a traditional Japanese work group may cause the productivity and morale of both the group and the promoted employee to fall:

> Japanese can be as embarrassed when they are singled out for praise as for blame. . . . Although more subtle, it is an act of giving exceptional attention to one individual, of separating one from the group. Also . . . failure to include people who expect, as members of the organization, to be included can cause a loss of face. (Condon, 1984, p. 32)

A similar promotion in the United States, by contrast, might be seen as a reward for the promoted employee and might even be viewed as encouraging the remaining members of the group to work harder for a goal that they too might attain. Thus, to communicate such a promotion openly may prove to be a poor policy in Japan but a good policy in the United States. As Boye DeMente explains, this also contributes to the Japanese disapproval toward changing companies, a common practice in North America and Europe:

> In a system in which promotion, income, prestige, etc., are primarily based on seniority, a new member coming in anywhere except at the bottom (or the very top) breaks the "chain" and throws everyone directly below the new member off schedule for life. (1981, p. 32)

As Clark notes: "Those who have joined from another company, 'mid-career entrants' (*chuto saiyo*), may not pass up the standard ranks at all, and certainly will do so more slowly than the 'school entrants' (gakusotsu)" (1979, p. 118).

Because the influence of social organization on behavior determines to a large extent the value system of a given culture, individuals wishing to avoid misunderstanding and pseudoconflict must take particular care to remain nonjudgmental when the values determined by their own social organizational patterns clash with those with whom they communicate.

For example, in many parts of the world, including the majority of the cultures of central Africa, southern Asia, and the Arab World, it would seem highly inappropriate to suggest to employees that you expect them to skip over hiring their relatives to hire a stranger. For people in these cultures, nepotism both fulfills personal obligations and ensures a predictable level of trust and accountability. In such societies, familial ties are presumed to be more reliable than, for example, the legal and contractual ties to which the cultures of northern Europe and North America generally adhere. The fact that a stranger appears to be better qualified based on a superior resume and a relatively brief interview would not, as it might, for example, in the United States, affect that belief. In such a cross-cultural situation, employers would need to adapt how they expressed their own culturally determined views on hiring employees. In the example discussed here, whether hiring practices were based on an employee's resume or on the strength of his or her family connections, the cross-cultural communicator wishing to avoid pseudoconflict would need to adjust the way in which this preference were communicated, so that what was indicated would accommodate those who would find such a preference distressing.

While it is the goal of the communicator to avoid pseudoconflict whenever possible, differences in social organization often create a situation in which the individual experiences a very real, rather than a perceived, conflict. It is often difficult to rid communication of a judgmental bias when social organization varies markedly.

For example, those from the United States—whose founding principles as a nation were based on egalitarian values—may find it difficult to remain neutral on class and role structures that prevent upward mobility.

The socially determined inferior role of blacks in South Africa, of women in much of the Islamic world, or of lower castes in India—just to name a few—may prove particularly disturbing to those from the United States. If the U.S. communicator cannot eliminate the attendant condemnation from his or her communication, however, then he or she cannot expect to function effectively in that society. As James Livingstone has observed, regarding communication in the workplace, "A society preventing upward movement may in time come apart at the seams, but in day to day terms it can make difficulties for the enterprise in limiting its choice of executives to those which will be acceptable in the role to the rest of the community" (1975, p. 199).

Contexting

The next area of thought processing pertinent to communication is contexting, which we may define as the *way* in which one communicates and especially the circumstances surrounding that communication. Virtually all communication depends on the context in which the communication is set. The more information sender and receiver share—the more homogeneous their shared experience and world view—the higher the context of the communication and the less necessary to communicate through words or gestures.

In a highly contexted situation much of what the communicator chooses *not* to articulate is essential to understanding the transmitted message. The communicator, however, expects that which is not said to be understood already. Thus, a spouse or longtime friend would be more likely than a stranger to know when a person was upset without that person actually saying so. Clues in the person's behavior or conversation would be more apparent to those who knew that person well because their greater familiarity and shared set of understandings would better allow them to place that person's behavior and communication in its proper context.

In cross-cultural settings those from the same culture would have more common experiences and shared understandings than those from different cultures. In such cases the seeds of unintentional conflict are often planted. For example, in the United States it is not particularly uncommon for a businessperson to invite a business associate to dinner. Once there, the host and guest might well expect to mix some business discussion with purely social small talk. In France, by contrast, an invitation to dine at someone's home is considered an honor and is extremely rare. Once there, the guest and host would go to great extremes to avoid discussing any business matters, as the dinner would be considered a strictly social occasion. Therefore, the French business executive visiting the United States who received an invitation to dine at his or her U.S. business colleague's home might entirely misunderstand the context of the invitation. The French executive would feel highly honored when, in fact, the host intended the dinner as nothing more than an attempt to introduce a measure of genial informality into the situation. Once the French executive arrived, she or he would be shocked if, as is fairly common in the United States, someone else had also been invited without the knowledge of the French guest. Moreover, the French businessperson would almost certainly be insulted were the U.S. host to raise business matters, when that may have been the actual reason the U.S. host had invited the French guest home to dinner. A pseudoconflict based on such misunderstanding could easily escalate to a real conflict because the U.S. host and the French guest did not realize the context in which each understood the invitation. They lacked an adequate set of understandings to place the communication in that context.

Such a shared set of understandings acts to reduce the inherent uncertainty present in all communication. As Berger and Calabrese have indicated, "When strangers meet, their primary concern is one of uncertainty reduction or increasing predictability about the behavior of both themselves and others in the interaction" (1975, p. 100). The degree of uncertainty among them is reduced to the extent that those within the same culture share more information in common with each other than with those from other cultures—that is, they approach their communication with a more greatly shared context.

Moreover, the level of contexting within the *same* culture depends on the nature of the culture itself. As Edward Hall in his seminal works on contexting (1961, 1966, 1976, 1983) has observed, some cultures rely more heavily on context than others. These cultures determine most or even all of the meaning in a message not from the actual words the sender uses but from how it is delivered and under what circumstances the message is conveyed. Other cultures, by contrast, rely more heavily on what is actually said or written than on the circumstances surrounding the delivery of the message. In effect, Hall has asserted, one can actually rank cultures along a context scale:

> It appears that all cultures arrange their members and relationships along the context scale, and one of the great communication strategies, whether addressing a single person or an entire group, is to ascertain the correct level of contexting of one's communication. (1984, p. 61)

Thus, there are high-context cultures whose members rely heavily on inferred meaning and low-context cultures whose members rely heavily on literal meaning. Additionally, evidence exists suggesting that members of low- and high-context cultures differ markedly in how they seek information to reduce the uncertainty that contexting attempts to eliminate. As William Gudykunst observes:

> While members of high-context cultures reduce uncertainty in intial inter-actions, the nature of information they seek and their level of attributional confidence appears to be different from the typical pattern . . . for a low-context culture like that of the United States. (1983, p. 50)

In high-context cultures such as Japan and China much of what is not actually said must be inferred through what seems (to those from low-context cultures such as Germany, Sweden, and the United States) to be indirection. To people from low-context cultures those in high-context cultures may seem needlessly vague or incomplete. Conversely, those from high-context cultures may view their low-context counterparts as imper-sonal and confusingly literal.

It is important for those people to assess the level of contexting inher-ent in the communication of the culture in which they conduct business to understand clearly what has been conveyed and to avoid conflict. To do so, one must examine any communication exchange closely. Being aware of the importance any given culture generally places on contexting will help the communicator determine how much of the message he or she is likely to receive directly. Still, as even the lowest-contexted cultures use context-ing to some extent, the communicator must be sensitive to its effects and not simply to the message as if in isolation.

In oral communication one must observe closely nonverbal signals. As discussed later in Chapter 3, and later in this chapter, however, this is not always readily possible. The communicator must become familiar with the nonverbal behavior of those from the culture with whom he or she speaks.

In written communication contexting is even more difficult. The com-municator must seek out the underlying message from the writer's choice of words alone. The reader must then place these words within the context of whatever it is possible to construe from the larger range of existing interaction between the message's sender and its receiver.

Authority Conception

One fairly common form of conflict grounded in communication is linked to how people view authority. Conflict in such cases often occurs when a person from one culture does not understand clearly the relative ability or inclination of an individual from another culture to act on his or her own initiative. For example, in cultures like the Philippines with a high respect for authority, a subordinate may never point out to his or her boss that an idea seems impossible to carry out. Instead, the subordinate will undertake the project his or her boss has ordered and fail. Additionally, the Filipino boss would be surprised and even displeased were the employee to bring up this concern. Conversely, in a culture like the United States, where people are more likely to question authority, the subordinate might be more likely to share his or her concerns with the boss before undertaking the project. The U.S. superior, in turn, would in many instances *expect* the subordinate to raise these concerns. In a cross-cultural situation conflict would likely occur when a Filipino boss received the unexpected feedback from a U.S. subordinate. Similarly, conflict might occur when a U.S. manager did *not* receive such feedback. Such conflict has its roots in an aspect of communication which could be called *authority conception*.

Different cultures often view the distribution of authority in their society differently. *Webster's New Collegiate Dictionary* defines authority as the "power to influence or command thought, opinion or behavior" (1974, p. 76). For our purposes, we will focus only on behavior, as that is the only one of these areas which the communicator can clearly recognize. Those in authority over others therefore can be said to have the power to influence or command behavior. Authority in any given culture is determined by the roles the individuals within that culture assume relative to one another. That system of roles may be called an *authority hierarchy*. *Authority conception* may be defined as the degree to which individuals believe those higher up in the authority hierarchy have the power to influence or command behavior.

Authority conception varies from culture to culture. Andre Laurent (1983) conducted a study of managers in 12 countries in which, among other things, he asked their views of authority conception. Laurent queried the managers regarding their reaction to the following statement: "The main reason for all hierarchical structure is so that everybody knows who has authority over whom." His responses varied greatly. The percentage of agreement with Laurent's statement in the United States was the lowest of those polled, with only 18%, while the percentage of agreement with the statement was highest among Indonesian managers, with 86%. In the same study Laurent asked the managers to what extent they agreed that it was necessary to bypass the hierarchical line to have efficient work relationships. Again, the managers showed great cross-cultural diversity in their responses. For example, 75% of the Italian managers disagreed with Laurent's statement, as compared to 32% of U.S. managers and a low rating of 22% disagreement among those from Sweden (Laurent, 1983).

Laurent's findings, though admittedly limited at present only to the workplace, have significant ramifications for all communicators. One can infer from Laurent's findings that those in the United States could communicate on a much more informal basis than would be appropriate in many other cultures. This is because those from the United States would feel much less need for an authority hierarchy than do those from nations such as Indonesia which have a much stronger authority conception. Consequently, most people—or at least most managers—from the United

States would be likely to believe that they can work in an organization with little or no formal authority hierarchy. Communication, therefore, could be assumed to be less formal, since people in the United States would be more likely than most cultures are to view each other as colleagues and relative equals rather than as superiors and subordinates in the authority hierarchy. The exact opposite, in turn, could be inferred regarding the level of appropriate formality in communicating with Indonesians.

Likewise, Laurent's study would imply that the flow of communication would vary greatly from culture to culture. The communicator, one can infer, would be much more able to communicate *directly* with his or her superior in Sweden than in Italy. Relatedly, a communicator should probably be prepared to receive considerably more requests for approval from subordinates in Italy than in Sweden.

Another dimension of authority conception affecting communication that varies across culture is *power distance*. Geert Hofstede, who coined the term (based on the work of M. Mulder, 1976; 1977), defined power distance as "the extent to which a society accepts the fact that power in insitutions and organizations is distributed unequally" (1980, p. 45). The flow of communication in those cultures with a larger power distance is more highly centralized in their authority hierarchy than in those with a smaller power distance.

Hofstede surveyed employees of a major multinational corporation in 40 countries on a number of issues, including power distance (1980). He found significant differences in the power distance common in various cultures. Using a power distance index on a scale of 1 to 100 with lower scores representing less power distance, Hofstede discovered an enormous variance. While most countries fell in the 30 to 60 range—Greece (with 60), Italy (with 50) and the United States (with 40)—Hofstede showed enormous overall variation. Those in the Philippines with a score of 94 and in Mexico and Venezuela (both with 81) topped the list, while those in Austria (with 11), Israel (13), and Denmark (18) were at the bottom of the list, showing significantly lower power distance.

Relative power distance in a given culture markedly affects communication and thus the likelihood that pseudoconflict will occur. Power distance shapes the view of how a message will be received based on the relative status or rank of the message's sender to its receiver. Thus, in a culture such as Austria or Israel, which has a low power index and which is therefore fairly decentralized, people would generally pay attention to a person based on how convincing an argument he or she puts forth, regardless of that person's rank or status within the organization or society at large. By contrast, in a culture such as Mexico or Venezuela, which has a high power index and which is consequently highly centralized, that which a relatively high-ranking individual communicates is taken very seriously, often overriding one's agreement or disagreement with that which is being communicated.

Similarly, in working with cultures such as Israel and Austria which have a low power distance, we might anticipate at the outset more acceptance of a participative communication model. Conversely, in working with cultures such as the Philippines with a large power distance, one might anticipate at the outset relatively less use of participative communication styles and more concern with who has the relevant authority.

That a culture has a centralized authority conception or large power distance does not necessarily, however, indicate that its members *prefer* one-way downward communication. As Bernard Bass and Philip Burger have shown in their 12-culture survey, "Participants tended to favor two-way over one-way communication everywhere. . . . [T]hey viewed two-way communications as less frustrating, more preferable, and more satisfying" (1979, p. 162). Rather, where the cultures differed was in the *degree* of preference, frustration, and satisfaction implict in one-way communication.

Temporal Conception

The final area in the checklist of thought-processing factors affecting cross-cultural communication is temporal conception, or how people view time. "A culture's concept of time," as Richard Porter and Larry Samovar have defined it, "is its philosophy toward the past, present, and the future, and the importance or lack of importance it places on time" (1982, p. 41). Those philosophies and assignations of importance regarding time are subject to great variation across cultures. In any communication, as Carley Dodd observes, "Time is a potent force, communicating as powerfully as verbal language" (1982, p. 236). Moreover, Dodd notes, "In intercultural communication encounters, an individual's sense of temporality, or that person's concept of time, may influence communication behavior" (1982, p. 236).

Arguably no factor in communication thought processing is more likely to create conflict based on misunderstandings rooted in cultural differences than how we conceive of time. Before proceeding, it might prove useful to provide an example that has been repeated in various forms on thousands of occasions in cross-cultural interaction.

A U.S. automaker is sent on a sales trip to Saudi Arabia. The prospective Saudi client has set an appointment to meet with her, but when she arrives at exactly the preappointed time, she is asked if she would mind waiting. She is made comfortable, but after waiting for over an hour she demands to know how much longer she must wait. She does not receive a definite answer but is assured that her Saudi contact will meet with her as soon as he is free. She accepts this answer with an edge of irritation in her voice that she makes no effort to conceal, since she sincerely believes that she has been treated shabbily. To her amazement she waits an additional 2 hours before she is finally admitted to meet with the man she has come to see. Her problems, however, do not go away once the meeting has begun. The Saudi, for reasons beyond her ken, simply will not get down to business, even though they are running so late. Instead, he inquires about various people back in the United States whom he knows and with whom she works. Next he discusses the entire history of his relationship with her company, a relationship which she not only knows already but which also takes almost an hour to recount because of his annoying habit of sidetracking his narration onto what she feels are all sorts of irrelevant details. Invariably these details are about the people with whom he dealt at each step. Moreover, the entire time they are meeting, various people interrupt them either in person or on the telephone, and while he handles each interruption relatively quickly, she resents the lack of his undivided attention after having waited so long herself. Finally, before they have even discussed the sale for which they had set the meeting, the Saudi observes that it is getting very late and suggests that they meet again the following day. Even then, he only hints that he will buy the cars she has come to sell.

At this point, the U.S. businesswoman is certain the Saudi has intentionally snubbed her. Frustrated and angry, she tells the Saudi that he has not treated her professionally. She is confused by how sincerely surprised the Saudi seems at her response.

Back at her hotel, the U.S. auto executive ponders why she would have been treated so rudely. First, she thinks that perhaps the Saudi was treating her so poorly because she is a woman, and she has been told that women may not be treated as equals in some cultures, including Saudi Arabia. Still, she is aware that the Saudi seemed to go out of his way in his conversation to assure her that he both respected her and understood the important role women played in the company she represented. Indeed, in the many stories he related of the various people he knew from her company, she was aware that several had been about other women executives, and in all instances he had seemed to show very little overt sexism. Next, she thought, she had been snubbed because he was not interested in the product. He did hint, however, that he was going to buy the product before she left, although, much to her irritation, he did not say so directly at the time. Moreover, she could not figure out why he would have invited her to fly all the way to the Middle East to meet him if the product did not interest him. She concluded at last that she had not been snubbed at all but instead, based on the many interruptions and the rambling conversation, that the man was simply very disorganized. Still, she could not help but wonder, how could a man be so disorganized and attain so important a position in so well-respected a company. In fact, none of these reasons seemed to explain the Saudi's behavior.

What the U.S. executive did not consider was that the reason the Saudi acted the way he did was because he handled time differently than she did. To the Saudi, it would be wrong to cut short a meeting with a person simply to adhere to a schedule. To him people are more important than schedules, so he had no choice but to finish his discussion with his previous appointment before he could meet with the U.S. businesswoman. He felt that, as would most people in his culture, she would understand that this was the reason why she had to wait but that she, in turn, would not be cut short by his next appointment. In fact, he ended the day with her, sending the person with the next appointment home before they even had a chance officially to meet. Of course, to be able to spend this much time with her, he needed to handle the various pressing issues that accounted for the various interruptions in the meeting, such as when he had to explain to the person with the next appointment that he would have to see him tomorrow. He also believed, as is common in many cultures, that time spent developing a good personal relationship is more valuable than rushing into the details of business or the like. Unless one has a good personal relationship with a business partner—or anyone, for that matter—one could never fully trust that person. Relatedly, if one had trust, then one need not go over details of a deal too closely, since a person whom one trusted would not likely betray that trust. This is why the Saudi spent time telling the U.S. businesswoman the long history of his ties to her company and all the people at her company with whom he had developed a good personal relationship. In fact, he was shocked when at the end of the day the auto executive told him that she felt he had treated her poorly. He was distressed that he might lose his ties to the U.S. company and thought perhaps her outburst represented the company's official stance. After all, they had chosen to send a virtual stranger to see him, rather than any of those people with whom he had spent so much time establishing a good personal relationship.

The above example is hypothetical, but the difficulties described there have been experienced regularly in U.S.-Saudi interactions (Almaney and Alwan, 1982; Snowdon, 1986). Moreover, although it is dangerous to oversimplify, the illustration just described could have taken place in varying degrees in any number of configurations: a German in Peru, a Canadian in Nigeria, a Swede in Portugal. How one uses time, consequently, may profoundly affect the way in which one needs to communicate with those from other cultures and can be a cause of considerable conflict (Hall, 1984), as we have just seen.

The cause of the conflict is rooted in two different forms of temporal conception. In general, most people from the United States, Canada, and northern Europe regard time as inflexible, a thing to be divided, used, or wasted (Hall, 1984). For people from these cultures, "[T]ime can be manipulated. It can be used as a tool: to communicate information; to inspire fear; to invoke uncertainty; to create anger; or to demonstrate power" (Borisoff and Merrill, 1985, p. 67). These people (to use Hall's terms, 1984) are said to have a *monochronic* temporal conception. The U.S. businesswoman in our example was demonstrating what we could call classic monochronic behavior. This is not, however, a universal view. Throughout most of the Arab World, Latin America, and Central Africa, people are more likely to conceive of time as fluid, ranking personal involvement and completion of existing interactions above the demands of preset schedules. These people are said to be *polychronic* (Hall, 1984). The Saudi in our example could be said to have demonstrated classic polychronic behavior.

Admittedly, not all cultures can be so easily divided into monochronic and polychronic systems. Often certain subsets within a society function monochronically, while others within the same culture function polychronically. For example, the employees of most major corporations in the United States follow a strictly monochronic system. Many physicians in the United States, however, follow a comparatively polychronic system. Still, on the whole, one might generalize that U.S. culture follows a monochronic conception of time.

Because people generally complete tasks at the expense of scheduling in polychronic societies, people in high authority may become easily overwhelmed with multiple tasks. To prevent overloading people in positions of high authority, those in polychronic societies often use subordinates to screen for them (Hall, 1984). Once a person can get past those screenings, the person in authority will generally see the task through, regardless of the comparative importance of the task.

Because a polychronic system encourages one-on-one interaction, such cultural organization usually allows for highly personalized relationships to flourish between the person in authority and the task bringer. The flow of information is open in both directions at all times. Indeed, for the system to work smoothly, it is to the advantage of both superior and subordinate to stay fully aware of all aspects—professional and personal— of each other's lives. This personal involvement makes it even harder for the person in authority to refuse to carry out a request once the task is presented. In such situations, being able to break through those who screen for the person in authority is often the hardest part of having the person in authority assist in a task.

One's communication strategy in polychronic cultures therefore centers in large measure on simply *reaching* the appropriate individual. No direct barriers exist between the leader and the subordinate; the superior will almost always welcome the subordinate. This develops a system in which influence and close circles of contacts among those screening for those higher up creates an informal and unofficial communication hierarchy.

In a monochronic system personal feelings are rarely allowed to flourish on the job. This is precisely because personal involvement must not be allowed to disrupt preset schedules if the system is to function smoothly. Personal relationships are prescribed by the terms of the job. Multiple tasks are handled one at a time in a prescheduled manner. People in authority are, in contrast to those in polychronic cultures, available by scheduled appointments. In such a system, time, rather than the authority figure's subordinates or the personal relationship among the people involved, acts as a shield or screen for the authority figures.

Pseudoconflict is likely to occur when those from polychronic and monochronic systems meet. The monochronic person, for example, feels the polychronic person is making him or her wait needlessly for a scheduled appointment. The polychronic person, in turn, feels slighted by the monochronic individual's ostensibly cold use of time to end a meeting to adhere to that schedule even though more discussion between the parties may be warranted.

The communication strategy for the individual facing a generally polychronic system of temporal conception would differ significantly from the individual facing a monochronic one. First, in a polychronic system one should be aware that people distinguish between insiders and those outside the existing personal relationships. Moreover, the accessibility of the person in authority is often a function of this relationship. One must therefore try to establish an inside connection to facilitate the effectiveness of his or her message. By contrast, in a monochronic society one needs only to schedule an appointment with the appropriate people. The communicator should not expect people in a monochronic system to prefer those they know over strangers. The outsider—at least in the sense of having access to those in power—is treated in a similar fashion as the close associate.

Second, the communicator should be aware of the relatively large amount of information shared among those in a polychronic culture that is not necessarily related to the job at hand. As Hall has observed on this point: "Polychronic people are so deeply immersed in each other's business that they feel a compulsion to keep in touch. Any scrap of a story is gathered in and stored away. Their knowledge of each other is truly extraordinary" (1984, p. 50). One should expect therefore to keep in constant communication with those in a polychronic system. The communicator diminishes the effectiveness of his or her communication if such contact remains limited to times of direct need. Moreover, the monochronic belief that one must keep to the task at hand and avoid straying from a given subject is likely to clash with the polychronic need to stay informed of all aspects of the people with whom one communicates. The monochronic individual will likely insist on limiting communication to one subject at a time. The polychronic individual approaches communication holistically, handling numerous and often ostensibly unrelated subjects simultaneously.

The influence on communication of temporal conception is extensive. This is further complicated by the fact that no culture is exclusively polychronic or monochronic. Members of any culture lean to one direction or the other, although the cultures as a whole often organize their thoughts and conceive of time more one way or the other. The central issue here is to remain alert to communication differences that would indicate that one culture was more monochronic or polychronic. Armed with this awareness, the individual can adapt his or her communication strategies to avoid the pseudoconflict that the clash of these two temporal systems often creates.

Nonverbal Behavior

As discussed earlier in Chapter 3, nonverbal behavior plays a key role in interpersonal communication. As might be expected from that discussion, one of the most markedly varying dimensions of intercultural communication is nonverbal behavior. Because the subject of nonverbal communication has already been examined in depth earlier in this book, the discussion that follows represents only a brief overview of some of the more prominent cross-cultural aspects of nonverbal communication.

Knowledge of a culture conveyed through what a person says represents only a portion of what that person has communicated. Equally important to full communication is, in the words of Edward Hall, "the nonverbal language which exists in every country of the world and among various groups within each country. Most Americans are only dimly aware of this silent language even though they use it every day" (1959, p. 10).

While the subject of nonverbal communication as a whole is broader, much of this "silent language" in cross-cultural situations may be broken down into six areas: dress; kinesics, or body language; oculesics, or eye contact; haptics, or touching behavior; proxemics, or the use of body space; and paralanguage. Any one of these areas communicates significant information nonverbally in any given culture.

The fact that individuals from different cultures may have different interpretations for identical nonverbal clues can easily lead to conflict based on misunderstanding. In the arena of dress, for example, a European or North American may interpret as somewhat less than civilized and competent an Arab or Malaysian in traditional garb. Conflict could arise in this case if the European or North American were, based on the difference in appearance, to patronize his or her Arabic or Malaysian counterpart. Conversely, an Arab or Malaysian may well consider as flagrantly immoral the bare face, arms, and legs of a European or North American woman in a standard business suit. Conflict in such a situation could arise if the Arab or Malaysian were to indicate a sense of disdain or even refuse to deal with her because of this perceived affront to social and religious standards.

Differences in kinesics are often more subtle. Still, how people walk, gesture, bow, stand, or sit are all, to a large part, culturally determined. Thus, the various interpretations of day-to-day gestures described earlier in Chapter 3 may well not prove valid when people communicating are from different cultures. Ruesch and Kees have asserted that not only do the types and frequency of gestures people use vary from culture to culture but also that even the underlying purposes for using gestures are culture bound. Thus, Ruesch and Kees have suggested that

> gesture among the Americans is largely oriented toward activity; among the Italians it serves the purposes of illustration and display; among the Germans it specifies both attitude and commitment; and among the French it is an expression of style and containment. (1964, p. 22)

Kinesics appear to be linked to the language of a culture as well. As Genelle Morain (1987) has noted, those who viewed Fiorello LaGuardia in newsreel films in which the soundtrack was off were able to tell whether New York's trilingual mayor was speaking English, Italian, or Yiddish based merely on the culturally linked kinesics he used while speaking.

In many cases a kinesic sign or emblem well understood in one culture is totally unknown in another. In Indonesia and in much of the Arab World, for example, it is offensive to show the soles of one's feet or shoes to another. This often clashes with behavior in the United States, where foot crossing is common and no attention is paid to where one's sole points. In Japan a relatively elaborate system of bowing at varying degrees is common but has no counterpart in Europe or the Americas. This entire system of very expressive nonverbal communication is therefore lost in much Japanese interaction with those from other cultures.

Conflict deriving from misunderstanding can occur in instances where (a) a person from one culture expects an individual from another culture to understand the message he or she delivers nonverbally and (b) the person receiving that message does not respond as the sender expects.

Much more serious conflict can arise, however, when sending a nonverbal message that is recognized but that means something quite different in the culture of the person receiving the message than in the culture of the sender. One rather famous example of such a cross-cultural misunderstanding of nonverbal messages took place during the cold war between the United States and the Soviet Union. The Soviet head of state, Nikita Khruschev, visited the United States on a state visit. When he was met at the airport, he clasped his hands together and raised them over his shoulder. This gesture was duly shown over the television and in papers and readily misinterpreted by the U.S. audience. For them, Khruschev's gesture looked like that of a victorious boxer, with all its connotations. Khrushchev as a Russian, however, intended the nonverbal message to symbolize the clasping of hands in friendship. Thus, in the 1987 Leningrad concert of the U.S. musician Billy Joel, the crowd of Russian youths filling the concert hall almost all clasped their hands over their heads in a similar gesture.

Haptics, or touching behavior, also reflects cultural values. For example, in a generally nonhaptic society such as Japan, touching another person for any reason in public is traditionally avoided. Thus, when non-

Japanese shake hands with the Japanese, the Japanese are using an essentially unfamiliar practice. Conflict can occur when a non-Japanese interprets the limp or stiff handshake of a Japanese as a sign of weakness or formality rather than merely as a sign of unfamiliarity or lack of practice. The southern U.S. practice of friendly back slapping or exchanging hugs would likely be even more unfamiliar and because of its increased use of touch might prove distasteful to the Japanese or persons of other less haptic cultures. The United States itself is a fairly nonhaptic society, particularly among men. In many cultures which behave more haptically, expressive men often walk with arms interlinked or hold hands, behavior which to U.S. males might appear effeminate or overly intimate.

The use and meaning of eye contact, or oculesics, also varies significantly depending on the culture involved. In several cultures, for example, it is considered disrespectful to prolong eye contact with those who are older or of higher status. In many cultures it may be considered improper for women—regardless of age or status—to look men in the eye. By contrast, studies have shown that eye contact in the United States has less to do with age or rank (Beebe, 1974; Ellsworth and Ludwig, 1972)—although not necessarily so with gender (Henley, 1977)—than with a person's sense of belonging or credibility. While fairly steady eye contact in the United States may indicate the listener's interest and attentiveness, intense eye contact may provide anxiety or imply a threat because we have learned to interpret a stare in such ways.

What is important for the communicator to recall is that such an interpretation is culturally determined. Hall notes, for example, that "Arabs look each other in the eye when talking with an intensity that makes Americans highly uncomfortable" (1966, p. 151). Similarly, Jensen observes that "the educated Briton considers it part of good listening behavior to stare at his conversationalist and to indicate his understanding by blinking his eyes, whereas we Americans nod our head or emit some sort of grunt, and are taught from childhood not to stare at people" (1982, p. 265). By contrast, Dodd observes that Cambodians believe that meeting the gaze of another is insulting—something akin to invading one's privacy" (1982, p. 14). The degree to which eye contact in these examples is either greater or lesser than the amount considered appropriate according to the culture perceiving it is often misinterpreted. A culture with relatively more eye contact would be considered overly aggressive or threatening by an individual from a culture with less eye contact. A culture with relatively less eye contact, in turn, may be stereotyped as aloof, bored, or cold by an individual from a culture with more eye contact. Such misinterpretation may serve as barriers to effective cross-cultural interaction.

Finally, how far apart we stand from one another—proxemics—carries significant information to people who share the same culture. Here, too, as with other nonverbal behavior, such information is likely to be misinterpreted or misunderstood across cultures (Hall, 1961; Mehrabian,

1981). Copeland and Griggs have observed that "Americans are most comfortable when standing a little over an arms's length apart" (1985, p. 17). In many Latin American, southern European, and Middle Eastern cultures, however, a comfortable distance would be much closer. Indeed, in many parts of the world friendly or serious conversations are conducted close enough to feel the breath of the speaker on one's face.

Conflict based on misunderstanding can arise from these proxemic differences when distance considered too far or too close in one's own culture is interpreted erroneously as being either too intrusive and aggressive or too distant and formal. For example, a U.S. or Norwegian communicator unaware of a different individual use of spatial distance among Greeks or Algerians will face a very discomforting situation with the Greeks or Algerians literally backing their Norwegian or U.S. counterparts into a corner, as one party continues to move closer to the other party, who in turn continues to retreat.

ACTION

We have now established that conflict deriving from misunderstanding often occurs when communicating across cultures. We have established that those areas where such misunderstandings are likely to occur are differences in language, environment and technology, thought processing, and nonverbal communication behavior. Merely recognizing and acknowledging such differences, however, is not enough to prevent the attendant pseudoconflict likely to occur.

The course of action for diminishing the possibility of pseudoconflict deriving from intercultural communication differences can follow the 12-point procedure described in the action-interaction portion of Chapter 1.

Establish credibility   As Triandis (1976) implies, the ability to understand and acknowledge the similarities and differences between cultures leads to mutual respect and credibility in dealing with those from that culture. Armed with knowledge of the appropriate culture, we are best able to establish credibility with those from that culture. To obtain that knowledge we should seek out as much information as possible on the culture in question not only through reading or films but also, through asking those from that culture or those who are familiar with it. The types of information we should seek are outlined in the preceding sections of this chapter. It is important to stress that rather than approaching a culture with a list of "do's and don'ts," it is best to ask questions along the lines of cultural differences in language, environment and technology, thought processing, and nonverbal behavior. This way we approach the culture from a foundation of understanding on which we can build a recognition of likely behavior. A catalog of differences may tend to reinforce foreignness, undermining the fact that people behave as they do precisely because it makes sense within their culture to act in that manner.

Establish trust   Understanding differences and similarities between cultures is the essential first step on which all cross-cultural communication conflict containment should rest—but understanding itself is not enough. We must at all times work to establish trust in intercultural interpersonal interaction. Singer has pointed out that particularly in intercultural situations, "people who attribute a statement to someone they trust are likely to believe it, while if they attribute the same statement to someone they distrust they tend not to" (1987, p. 152). The difficulty is that that which conveys trust is itself often culturally determined. Thus, in a low-context society, a signed contract may provide evidence that an individual can trust another. In a high-context society, by contrast, a contract is only as valid as the relationship between the people involved—if the people do not know one another enough to trust each other before signing the contract, the contract itself will do little to offset that inherent lack of trust. Thus, to establish trust in a multicultural setting, it is necessary to recognize and then act on the principles that convey trust within the specific cultures involved.

Express problem   While we need to express the existence of a problem enough to recognize that a problem needs solving, it is important to remember that not all cultures respond identically to having a matter directly stated. The way a problem is expressed may prove difficult as well. As Stewart points out, "The conceptualization of the world in terms of problems" (1987, p. 55) to be solved in a rational way is a cultural tendency among those from the United States that is not widely shared. While the United States is not the only culture to emphasize rational, means-oriented problem solving, it is important to remember that in dealing with other cultures, particularly those in Asia and the Middle East, other perfectly acceptable means for conceptualizing conflict exist. Thus, the need to save face or the willingness to bow to the hand of God or fate may well prove more important than rational analysis. As Graham and Herberger (1987) observe, the standard U.S. approach to problem solving is to "lay your cards on the table." This approach demands a straightforward statement of points of view on a seemingly immutable truth. New conflict can easily arise from trying to solve existing conflicts if such a problem-solving style is not adapted to the way in which problems are raised in other cultures. For example, being intentionally deceptive about the facts of a matter or making another person expend a great deal of effort merely to determine the accurate facts of an issue are both considered abhorrent in the United States. Indeed, such behavior may be enough to bring conflict negotiation to an end. However, as Graham and Herzberger notes, "in Brazil, being tricky is a less serious transgression of negotiation ethics. It's even expected if a strong personal relationship between negotiators does not exist" (1987, p. 80).

Accurate communication   "The more culturally different the individuals are," Marshall Singer writes, "the more likelihood there is of distortion" (1987, p. 145). The problem in communicating across cultures is twofold. First, as with any interpersonal communication, a degree of error exists between what the sender of a message believes he or she has communicated and the way the person receiving that message interprets it. Here, the principles described in Chapter 2 on verbal communication should be applied. This problem, however, is compounded in communication across languages, as discussed earlier, by the inexactness inherent in any translation. We can offset this by choosing a translator or interpreter with great care. Thus, we would not trust an acquaintance with some high school French to translate an important letter. Nor should such a person with a few phrases of Vietnamese be viewed as particularly qualified to act as a crisis center interpreter for a substantial Vietnamese-speaking community. While some language knowledge is better than none in many instances, we should not underestimate the importance of finding the best qualified translator or interpreter in any situation in which accurate communication is important.

Recognizing status   The role of status has a great deal of variance across cultures. For example, the United States as a culture places far greater emphasis on egalitarianism than most cultures (Adler, 1986; Fisher, 1980; Graham and Herberger, 1987). This takes the form of using first names, downplaying titles, and viewing status-related ceremonies as a waste of time. Such behavior, much to the amazement of those from many other cultures, actually places people from the United States at ease. However, as Nancy Adler notes, "Most countries are more hierarchical and more formal than the United States, and most foreigners feel more comfortable in formal situations with explicit status differences" (1986, p. 163). Thus, people in Japan exchange business cards upon meeting each other not so much to keep in touch as in the United States but to allow one another to know their official status, and people in Germany would no sooner call each other by their first names in a business meeting than they would show up to that meeting in beach attire. The use of formal titles and the following of ceremony are not the only means to confer status however.

Cultural values toward age, gender, and the social class into which we are born all play a strong role in many cultures' view of status. While we cannot change these characteristics to accommodate another culture's values, it is possible to substitute others who are older, male, of a different social class, and so forth. Accommodating a culture's different beliefs on these characteristics, however, in itself raises ethical issues likely to create other types of conflict. What is important to the communicator hoping to lessen the possibility of avoidable negative conflict is to be aware that such status-linked differences exist for various cultures and to try, through recognition, to offset to whatever degree possible the conflict arising between differing views of these variant values. Thus, a young person representing her university at a conference in a culture such as China which confers greater status on those who are older would be advised to emphasize those areas of status—rank, accomplishments—qualifying her to represent her university. At the same time, she would be advised to show respect for those Chinese older than her and not to diminish their values even though by her very presence as university representative she does not adhere to those values.

Establish goals   In the cross-cultural arena, as with the other forms of communication-based conflict management discussed in this book, the establishment of goals is necessary to work toward objectives for overcoming the conflict at hand. In cross-cultural communication, though, the form that those goals may take is shaped by the process a culture prefers in reaching those goals. The way in which a culture processes thought, as we have discussed, influences the way in which its members communicate. Thus, while members of different cultures may agree to the same end goals, the way in which those goals are understood may prove to be so dissimiliar that the identical goals may not be *perceived* as being the same. For example, if a person from New York were working with one individual from Moscow and a third from Tunis on how to solve world hunger, all three might agree on the end goal of eliminating hunger, but in the process of articulating the belief in that end goal might convince each other that they actually *dis*agree with each other. Adler (1986) has chacterized North Americans as factual, Arabs as affective, and Russians as axiomatic. In an admittedly oversimplified version of this situation, the New Yorker might stress the factual: the number of hungry, the amount of money it would take to feed them, the system needed to transport the food, the organization of the people administering the program, and so forth. The Muscovite, in turn, might more likely appeal to the ideals at issue: Would all the hungry receive equal shares of food, would the food be used as a means of one group to impose their will on another, or what would be the long-term ideological consequences of feeding the hungry. The Tunisian, in turn, might choose to stress the affective details of the situation: the hardship the hungry experienced, the importance that the hungry not be forced to lose their essential human dignity in accepting the food, the long-term relationships and bonds that such a program would initiate. Moreover, disagreements on these issues could arise only if the three could reach a consensus to work together at all. Thus, the New Yorker with a factual bias may feel justified in knowing in advance how much each of the others would contribute and when they would do so. The Tunisian, in turn, could conceivably interpret the demand for hard figures as a lack of good faith. The Muscovite might feel suspicious as to the asserted ideals behind such a request. This triangle of misinterpretation could take almost endless permutations as well.

Consequently, the communicator should establish goals to reach consensus in conflict resolution. The communicator must, however, in the process of establishing those goals, constantly be aware of the cultural factors discussed in this chapter already.

Anticipate reactions   As in all communication, it is important in intercultural exchange to assess the likely reaction of the audience with whom one communicates. The less we know about the culture to which another belongs, though, the more difficult it is to anticipate that individual's likely reactions. In addition to acquiring as much information as possible before entering into an intercultural communication situation, we must actively attempt to seek out information even as the communication occurs. It is helpful to generalize about probable reactions, but such anticipated responses can easily transform into stereotypes if they are not continually modified. A broad range of behavior exists from person to person within the parameters of any given culture. We should therefore make generalizations regarding anticipated reactions with the express intent of disproving them.

Give and receive feedback   Several experts (Couch and Hintz, 1975; Ruben, 1987; Sarbaugh, 1979) suggest that among the most important dimensions of successful cross-cultural communication is the willingness to give and receive feedback. Ruben (1987) indicates two benefits of taking turns. First, reciprocity in communication implies interest in and concern for the other party. This contributes to building both the credibility and trust discussed above. The second benefit is the opportunity that, giving and receiving feedback allows the communicator for collecting more information about the other party's culture, way of thinking, and communicational framework.

Maintain adaptability   To accommodate cultural differences, the ability to adapt to unfamiliar ways of doing things and of thinking of the world is necessary. Flexibility and the ability to remain nonjudgmental are keys to open and effective cross-cultural communication.

Seek out creative means of problem solving   While creativity is generally a useful attribute in attempting to resolve any conflict situation, in cross-cultural problem solving the need to seek creative solutions is particularly important for two reasons. First, seeking creative solutions to perceived conflict allows for greater opportunity to detour perceptual difficulties blocking a common solution. That is, by seeking nonconventional approaches to conflict resolution, it is possible to work around those pseudoconflicts which are based less on the facts of the situation at hand than on the culturally based differences in the *perception* of those facts.

Second, agreeing on common solutions in problem solving is important, but approaching a problem from our own perspective is often unacceptable in reaching consensus with those from other cultures. The culture to which we belong directly affects the manner of thinking about, outlook toward, and the way in which problems are solved. The strategies a culture uses as well as its institutions for dealing with conflict reflect the basic values of that society (Likert and Likert, 1976; Moran and Harris, 1982). Seeking creative approaches to conflict management and problem solving allows for the members of all cultures concerned to create a new method of handling the situation at hand drawn from the principles on which the various cultures involved are based, but not bound to any one culture's way of handling the problem. The creative combination of culturally divergent approaches to the same problem reduces the risk of antagonizing members of any of the cultures involved because their own cultural input has been respected and in part used. Moreover, this creative combination of culturally divergent approaches to the problem allows for the opportunity for cultural synergy, in which the contributions of the various cultures involved in a problem create a stronger solution than any existing solutions to similar problems within a single culture (Adler, 1986; Moran and Harris, 1982). In such cases the sum of the parts is greater than the whole, as in the cultural synergy which came about in Japan in the 1960's by creatively combining aspects of U.S. and Japanese management approaches to create the so-called Theory Z management style (Ouchi, 1981).

Maintain open channels of communication   In all conflict management keeping the channels of communication open is important. In cross-cultural situations, however, as we have seen, this may at times prove to be particularly difficult. How to keep the channels open is itself culturally determined. For example, many cultures—most notably in Asia—do not value the airing of ideas and the expression of feelings; in the United States and much of Europe such behavior is often considered the *only* way to keep the channels of communication open. Similarly, U.S. communicators tend to think in individualistic terms when keeping the channels of communication open. Indeed, the central role of the individual has been suggested as being the most quintessentially characteristic of U.S. culture (Rogers, 1964; Stewart, 1987). Yet such an outlook may actually close down communication channels in collectivistic cultures which would not define problems in individualistic terms. Nevertheless, no matter what the cultural norms, it is possible to maintain open channels of communication once the communication process has been adjusted to accommodate those cultural norms.

Summarize decisions   Once conflict solutions have been decided, it is important to summarize those decisions for clarity and to ensure agreement. This would hold true whether dealing within a single or a multiple cultural setting. In a multicultural setting, though, summarizing decisions is particularly important, since the odds for inexact communication are higher. Just as pseudoconflict can occur when parties from different cultures perceive an irreconcilible difference where none exists, so too can *pseudoagreement* occur, when those parties incorrectly perceive that a common solution exits. Summarizing decisions increases the opportunity for discovering such cross-cultural pseudoagreement.

ANALYSIS

To increase our skills at communicating in a cross-cultural situation, it is necessary to analyze what has transpired once the 12 points of the action phase have been implemented. By reexamamining what occurred in any given cross-cultural interaction, the communicator can adjust his or her behavior in future encounters.

The analysis process may be divided into three steps. First, the communicator should review the expectations he or she held before the cross-cultural encounter took place. By examining which expectations were met and which did not materialize, the communicator can gain valuable insights into how he or she sterotypes those from the culture in question.

Second, the communicator can sharpen his or her skills in communicating with those from the cultures in question by noting in the cross-cultural encounter that behavior which was unexpected both on his or her own part and on the part of the person from the other culture. Moreover, the communicator would do well to try to determine why the behavior he or she has observed has taken place. Within this, it is advisable as well for communicators to remain aware of their emotions and feelings regarding the cross-cultural encounter. Even though these emotions and feelings may not surface as observable behavior, they provide valuable clues to analyzing how we approach cross-cultural interactions.

Finally, the communicators are advised to record their observations in writing. Then immediately before and after future cross-cultural encounters, they should review these notes, not only to determine how much they have remembered but also, more important, to establish to what extent their views may have changed. They can further understand their thought processing by establishing why these views have altered. They should try to determine whether these changes are due to the distancing effect of time or through reading or through other cross-cultural experiences and why factors affected their beliefs.

By analyzing his or her cross-cultural experiences in this manner, the communicator can learn to adjust behavior in future encounters. This way she or he can develop a truly multicultural understanding and in so doing greatly reduce the risk of future culturally based conflict.

SUMMARY

In situations involving parties from two or more cultures, the differences in those cultures can seriously affect communication. This chapter has discussed the role misunderstandings and perceived conflict—or pseudo-conflict—plays in cross-cultural communication. Ways to reduce the negative effects of communication-based pseudoconflict derived from cultural differences were also discussed.

It has been asserted here that we need to follow several steps in managing cross-cultural misunderstandings. The first step is assessment of the unique features of cross-cultural communication. This involves both the recognition of the importance of culture in communication and basic understanding of culture in the abstract. Only then is it possible to see the climate in which communication-based cross-cultural conflict takes place clearly enough to manage conflict situations likely to occur in a multicultural setting.

The second step is acknowledgment. This involves examining why culturally caused misunderstanding occurs. To do so, the communicator must grapple with his or her own ethnocentrism and develop empathy for the other party. Understanding the other party's perspective reduces the level of uncertainty in any cross-cultural communication.

The third and most difficult step is attitude adjustment. This step involves analyzing the possible sources of cross-cultural pseudoconflict in both the communicator's own behavior and the behavior of the culturally different parties with whom he or she interacts. To this end, a cross-cultural communication checklist was discussed covering the four main factors likely to create pseudoconflict in such situations: language, place, thought processing, and nonverbal communication behavior. To some extent, all four of these factors appear to be deceptively universal while changing—often dramatically—from culture to culture.

A fourth step, action, was next discussed. The 12-point plan of action for reducing communication-based conflict—as discussed throughout this book—was adapted to meet the needs of the cross-cultural communicator. Applying this plan of action will not necessarily eliminate all culturally derived pseudoconflict but is nonetheless a means to actively reduce the barriers to cross-cultural communication that cause pseudoconflict.

Finally, a last step—analysis—was suggested. By analyzing what occurred in each cross-cultural interaction to reexamine what transpired, the communicator can learn to adjust behavior in future multicultural encounters and, through this, lessen the chance for future culturally based conflict.

SUGGESTED ACTIVITIES

A. Focus on stereotyping

Students or seminar participants are each given a piece of white chalk taken from a box of chalk in which the pieces look as similar to one another as possible. The students are then given 5 minutes to examine their particular piece of chalk closely, selecting features that give their piece of chalk its own unique characteristics. At the end of the 5-minute examination period, the students are asked to write down their observations regarding their piece of chalk. Selected students read their observations aloud. The class should discuss the differences observed in the chalk pieces. A comparison between chalk and people should lead to a discussion of stereotyping and to the power to observe differentiating details among seemingly like elements.

The instructor should next collect the chalk, taking care to note where the chalk pieces belonging to two or three students have been placed. Laying the chalk pieces out on a table or desk, the instructor should call on the students who laid down the chalk pieces whose placement he or she had noted. A discussion may then follow depending on whether the students were or were not able to pick out the pieces that they had studied.

B. Focus on self-awareness

Each student or seminar participant should be asked to recall an encounter with a person from another culture. If a student knows no person from another culture, he or she should be asked to recall such an encounter with a person from another ethnic group. Students should then divide a piece of paper into three columns, marking the first column *before*, the second as *during*, and the third *after*, then number each column from 1 to 5 as shown below:

Before	During	After
1	1	1
2	2	2
3	3	3
4	4	4
5	5	5

Students should next record in the *before* column five expectations they remember having had before their encounter regarding people from that culture. They should then record their thoughts while the encounter occurred regarding that expectation in the *during* column. Then the students should indicate their current feelings toward each of the expectations they listed regarding the culture in question in the *after* column.

Students should then discuss or write a short analysis regarding why their expectations changed or remained constant. They should also comment on how those expectations might have created or avoided possible points of conflict depending on the inconsistency or consistency of those expectations.

An illuminating extension of this exercise is to have the students share these observations with someone from the culture in question. Does the person from that culture share the views of his or her culture that the student's evaluation suggests?

C. Focus on language and context

Students or group participants should be broken into an even number of small groups. Each small group should be instructed to select three nonsense phrases with which to replace three common expressions. For example, the nonsense word *quibblezip* might be used to replace the phrase *Do you know what I mean?*

The small groups should then be paired off. The class should then be given a subject to discuss, perhaps the ways in which language and contexting may create pseudoconflict in cross-cultural communication. In the discussion group members should use the common expressions they have selected, replacing the expression with the nonsense phrases they have selected.

The discussion should be allowed to run at least five minutes or more so that adequate time has been allowed for the expression to be used several times.

At the close of the discussion students should see if they were able to identify the meaning of the nonsense phrases from context alone.

The class should then be polled as to how many people were able to identify all three phrases.

A discusssion should then follow on several subjects:

a. How did the students feel about the use of the nonsense phrases? Was it disruptive? Annoying? Stupid?
b. In what way could the way students felt about the use of the nonsense phrases lead to conflict?
c. What role did contexting play in determining the meaning of the nonsense phrases?

D. Focus on environment

Provide students or group participants with a photograph of a typical U.S. kitchen, a typical Japanese kitchen and a typical West German kitchen. (These may be obtained from advertisements, from actual photographs, or from books on interior design or architecture.)

Students should answer several questions to determine that the role the environment plays in shaping the outlook a person holds to be universal or at least normal:

a. How big is each kitchen compared to the others?
b. What sort of appliances or objects do the three share? Are any of these appliances or objects different in any notable way? Why or why not?
c. Would cooking in the three kitchens differ? Would eating in the kitchens differ?
d. How would the differences in the three kitchens affect an advertising campaign for a microwave oven? For a dishwashing machine? For plastic storage containers?
e. Could differences in how the kitchen environment is used create a conflict between advertising executives determining the appropriate

promotional campaign for these three cultures? For guests from one of these cultures in the homes of the other cultures? For others?

E. Focus on social organization

Students should select several magazines from the United States and several magazines from another country of their choice (obtainable through the library or an international magazine vendor).

Students should examine advertising in the magazines for major items affecting the family (life or medical insurance, savings accounts, financial planning, and so on).

A discussion should follow regarding what these advertisements imply about the social organization of the culture from which they are taken by answering questions such as those that follow:

    a. Do the advertisements show pictures of a single man making a decision for his family? Are they shown with a husband and wife jointly making the decision? What does this say about the role of men in the society? Of married couples?

    b. Are there children in the advertisements? If so, what role do they play? What does this say about the role played by family in these cultures?

    c. Do the advertisements use animation or humorous pictures, or is the subject seriously handled? How much of the advertisement is devoted to printed material? How much is devoted to illustrations? Are the illustrations pertinent to the information or are they intended to set a mood? What might this say about how the subjects of these advertisements are viewed in their respective cultures?

    d. Could what the differences implied in these lead to conflict in other situations? Explain.

F. Focus on nonverbal behavior

Have participants or students watch a foreign film. What differences from the United States do they observe in kinesics? In proxemics? In eye contact? In touching behavior?

A discussion should follow on how these differences could lead to misunderstanding and pseudoconflict.

G. Focus on temporal conception

Students or participants should divide into groups of three and hold a conversation on a topic of their choice, perhaps on the role temporal conception plays in communication. One person in each group should be instructed to count silently to 25 before responding to any comment or question. The other two members of the group should speak normally.

Following this conversation, students should examine how they felt about the delayed response time. Specifically they might find it useful to discuss some of the following questions.

(For the student who employed the delayed response time)

    a. Did you find it difficult to participate in the conversation?

    b. Did you find any advantages to employing a delayed response time?

    c. In the United States many people consider a quick response time a sign

of high intelligence. This belief is not universally held. How does this make you feel about a culture that values a slower response time? Why do you think, based on your experience in this exercise, people in some cultures would think that a slow response time was favorable?
d. How might a delayed response time when used in the United States create conflict, particularly in a pressuresome or tense situation?

(For the students who did not employ the delayed response time)
a. Did you find it difficult to converse with the person employing the slow response time?
b. What disadvantages did you observe about a person using a delayed response time? Did you see any advantages?
c. How might conflict result when people from the United States deal with someone from a culture in which a delayed response time was customary in pressuresome or tense situations?

SIX
HOW WRITING STYLES
CAN CREATE CONFLICT

Writing is an *unnatural* activity. It must be taught formally and studied deliberately. And many of the problems that arise in learning to write are simply problems in finding the proper written equivalent for the materials of speech. The spelling of our words is a clumsy attempt to reproduce the sounds of our voices. The punctuation of our sentences and setting off of paragraphs is designed to give some approximation of the pauses and intonations we use automatically to give shape and point to our speaking. . . . If there were no compensations for all these disadvantages, then communicating with other people through the medium of squiggles on paper would be as unsatisfactory as trying to wash your feet with your socks on. Fortunately, there *are* compensations (even though that word *are* has to be printed in italic type in order to capture an intonation that would be conveyed effortlessly in speech). (Scholes and Klaus, 1972)

Few communication tools serve to manage conflict as effectively as an appropriately chosen writing style. Unlike speech, writing allows the luxury of one-sided communication—a monologue weighted in the writer's favor. While writing well can prove to be among the strongest of tools to reduce the likelihood of conflict, inappropriate writing styles may not only increase existing levels of conflict but also, often create conflict where none existed before. How effectively a writer increases or reduces conflict is based largely on the tone and style the writer chooses, the situation at hand, and the perceived needs of the reader.

As discussed throughout this book, not all conflict is nonproductive. Controlled conflict that increases resourcefulness, competitiveness, or the testing of alternative viewpoints can provide an important managerial tool. However, conflict deriving expressly from the way in which something is written rather than from an underlying, intentional, and controlled source of conflict is almost always negative in its consequences. Such conflict arises from chance rather than choice and frequently escalates into damaging interpersonal relationships. Consequently, many authors—particularly in the field of business—have stressed the importance of clear and accurate writing as a means of avoiding negative conflict (Bovee and Thill, 1986; Brown, 1982; Harcourt, Krizan and Merrier, 1986; Hatch, 1983; Lewis, 1987; Murphy and Hildebrandt, 1984; Pearce, Figgins and Golen, 1984; Smeltzer and Waltman, 1984; Wolf and Kuiper, 1984).

To avoid the adverse consequences of unclear or unintentionally inflammatory writing style, it is important to take into account the three basic steps of writing: conceptualization, transmittal, and reception (Victor, 1986). Writing style conflict comes from a misjudgment of one of these steps.

ASSESSMENT: A MATTER OF CONCEPTUALIZATION

The conceptualization process parallels the assessment step in the "five A" model decribed earlier. Conceptualization requires that the writer firmly assess the purpose of his or her writing. Unless the writer clearly understands at the outset which objectives he or she wishes to accomplish through the piece of writing, it is unlikely that the reader will be able to understand fully what the writer intended to convey. The transmittal step is the actual process of putting words on paper. Several difficulties inherent in language itself may undermine, at times, even the best intentions. Finally, unless those words are chosen with the reader in mind, no matter how clearly the writer understands the message and its objectives, the reader may not receive them in the manner the writer desires. When the writer gives insufficient attention to any of these basic steps—conceptualization, transmittal, or reception—the writer risks creating nonproductive writing-style conflict.

At the core of a great deal of conflict deriving from writing style is the writer's failure to conceptualize the purpose of the piece of writing. Unless the writer clearly understands the precise purpose of what he or she writes, the chance is greatly reduced that the reader will act in the intended manner after reading the message. The difference between the desired action and the actual outcome creates unecessary and nonproductive conflict.

When the written communication attempts to solve a problem, it might seem that the purpose of the piece would be obvious—to resolve the problem. Yet often before writing, the writer fails to anticipate precisely the nature of the problem. For example, a company president may observe an increase in absenteeism in a certain company division. The president may then send a memorandum requesting a report from the division head. This might read:

> Please summarize the performance of the personnel in your division.

This request, in turn, could prove inadequate because it fails to explain the president's underlying purpose of gauging absenteeism. If the division head does understand *why* the president has asked for the report, the report may inadequately describe, or even ignore, the absenteeism problem. Indeed, in attempting to place the division in the best possible light, the division head may not address the absenteeism problem at all, focusing instead on the division's increased production over the last quarter. Without direction from the president, the division head can only surmise the purpose of the report. Consequently, the report does not solve the problem, and the president, by failing to specify a purpose, has wasted the division head's time, and cost the company an unnecessary expense, and he still has no solution to the absenteeism problem.

Conceptualization, however, often goes beyond determining the purpose of the communication. Generally, writers attempt to maintain a certain attitude in their writing. They may wish to persuade a reader to follow a certain suggestion, as in a sales letter, or they may wish simply to inform the reader while appearing as objective as possible, as in a financial statement. In other instances a writer's primary purpose may center on avoiding blame and only give secondary importance to explaining fully the facts of a situation.

Further difficulties may arise when writers fail to balance the content of their communication. Indeed, writers may lose sight of the ostensible purpose of what they write if they become overly concerned with a secondary aim or with a purpose which for them is more important than it is for their readers. In turn, by attending only to the ostensible purpose, a writer may alarm the reader. For example, the company president in the preceding example could have written a direct request for information regarding absenteeism in the division:

> Please provide a report to me on the high rate of absenteeism in your division.

In such a memorandum the president makes clear that the absentee rate in the division is of concern. In response the division head may well have written a different report but not necessarily a report which would prove any more useful to the president. The division head, for instance, may have felt threatened by the president's inquiry. As a result a large part of the report might attempt to deny direct responsbility for the absenteeism or divert the president's attention from the problem of absenteeism to some positive aspect of the division such as the increased productivity. The ostensible purpose of the report in such a case would be to inform the president about absenteeism in the division. The division head's primary purpose, however, is not the same as the ostensible purpose. Indeed, the division head's primary purpose most likely is to avoid blame for the problem. If the division head were to concentrate too heavily on the attempt to deny responsbility, the report might still not contain the information the president needed. Ideally, the division head would have balanced the need to inform the president against the need for protection. The president, however, could have saved time and might have received a more direct reply had the request indicated that no blame would be assigned or that the report should contain only information regarding the absenteeism rate.

When writing in a potentially explosive situation, writers must identify and address the potential conflict in the least antagonizing manner possible. Although anger or other strong emotional entrenchments often characterize a conflict situation, the expression of such feelings should rarely serve as one's purpose for writing. In particular, a number of experts have shown that threats or attempts to intimidate others through hostile or antagonizing statements reduce the ability to achieve consensus among parties in conflict (Bales, 1970; Burke, 1970). Rather, writers in potentially explosive situations should attempt to maintain as objective a tone as they can. To do so, they should stress objectively concrete goals or suggestions. William Brooks and Philip Emmert note that "When messages are orientational and substantive, when they clarify and emphasize expectations, procedures, sanctions, and promises of reward, then cooperative behavior is likely to be facilitated" (1976, 230). Bearing this in mind, the writer may have to alter the very nature of the content (that is, the ostensible purpose) of the message if one of the primary purposes for writing is to avoid or to manage conflict.

In any case, for the writer to write as if no factors outside of the ostensible purpose mattered in a conflict situation will increase the inherent tensions needlessly. Only after the writer adjusts the tone and focus of the message to reduce as much as possible any inherent tension can he or she safely address the ostensible issue at hand.

ACKNOWLEDGMENT: RECEPTION

To reduce effectively the possible tensions inherent in a message, the writer must thoroughly analyze how the reader may receive the message.

Reception is the acknowledgment step in our "five-A" model. To analyze the way a reader receives a given message, then, is to acknowledge or to attempt to understand the reader's perception. Arguably the most dangerous conflict-causing error a writer can make is to write a message as if it were intended for the writer alone, without consideration for the reader. At the source of such an error is the failure of the writer to recognize that writing is only as effective as its ability to influence the message's reader in the manner the writer envisions. Unless the writer *anticipates* the message's reception—that is, the likely reaction of the reader—the ability of the writing to influence the message's reader in the desired manner will rest on chance rather than on choice. In short, writing which does not consciously attempt to accommodate the likely reactions of its recipient seriously diminishes its reliability and may provoke conflict. For example, a letter to a union's membership regarding a less than favorable collective bargaining agreement with an employer requires a different approach from the same letter directed to the employer's management team. The membership's letter may read as follows:

> The following letter details the results of our union's recent collective bargaining session. Though all our demands were not met, we believe that the members will find that the key issues are addressed.

The management team may receive a message stating:

> The following letter details the results of the negotiation with Local 123 of the XYZ Union. Unfortunately, several points had to be conceded to reach a settlement. The consequences should be mitigated by avoiding a lengthy strike which may have severely affected production and long term profits.

While the content in both letters is essentially the same, the writer has adjusted each letter's tone and format to account for the fact that one audience would read such information as bad news, while the other would see it as potentially good news. Still, writers in such situations all too frequently consider only their purpose at hand—to indicate the results of the new labor-management collective-bargaining agreement.

The need to analyze and acknowledge one's audience before actually writing, however, holds even when dealing with less obviously inflammatory situations than that just described. By attempting to visualize a specific picture of the recipient of their communication, writers can reduce many potential conflicts inherent in a one-sided communication medium such as writing, which does not allow the reader to respond quickly.

Those writers least likely to create unproductive conflict among their readers visualize their receivers in detail—a process we may call *audience analysis*. They acknowledge the attitudes, rank, age, gender, experience, area of expertise, or whatever pertinent data they can accumulate about those to whom they write. Even if they send a message of some sort to an unknown recipient, such writers attempt to construct some concept of a plausible recipient. If the piece of communication is written for a group, an effective writer will focus on as specific a representative sampling as possible and write for that particular audience. Above all, those writers least likely to create unproductive conflict among their readers attempt to anticipate and adjust their writing for the possible response their communication is likely to provoke.

ATTITUDE: TRANSMITTAL

The analysis of purpose and audience addresses what may well be possible sources of true conflict. The interim step in the communication process in which the conceptualization (purpose) is *transmitted* to the recipient (audience) often does not represent a true conflict at all, however. To the extent that conflict-free transmittal of a message hinges on the consideration of behavior and perspective from the point of view of both writer and reader, it parallels the "attitude" step of our "five-A" model. Transmittal problems in writing often represent perceived disagreements or pseudo-conflicts on the part of parties who actually do agree.

While such superficial conflict may initially appear easy to control, frequently it remains deceptively hard to contain at the simplest stage. As Miller and Steinberg observe, "pseudoconflicts are quite difficult to manage effectively. People frequently jump to conclusions about the reality of the perceived conflict and never think to verify their perceptions" (1975, p. 267).

These assumptions or false conclusions may readily escalate to the level of what Miller and Steinberg term ego conflict (1975, p. 267). Ego conflict is the state in which conflicting parties become so involved emotionally in their perception of the conflict that they can no longer divest themselves of inherently hostile relational transactions without losing face or feeling deep resentment. Ego conflicts often occur in contract negotiations in which each party represents his or her interests. Fees and terms offered may be viewed as an affront by the potential contractee, while the contractor may solely be attempting to make the best possible deal for her or his organization without considering how his or her actions may affect the quality of the work of the contractee. Even if a neutral arbiter points out that the difficulty is only a pseudoconflict based on a misunderstanding, the parties are often too deeply involved at that point to allow cooperative communication to resolve their differences.

In writing, pseudoconflict normally arises from two causes. The first derives simply from errors in writing style, which we may term *unrecognized linguistic communication conflict.* The second cause, tonal error, rests not in the misuse of the language but in the miscalculation of the wording required to address best the reader's needs while fulfilling the purpose intended.

Transmissional—or linguistic communication—conflict has at its root the fact that language is itself a faulty means of communication (Whorf, 1952). As discussed throughout this book, all languages are, at best, approximate media for conveying information. Three basic factors contribute to the inability to communicate in differing degrees:

1. Vocabulary variation
2. Language misusage
3. Semantic unclarity

Vocabulary Variation

Vocabulary variation takes two forms: dialect differences and professional jargon. Both of these tend to limit the number of readers who can understand fully what is written. A reader's inability to follow the meaning of a message due to vocabulary variation can in itself cause conflict through misinterpretation. Moreover, preconceived attitudes toward particular variants may isolate or even antagonize those who do not share those variations.

Dialect Differences

Of the two forms vocabulary variation takes, dialect differences in formal writing are the least likely to produce conflict through actual misinterpretation. Regional slang or colloquialisms, however, are still often limited enough to mislead or alienate those who do not belong to the group, and consequently most writers should take care to avoid such phrasing.

Nevertheless, even though most readers can understand dialect differences, conflict often arises from their use for a secondary reason. Sociolinguistic biases regarding certain uses of the language often encourage some groups to look down on those using forms they consider substandard (Trudgill, 1974). Thus, a reader accustomed to standard American English may look down on the language of a writer using an Appalachian or other nonstandard dialect. Although the reader understands what the writer means, the reader may not give full credit to the writer's ideas because the dialect of the writing may not appear educated enough to merit full credibility.

In return, emotional defensiveness might arise on the part of those groups whose dialects may have been viewed, for whatever reason, in a negative light. The consequent emotional investment could then easily lead to ego conflict based on the variant dialect users's indignation. Similarly, the standard dialect user is likely to view the variant dialect as wrong (rather than different) and so may become emotionally invested in maintaining what he or she perceives to be correct usage.

Professional Jargon

Still, vocabulary variation does not manifest itself most problematically in dialect differences but in the use of professional jargon. In an age of increasingly specialized labor and complicated technology, many professions have developed their own vocabulary variations, a sort of occupational dialect.

As with all vocabulary variation, jargon risks confusing the reader who is unfamiliar with it. Worse than this, jargon often acts as a profession's passwords to exclude those who do not belong to the group. Thus, jargon often intimidates those unfamiliar with it, especially newcomers to the profession or those outside it. This in turn may lead to open conflict if the readers unfamiliar with the jargon feel patronized, isolated, or less intelligent. In turn, they attempt to equalize the perceived power imbalance by, for example, making the jargon user feel incompetent. Similarly, uninitiated readers may believe that their lack of understanding diminishes their credibility in the organization or in the specialized field that uses the jargon. Subsequently, they may react rashly to protect themselves and, by failing to take the necessary time and care in their actions, unnecessarily create conflict situations. Finally, readers may feel hostile toward the writer who uses jargon as they believe—often justly—that the writer deliberately uses such language either to belittle or to confuse them. For example, house buyers may grow irritated with a mortgage company when the company has written the mortgage agreement in language they cannot understand. This sense of irritation is likely to stem from a feeling that the company is deliberately obfuscating the agreement to take advantage of them. The resultant ego conflict involved in such a reaction may be very difficult to overcome.

Language Misusage

Language misusage, the second element in written linguistic communication conflict, falls into either usage ignorance or ambiguity. Many writers, even successful politicians and executives and respected educators and scientists, are ignorant of the basic rules governing their language. They misconjugate verbs or vary their verb tenses without reason. They misspell words (some classics are "seperate" rather than "separate", "definate" rather than "definite") or choose words which do not mean what they intend. They use double negatives or indecipherably entangled syntax. To compound the matter, many of these people are wholly unaware of their errors. Like vocabulary variations, errors due to grammatical ignorance may lead to conflict when the writer's words become so unclear as to be incomprehensible.

Similarly, readers who catch the writer's mistakes may consider themselves superior to the writer and either disregard or look down on the content of the message.

Conflict arises because the grammatical errors reflect only on the writer's ability to handle the language and not on the reasoning behind the message. Such emotional overtones and prejudice, as with dialect differences, are deeply rooted in the reader's preconceptions about education, language, and competency. Still, the reader must attempt to see beyond such superficial difficulties to the actual message at hand. Only in this way can the reader prevent escalating the situation from one based on inaccurate communication (but one in which both parties essentially agree) to real conflict, potentially involving the emotional entrenchment of both parties.

Ambiguity is language misusage that is technically correct but carries more than one acceptable meaning. As language itself is an imperfect medium to convey ideas, such situations are relatively common. At times, ambiguity adds power to the language. Ambiguity is a favorite device of poets. For example, in Wallace Stevens's famous poem, "Anecdote of the Jar," he opens as follows:

I placed a jar in Tennessee
And round it was, upon a hill.

Here the phrase, "And round it was," can refer both to the poet who stayed "'round" the jar and to the shape of the jar itself. The ambiguity adds resonance to the poem and makes it amusing to read. Imagine such ambiguity in a business situation, however, and the results can become disastrous. One employee might write the following in a memorandum:

I have discussed planting the landscape with managers.

Like the ambiguous line in the poem, this statement carries more than one meaning. The employee might seem to say that she had discussed *using* the managers—rather than gardners—to plant the landscape. A reader might even read such a statement as meaning that the employee intends to plant the landscape *with* managers (rather than bushes or trees). Still, as these two meanings are somewhat nonsensical, most readers will understand the writer's intended statement that she had discussed with managers her ideas regarding the landscape. She will be understood, although she will likely lose credibility as an effective communicator.

Unfortunately, many ambiguities are not so clearly unraveled. For instance, readers would more likely feel confused if the same employee had written a statement such as the following:

I discussed running the program with the temporary workers.

As in the previous example, the reader may infer more than one meaning from this sentence. In this case, though, both meanings make sense. On the one hand, the writer might have meant that she had discussed with the temporary workers a way to run the program. Just as plausibily, though, a reader might interpret her to mean that she discussed a way to use temporary workers for running the program. As readers have no way of knowing which interpretation is correct, they may act in a manner that the writer did not intend. The resulting misinterpretation, depending on its seriousness, could easily escalate to open conflict as both writer and readers would feel fully justified in the actions they took.

Semantic Unclarity

The last category of linguistic communication conflict is semantic unclarity. Semantics, the meanings or connotations of words, vary in the emphasis different words have for different readers. As discussed in Chapter 2, readers bring their own experiences to bear when interpreting any communicative act. Different environmental, social, and cultural influences shape each reader's understanding of the world. These different views of the world, in turn, tend to influence the subtle variations alternate readers associate with the same word. The word *pet*, for example, may mean a dog to one reader, a cat to another, or may bring to mind first a rabbit, horse, hamster, or any other tame animal kept for companionship or affection's sake. Such different conceptions on first reading any given word reflect the different perceptions of reality each person brings to bear in any communication process. Such a process, admittedly, is not particularly problematic when dealing with the semantics of such a word as *pet*, as this word is relatively concrete.

By contrast, when words do not describe something that can be understood through the senses—when they must be understood in abstract terms—the difficulty of semantics increases. When words describe concepts which the reader comprehends only through comparative analysis, the reader's experience with the range of comparison for that term dictates his or her feelings regarding its meaning. Such terms as *efficient* or *expansive* vary according to the reader's experience. Managers who have transferred from a division of the company accustomed to completing its inventory of supplies over a 3-week period to a division which customarily completes the same task in 1 week will find that their conception of the word *efficient* is highly subjective. Similarly, an executive whose travel budget averages over $2,000 each trip may regard a month's business trip costing $1,500 as comparatively inexpensive, whereas a worker whose travel budget is only $500 each year may see such a trip as impossibly expensive.

As discussed in Chapter 2, to some extent the subjectivity of the meaning of words described here holds true for all communication, spoken or written. In spoken communication, however, the speaker may be cued to misunderstanding by nonverbal signals or by the immediate response of the listener. In writing, the word stands by itself with no external clues regarding interpretation. Consequently, the chances for such miscommunication and attendant conflict increase with written communication.

If writers realize the inherent conflict involved in comparative terminology, they can attempt to surmount such impediments to accurate communication by stating their ideas more concretely. Rather than ordering an employee to perform a job more effectively, the writer would do better to specify what he or she believes is effective. To do this the writer must spell out in precise terms that degree of impact regarding time, audience reaction, or amount of profit which he or she expects from the employee for the given job.

Semantic misunderstandings increase even further when the abstract terms the writer chooses lack even a comparative base. Such terms as *liberty*, *friendship*, *morality*, or *happiness* have vastly different meanings for each person with little or no common base of comparison. Assuming that others automatically share our understanding of a comparative or abstract term openly invites conflict. As discussed in Chapter 5, such abstract terms depend largely on culturally learned attitudes and values as well. Consequently, semantic difficulties in dealing with abstract terms are compounded when interacting with those from different cultures. A Japanese, a British, and a U.S. concept of such a term as *politeness* would vary extensively depending on its cultural milieu. Because no absolute notion of politeness exists, the writer must carefully gauge the meaning of the word within its cultural context.

A final reason that semantic difficulties often lead to conflict, even when readers share an essentially similar conception of reality, is that many words carry more than one meaning. For example, the English word *sensitive* has varying shades of meaning, which differ depending on the context of the sentence. An employee reading his company file may understand a report calling him a *sensitive person* to mean that his superiors viewed him as one who is alert and considerate about other persons' feelings. At the same time, the superior who wrote the evaluation may have viewed him as one who becomes easily hurt or offended. The former meaning would usually be recognized as a positive statement; the latter, a negative one. Even in the same context this subtle but important shading of the word could connote two contrasting meanings. The result of reading the positive evaluation of *sensitive* in the more negative sense of the word might well produce a pseudoconflict with enough emotional overtones to escalate readily to a state of ego conflict.

Tonal error is the other factor which frequently contributes to pseudoconflict in writing style. Tone in writing may be roughly defined as the manner of expression of character prevailing in a given piece of writing. If that manner of writing antagonizes the reader, even if both reader and writer agree on the issue at hand, pseudoconflict will arise and can easily escalate into full-scale interactional opposition.

Tone generally rests in choosing the best use of emotion for a particular situation. All writing carries within it an emotional balance. Even writing which might be considered wholly objective holds its place on the emotional spectrum as disinterested or lacking in feeling. Were a letter expressing closeness to be written in a purely objective tone, for example, it might appear cold or distant. A termination letter reading:

> We no longer have use for your services. You may pick up your final check this Friday.

would have a significantly different effect from one stating:

> We cannot renew your contract at this time. Your services have been highly valued by this firm, but economic realities have caused us to cut back and to eliminate all but essential services. We wish you the best in your future endeavors and hope to join forces again at some more prosperous time.

No formula exists for choosing the best tone. It must be selected to match each situation. To best choose the right tone, we should judge it as the ideal spot on a scale between two opposites. Thus, to determine how accepting a tone we should adopt, it would be best to estimate the most appropriate degree between openly hostile and uninhibitedly happy. Similarly, we must gauge on such a scale of opposites the best tone for all emotions that seem pertinent to the situation.

Conflict arises from tone when the emotions intended do not match the emotions for which the situation calls. Certain tonal stances, however, are more likely than others to produce resistance or to plant the seeds of conflict in readers.

Immoderation in word choice, for example, is generally provocative. Calling a new marketing scheme *putrid* or *disgusting* would create so much hostility on the part of the designer of the scheme that the designer would likely ignore whatever reasoning supported such a conclusion. Even if the writer could have convinced the scheme's originator that problems existed in the plan, the antagonism of the immoderate *tone* would produce an ego conflict even though the *substance* of the objections provided no such impediment.

Similarly, patronizing tones often produce ego conflict where substantive disagreements may not have existed. For instance, such phrases as "of course" or "obviously" mildly imply that the reader should know something he or she may not know, since the writer would not have stated the material if it were already understood. The patronizing phrases, inserted usually because the writer has failed to gauge accurately the knowledge level of the audience, may easily make the reader defensive. If such phrasing is combined with immoderate language—"obviously, as any fool would know"—the defensiveness is compounded and can produce an explosive conflict situation.

Finally, overly general or simplified tones commonly cause conflict. Generalizations such as "always", "every," or "all" frequently inspire resistance unless empirical evidence supports them. Similarly, oversimplification, although effective in rapidly conveying a complex idea, often antagonizes those who feel the subject merits fuller discussion because the simplified handling does not clearly apply to their situation.

ACTION

The factors of tone and types of linguistic communication that may produce conflict are admittedly numerous. Still, one must remember that the factors together comprise only one of the three steps in the communication process, transmittal. Transmittal, in turn, should be weighted equally in importance with the conceptualization and reception steps that it connects.

To avoid undesired conflict the writer should carefully consider the points raised thus far in this chapter. Still, the writer may wish to employ as guidelines the following writing checklists, which reflect a consolidation of the conceptualization, transmittal, and reception stages discussed earlier.

To remain conflict free in the conceptualization process or assessment step, the writer should answer the following four questions:

1. What is my *ostensible* purpose for this message?
2. What are my *underlying* reasons for writing?
3. How do I want the reader to react?
4. Is there a possibility of real conflict here rather than pseudoconflict?

To reduce the chance of negative conflict in the reception process or acknowledgement and attitude steps, the writer should answer the following four questions:

1. How do I anticipate the reader will react?
2. To whom am I writing?
3. What details—age, rank, sex, attitudes, area of expertise, experience—do I know about the reader?
4. If the reader is unknown, what can I fairly guess about him or her?

To reduce unwanted conflict in the transmittal process or action step, the writer should answer the following 10 questions:

1. Am I using any dialectical variations in my language that the reader may not understand or might misjudge?
2. Am I using any professional jargon that is not absolutely needed?
3. If I am using needed jargon, can the reader understand it?
4. Am I writing in a technically proper manner with good grammar, spelling, punctuation, and mechanics?
5. Can the reader construe what I have written in more than one way?
6. Am I being concrete—that is, am I semantically clear?
7. Am I moderate in tone?
8. Have I avoided patronizing the reader?
9. Have I avoided oversimplification?
10. Have I eliminated any generalizations?

Even if the writer follows these three checklists before composing each written message, miscommunication that leads to pseudoconflict may still occur. Nonetheless, a careful review of the answers to the questions in these three checklists should help the writer avoid much of his or her communication-based conflict in writing.

ANALYSIS

As we have just seen, the communication process of writing is complex and requires great care if the writer wishes to avoid nonproductive conflict. Still, it is important to note that although nonproductive conflict is created through writing, conflict is also resolved by writing. Indeed, although the amount one writes admittedly increases the opportunity to miscalculate a step in the writing process and thus increase the chance of causing conflict, frequent communication more often leads to positive behavior and cooperative interaction.

A substantial amount of research indicates that the very existence of some attempt to communicate reduces behavior that causes conflict (Deutsch, 1958; Swingle, 1976). Brooks and Emmert state that "the presence of a channel in which worded messages can be sent and exchanged, in contrast with the absence of such a channel, clearly increases the amount of cooperative behavior" (1976, p. 228). For all the possible sources of conflict in writing style and communication in general, the failure to write or to communicate is a much greater source of conflict. Rather than not writing to avoid conflict, we would do better to avoid conflict through writing carefully.

SUMMARY

Many individuals are aware that their nonverbal and verbal communication directly affects the way others react to them. This awareness is increased by the fact that the person communicating can *see* the respondent's or listener's reactions.

The act of writing, however, removes the reader from view. Therefore, the physical distance often coincides with a lack of adequate concern for how the written message is received and interpreted.

In this chapter we presented the three basic steps of the writing act: conceptualization, transmittal, and reception. We have explored how the lack of attention to any or all of these areas can create nonproductive conflict.

Three key areas exist where writer error or misperception can lead to potential problems with the reader. These areas include:

1. Analysis of the purpose of the written communication;
2. Accurate analysis and consideration of the reader's capabilities and expectations; and
3. Maintenance of a proper tone and style appropriate for the content and for the reader.

The failure to adhere to these three areas can lead to a pseudo-conflict, which is a conflict caused by a misunderstanding. Equally destructive communication can create an ego conflict, whereby an individual may feel cornered, threatened, or defensive and may respond accordingly.

This chapter presented the ways in which writing can cause or sustain conflict. By attending to the above issues, writers can assume their share of the responsibility for effective communication.

SUGGESTED ACTIVITIES

A. Focus on clarity
Read the following memo:

To: All Division 5 Employees
From: Charles W. Selrachny
Date: January
Subject: No Smoking

In the near future, we will start a new policy of no smoking in hazard areas. Only the cafeteria and some bathrooms are not hazardous. Consequently, do not smoke cigarettes except there.

Be prepared to discuss the following questions:
1. How is the ambiguity of the subject line misleading?
2. What are the hazard areas? How could the lack of specificity lead to danger or conflict?
3. When does the new policy begin? What difficulties could the lack of specificity of a starting point for this new policy cause?

4. In the last sentence of the memorandum, only cigarettes (not, for example, cigars, or other smoking materials are forbidden. How could this specificity lead to danger or conflict?

B. Focus on audience analysis: Neutral subject

Choose or imagine a position at your place of work that you would like to have someone fill. Then write the three following items:

1. A memo to your boss asking her or him to permit you to hire someone for that position.
2. An advertisement for the position and accompanying letter to the appropriate newspaper or professional publication.
3. A memo to the Human Resources or Personnel Department, giving them an offical job description to place in the new hire's file.

The way in which we write changes dramatically depending on the message's intended reader, even when the general subject of that message remains constant. The three written messages you have just completed have very similar purposes but very different audiences. How does each of these three audiences differ? How did you adjust your writing of each to adapt to these differences?

C. Focus on audience: Emotional subject

Consider the following situation:

You discover that a colleague from another department in your organization has used *your* ideas in her area. At the directors' meeting, she reports her "new" idea to the vice-president in front of you. She fails, however, to acknowledge the fact that her unique idea was in fact yours. It is raise and promotion time, and you refuse to sit back and allow her to garner all the credit.

You decide to write the two following letters:

1. A letter to your colleague and former friend indicating your displeasure with the way she handled your confidence.
2. A letter to the vice president explaining your concern about the situation.

Analyze both responses. What similarities and differences did you experience when writing about the same situation to the two distinct readers? Explain the conceptualization, transmittal, and reception processes in both cases. Explain how your letter might affect the likelihood of conflict.

D. Focus on dialect differences

Read the text of the following complaint letter to a U.S. hotel written by an unhappy patron.

> Dear Mr. Lawson:
>
> I wish to inform you that I was very unhappy during my last stay at your establishment for several reasons.
>
> On my arrival, the lifts were not functioning properly, so I was forced to use the stairs. On the staircase, one of your charwomen refused to let me pass and insulted me. Attempting to step around her, I got a ladder in my stockings and snagged my pullover. Once in my room, I attempted to

repair my pullover, but found that the sewing repair kit the hotel had provided had no reel of cotton in it. I was so distressed by this that I felt a bit ill so I went back to your main lobby only to find the hotel chemist's shop closed.

Thinking it best at this point to relax, I decided to have dinner at the hotel restaurant. However, even there the service was poor. I ordered an underdone undercut with French beans but received a nearly burnt joint with sauteed auberge.

When I returned to my room I attempted to make a trunk call home unsuccessfully. Finally, I called the front desk to ask them to knock me up in the morning and your clerk responded with a rude remark.

I am a solicitor of, if I must say so myself, some note in England. Perhaps this sort of service is acceptable for the average commerical bagman you host at your hotel but it is not what I would have expected from an establishment of your reputation. I have already shared my views on this with my booking clerk, but I felt that it would only be proper to share my views with you as well.

Sincerely,
Francine Farquhar

1. Although Mr. Lawson and Ms. Farquhar share a common language, Mr. Lawson may have difficulty understanding many of the words Ms. Farquhar uses that reflect her British dialect. How many of the British English words used by Farquhar listed below did you know?

British English	U.S. English
lift	elevator
charwoman	cleaning lady
ladder	run in stocking
pullover	sweater
reel of cotton	spool of thread
chemist	pharmacist
undercut	tenderloin
joint	roast
underdone	rare
French bean	string bean
auberge	eggplant
trunk call	long distance telephone call
knock me up	wake me up
commercial bagman	traveling salesperson
booking clerk	ticket agent

2. The difficulties attendant on the dialect differences in the letter might have been less substantial if Ms. Farquhar had *spoken* her complaint before leaving rather than having *written* her complaint. Why would this be so?

SEVEN
CONCLUSION

In his address at American University, John F. Kennedy spoke about the importance of confronting differences between people:

> Let us not be blind to our differences—but let us also direct attention to our common interests and the means by which those differences can be resolved. And if we cannot end now our differences, at least we can help make the world safe from diversity. (June 12, 1963)

Conflict as it routinely occurs in personal and professional settings can either be regarded as a very negative force or as a source of great potential and productivity. The differences between and among people can readily destroy relationships and hinder personal development or nourish those same relationships and foster personal growth. The outcome rests in how the individuals manage the conflict they face.

In this book we have described an approach for managing conflict productively through directed communication skills. We have discussed the specific verbal and nonverbal communication skills needed to handle conflict-producing behavior effectively. We have considered ways to defuse negative pseudoconflict and to establish a supportive communication environment for managing actual disagreements. Finally, we have described a five-step model of assessment, acknowledgement, attitude, action and analysis designed to allow the reader systematically and straight-forwardly to put into use these communication skills.

In this book we have introduced specific sources of conflict as well. While it would be impossible to address adequately all possible communication-based sources of conflict, we have applied our communication skills approach to conflict management in the contexts of three important and nearly universal sources of conflict: gender as a factor affecting communication; cross-cultural communication; and writing as a means of communication that is at once interactive and performed in isolation.

It is hoped that you will be able to apply the five-step communication model presented in this book not only to the specific conflict situations examined in this book but also to other conflict situations you may face. The communication skills approach delineated in this book is designed to encourage people to face rather than flee from conflict because for them conflict will represent an opportunity to engage in an open-minded exchange of ideas by which the synergy of different views of a common situation represent the possibility of strengthening relationships and self-developement.

At the beginning of this book, we observed that conflcit will not go away simply because individuals are reluctant to deal with it. Those who have considered conflict as something to be avoided, we noted, are often ill equipped to deal with those conflict situations from which they cannot hide. We also noted that those who attempt to deal with conflict solely in a competitive manner in which one side loses and the other wins are often unable to strengthen the interpersonal relationships out of which the conflict arises. Only the ability to develop a flexible and appropriate attitude to conflict can transform a potentially destructive situation into a positive interaction.

It is our hope that the communication skills approach to handling conflict we have described will provide you with the means to view conflict not as a counterproductive and negative encounter to be overcome but as a potentially productive interaction that can be managed effectively and appropriately. In doing so, you will open up a future of opportunity that will allow you to participate in and even embrace conflict situations as a source of change and growth.

REFERENCES

ADLER, N.J. *International Dimensions of Organizational Behavior*. Boston: Kent Publishing Co., 1986.

ADDINGTON, D.W. The relationship of selected vocal characteristics to personality perception. *Speech Monographs*. pp. 492–503, 1968.

ALMANEY, A. Intercultural communication and the MNC executive. *Columbia Journal of World Business*. Vol. 9, No. 4, 1974.

ALMANEY, A.J., AND ALWAN, A.J. *Communicating with the Arabs*. Prospect Heights, IL: Waveland Press, Inc., 1982.

ARGYLE, M., AND FURNHAM, A. Sources of satisfaction and conflict in long term relationships. *Journal of Marriage and the Family*. No. 45, pp. 418–93, 1983.

ARGYLE, M., INGHAM, R. ALKEMA, F., AND MCCALLIN, M. The different functions of gaze. *Semiotica*, 7, pp. 19–32, 1973.

BALES, R. *Interpersonal Communication*. Dubuque, IA: William C. Brown, 1970.

BALL, D.A., AND MCCULLOCH, W.H., JR. *International Business: Introduction and Essentials*. 2nd ed. Plano, TX: Business Publications, Inc., 1985.

BANDURA, A., AND WALTERS, R.H. *Social Learning and Personality Development*. New York: Holt, Rinehart & Winston, 1963.

BARNLUND, D.C. *Interpersonal Communication: Survey and Studies*. Boston: Houghton Mifflin, 1968.

BARNLUND, D.C. Communication: the context of change. In *Basic Readings in Communication Theory*. 2nd ed. C. David Mortensen, ed. New York: Harper & Row, pp. 6–26, 1979.

BARRY, W.A. Marriage research and conflict: an integrative approach. *Psychological Bulletin*. Vol. 73, No. 1, pp. 47–54, 1970.

BASS, B.M., AND BURGER, P.C. *Assessment of Managers: An International Comparison.* New York: The Free Press, 1979.

BEEBE, S. Eye contact: a nonverbal determinant of speaker credibility. *Speech Teacher.* Vol. 23, pp. 21–25, 1974.

BELLOW, S. *More Die of Heartbreak.* New York: William Morrow & Co., 1987.

BEM, S. The measurement of psychological androgyny. *Journal of Consulting and Clinical Psychology.* Vol. 42, pp. 155–162, 1974.

BENEDICT, R. *Patterns of Culture.* New York: New American Library, 1934.

BARELSON, B., AND STEINER, G.A. *Human Behavior: An Inventory of Scientific Findings.* New York: Harcourt, Brace & World, 1964.

BERGER, C., AND CALABRESE, R. Some explorations in initial interactions and beyond: toward a developmental theory of interpersonal communication. *Human Communication Research.* Vol. 1, pp. 99–112, 1975.

BERNARD, J. *The Female World.* New York: The Free Press, 1981.

BIRDWHISTELL, R.L. *Kinesics and Context: Essays on Body Motion Communication.* Philadelphia: University of Pennsylvania Press, 1970.

BLAKE, D.H., AND WALTERS, R.S. *The Politics of Global Economic Relations.* Englewood Cliffs, NJ: Prentice-Hall, Inc., 1976.

BLAKE, R.R., AND MOUTON, J.S. The intergroup dynamics of win-lose conflict and problem-solving collaboration in union-management relations. In *Intergroup Relations and Leadership.* M. Sherif, ed. New York: Wiley, pp. 94–142, 1962.

BLAKE, R.R., AND MOUTON, J.S. *The Managerial Grid.* Houston, TX: Gulf Publishing Co., 1964.

BLUMSTEIN, P., AND SCHWARTZ, P. *American Couples: Money, Work, Sex.* New York: William Morrow & Co., Inc., 1983.

BORISOFF, D., AND MERRILL, L. *The Power to Communicate: Gender Differences as Barriers.* Prospect Heights, IL: Waveland Press, 1985.

BORISOFF, D., AND MERRILL, L. Teaching the college course on gender differences as barriers to conflict resolution. In *Advances in Gender and Communication Research.* L.B. Nadler, M.K. Nadler, and W.R. Todd-Mancillas, eds. Lanham, MD: University Press of America, Inc., pp. 351–363, 1987.

BORISOFF, D., AND VICTOR, D. Cross-cultural communication barriers: Implications for acknowledging differences on issues of gender, ethnicity, religion, and political ideology. Paper presented at the American Business Communication Association. New York City, April, 1987.

BOVEE, C.L., AND THILL, J.V. *Business Communication Today.* New York: Random House, 1986.

BRADLEY, P.H. Sex, competence and opinion deviation: an expectation states approach. *Communication Monographs.* 47, pp. 105–110, 1980.

BRIEF, A.P., SCHULER, R.S., AND VAN SELL, M. *Managing Job Stress.* Boston: Little, Brown, & Co., 1981.

BROCKRIEDE, W., AND EHNINGER, D. Toulmin on argument: an interpretation and application. *Quarterly Journal of Speech.* Vol. 46, pp. 44–53, 1960.

BROOKS, H. Technology as a factor in U.S. competitiveness. In *U.S. Competitiveness in the World Economy.* B.R. Scott and G.C. Lodge, eds. Boston: Harvard Business Press, pp. 328–356, 1985.

BROOKS, W., AND EMMERT, P. *Personality and Interpersonal Behavior.* New York: Holt, Rinehart & Winston, 1976.

BROWN, L. *Communicating Facts and Ideas in Business.* 3rd ed. Englewood Cliffs, NJ: Prentice-Hall, 1982.

BURGOON, J., AND SAINE, T. *The Unspoken Dialogue.* Boston: Houghton Mifflin, 1976.

BURKE, R.J. Methods of resolving superior-subordinate conflict: the constructive use of subordinate differences and disagreements. *Organizational Behavior and Human Performance*, 5, pp. 393–411, 1970.

BURLING, R. *Man's Many Voices*. New York: Holt, Rinehart & Winston, 1970.

CAHN, D.D., JR. *Letting Go: A Practical Theory of Relationship Disengagement and Reengagement*. Albany: State University of New York Press, 1987.

CASMIR, F.L. Stereotypes and schemata. In *Communication, Culture, and Organizational Process*. W. Gudykunst, L. Stewart, and S. Ting-Toomey, eds. Beverly Hills, CA: Sage Publications, pp. 48–67, 1985.

CHESANOW, N. *The World-Class Executive*. New York: Rawson Associates, 1985.

CHOMSKY, N. *Language and Mind*. New York: Harcourt Brace Jovanovich, 1968.

CLARK, R. *The Japanese Company*. New Haven: Yale University Press, 1979.

CONDON, J.C., JR. *Semantics and Communication*. New York: Macmillan, 1965.

CONDON, J.S. *With Respect to the Japanese: A Guide for Americans*. Yarmouth, ME: Intercultural Press, Inc., 1984.

CONDON, J.S., AND YOUSEF, F. *An Introduction to Intercultural Communication*. New York: Macmillan, 1985.

COPELAND, L., AND GRIGGS, J. *Going International: How to Make Friends and Deal Effectively in the Global Marketplace*. New York: Random House, 1985.

COSER, L.A. *The Functions of Social Conflict*. New York: The Free Press, 1956.

COUCH, C., AND HINTZ, R.A. *Constructing Social Life*. Champaign, IL: Stypes Publishing, 1975.

CROSS, G.P., NAMES, J.H., AND BECK, D. *Conflict and Human Interaction*. Dubuque, IA: Kendall Hunt, 1979.

CUMMINGS, L.L., HARNETT, D.L., AND STEVENS, O.J. Risk, fate, conciliation and trust: an international study of attitudinal differences among executives. *Academy of Management Journal*. Vol. 14, No. 3, pp. 285–304, Sept. 1971.

DANIELS, H. Nine ideas about language. In *Language*, 4th ed., V.P. Clark et al, eds. New York: St. Martin's Press, pp. 18–42, 1985.

DAVITZ, J.R. *The Communication of Emotional Meaning*. New York: McGraw-Hill, 1964.

DEAUX, K. Internal barriers. In *Women in Organizations*. J. Pilotta, ed. Prospect Heights, IL: Waeland Press, pp. 11-22, 1983.

DeMENTE, B. *The Japanese Way of Doing Business: The Psychology of Management in Japan*. Englewood Cliffs, NJ: Prentice-Hall, Inc., 1981.

DEUTSCH, M. Conflict and its resolution. In *Conflict Resolution: Contributions of the Behavioral Sciences*. C.G. Smith, ed. Notre Dame: University of Notre Dame Press, pp. 36–57, 1971b.

DEUTSCH, M. Toward an understanding of conflict. *International Journal of Group Tensions*. 1, pp. 42–54, 1971a.

DEUTSCH, M. Conflicts: productive and destructive. In *Conflict Resolution Through Communication*. F.E. Jandt, ed. New York: Harper & Row, 1973a.

DEUTSCH, M. *The Resolution of a Conflict: Constructive and Destructive Processes*. New Haven: Yale University Press, 1973b.

DeVITO, J.A. *The Communication Handbook: A Dictionary*. New York: Harper & Row, 1986.

DeWINE, S. Female leadership in male-dominated organizations. *ACA Bulletin*. 61, pp. 19–29, 1987.

DODD, C.H. *Dynamics of Intercultural Communications*. Dubuque, IA: William C. Brown, Co., 1982.

DOUGLAS, M. *Implicit Meanings*. London: Routledge & Kegan Paul Ltd., 1975.

DOUVAN, E., AND ADELSON, J. *The Adolescent Experience*. New York: John Wiley, 1966. Cited in J. Pearson, *Gender and Communication*. Dubuque, IA: William C. Brown, 1985.

EAKINS, B.W., AND EAKINS, R.G. *Sex Differences in Human Communication.* Boston: Houghton Mifflin Co., 1978.

EDELSKY, C. Question intonation and sex roles. *Language and Society.* 8, pp. 15–32, 1979.

EKMAN, P. Movements with precise meanings. *Journal of Communication,* 26, pp. 14–26, 1976.

EKMAN, P., AND FRIESEN, W.V. The repertoire of nonverbal behavior: categories, origins, usage and coding. *Semiotica.* 1, pp. 49–98, 1969.

EKMAN, P., AND FRIESEN, W.V. Hand movements. *Journal of Communication.* 22, pp. 353–354, 1972.

EKMAN, P., AND FRIESEN, W.V. Nonverbal behavior and psychotherapy. In *The Psychology of Depression: Contemporary Theory and Research,* R.J. Friedman and M.M. Katz, eds. Washington, DC: Winston & Sons, 1974.

EKMAN, P., AND FRIESEN, W.V. *Unmasking the Face.* Englewood Cliffs, NJ: Prentice-Hall, 1975.

ELLSWORTH, P., AND LUDWIG, L. Visual behavior in social interaction. *Journal of Communication.* Vol. 22, pp. 378–381, 1972.

ELLUL, J. *The Technological Society.* J. Neugroschel, trans. New York: Vintage, 1964.

FAGOT, B. The influence of sex of child on parental reaction. *Developmental Psychology.* 10, pp. 554–558, 1978. Cited in J. Pearson, *Gender and Communication.* Dubuque, IA: William C. Brown, 1985.

FAST, J. *Body Language.* New York: M. Evans & Co., 1970.

FEIGENBAUM, E.A., AND MCCORDUCK, P. *The Fifth Generation: Artificial Intelligence and Japan's Computer Challenge to the World.* New York: New American Library, 1983.

FIELDS, G. *From Bonsai to Levis, When West Meets East: An Insider's Surprising Account of How the Japanese Live.* New York: New American Library, 1983.

FILLEY, A.C. *Interpersonal Conflict Resolution.* Glenview, IL: Scott, Foresman & Co., 1975.

FILLEY, A.C. Conflict resolution: the ethic of the good loser. In *Readings in Interpersonal and Organizational Communication,* 3rd ed. R. Huseman, C. Logue, and D. Freshley, eds. Boston: Holbrooke Press, pp. 234–252, 1977.

FISHER, G. *International Negotiation: A Cross-Cultural Perspective.* Chicago: Intercultural Press, 1980.

FISHER, R. AND URY, W. *Getting to Yes: Negotiating Agreement Without Giving In.* Boston: Houghton Mifflin, 1981.

FISHMAN, P.M. Interaction: the work women do. *Social Problems.* 25, pp. 397–406, 1978. Cited in C. Kramarae, *Women and Men Speaking.* Rowley, MA: Newbury House, 1981.

FISHMAN, P.M. Interactional shitwork. *Heresies: A Feminist Publication on Art and Politics.* 2, pp. 99–101, 1977. Cited in C. Kramarae, *Women and Men Speaking.* Rowley, MA: Newbury House, 1981.

FOLGER, J.P., AND POOLE, M.S. *Working Through Conflict: A Communication Perspective.* Glenview, IL: Scott, Foresman & Co., 1984.

FREEDMAN, R. *Beauty Bound.* New York: Basic Books, 1986.

GAHAGAN, J.P., AND TEDESCHI, J.T. Strategy and the credibility of promises in the prisoner's dilemma game. *Journal of Conflict Resolution.* 12, pp. 224–234, 1968.

GARVIN, G. International English: some strings attached. In *Communication at Work,* H. Smith, ed. Toronto: Proceedings of the Combined Eastern/Canadian ABCA Canadian STC Meeting, pp. 53–63, 1985.

GIBB, J. Defensive communication. *Journal of Communication.* 11, pp. 141–148, 1961.

GILKEY, R., AND GREENHALGH, L. Developing effective negotiating approaches among professional women in organizations. Submitted to the Third Annual Conference on Women and Organizations, Simmons College, August 1984.

GILLIGAN, C. Woman's place in man's life cycle. *Harvard Educational Review.* Vol. 49, No. 4, pp. 431–446, November 1979.

GOFFMAN, E. *The Presentation of Self in Everyday Life.* Garden City, NY: Doubleday Anchor Books, 1959.

GOFFMAN, E. *Behavior in Public Places.* New York: The Free Press, 1963.

GOLDMAN-EISLER, F. A comparative study of two hesitation phenomena. *Language and Speech.* 4, pp. 18–26, 1961.

GOLDSTEIN, J.R. Trends in teaching technical writing. *Technical Communication.* Vol. 4, pp. 25–34, 1984.

GOODMAN, E. Processes of conflict resolution. Lecture at New York University, Summer, 1983.

GRAEBNER, A. Growing up female. In *Intercultural Communication: A Reader.* L.A. Samovar and R.E. Porter, eds. Belmont, CA: Wadsworth Publishing Co., 1982.

GRAHAM, J.L., AND HERBERGER, R.A., JR. Negotiators abroad: don't shoot from the hip. In *Toward Internationalism: Readings in Cross-Cultural Communication.* 2nd ed. L.F. Luce and E.C. Smith, eds. Cambridge, MA: Newbury House Publishers, pp. 73–87, 1987.

GREGORY, G. Japan: new center of innovation, evolving from imitator to inventor. In *Speaking of Japan.* Vol. 3, No. 18. Keizan Koho Ctr, Japanese Institute for Social and Economic Affairs, pp. 2–9, June, 1986.

GUDYKUNST, W.B. Uncertainty reduction and predictability of behavior in low-context and high-context culture: an explanatory study. *Communication Quarterly.* Vol. 31, no. 1, p. 50, Winter 1983.

GUMPEREZ, J.J., AND HYMES, D. The ethnography of communication. *American Anthropologist.* Vol. 66, no. 6, part 2, December, 1964.

HAIRE, M., GHISELLI, E.E., AND PORTER, L.W. Cultural patterns in the role of the manager. *Industrial Relations.* Vol. 2, no. 2, pp. 95–117, February 1963.

HALBERSTAM, D. *The Reckoning.* New York: William Morrow & Co., Inc., 1986.

HALL, E.T. *The Silent Language.* New York: Doubleday, 1959; Fawcett Publications, 1961.

HALL, E.T. *The Hidden Dimension.* New York: Doubleday, 1966.

HALL, E.T. *Beyond Culture.* New York: Anchor Press, Doubleday, 1976.

HALL, E.T. *The Dance of Life: The Other Dimensions of Time.* Garden City, NY: Anchor Press, Doubleday, 1983.

HALL, J. *Nonverbal Sex Differences: Communication, Accuracy and Expressive Style.* Baltimore, MD: The Johns Hopkins University Press, 1984.

HARCOURT, J., KRIZAN, A.C., AND MERRIER, P. *Business Communication.* Cincinnati: South-Western, 1986.

HARRISON, R.P. *Beyond Words: An Introduction to Nonverbal Communication.* Englewood Cliffs, NJ: Prentice-Hall, 1974.

HATCH, R. *Business Communication: Theory and Technique.* Chicago: Science Research Associates, 1983.

HEILBRUN, A.B. Measurment of masculine and feminine sex role identities as independent dimensions. *Journal of Consulting and Clinical Psychology.* 44, pp. 183–190, 1976. In J. Pearson, *Gender and Communication.* Dubuque, IA: William C. Brown, 1985.

HELLWIG, B. The breakthrough generation: 73 women ready to run corporate America. *Working Women,* April 1985.

HENLEY, N.M. *Body Politics: Power, Sex and Non-Verbal Communication.* Englewood Cliffs, NJ: Prentice-Hall, 1977.

HESLIN, R. Steps toward a taxonomy of touching. Paper presented to the Mid-western Psychological Association, Chicago, May 1974. Cited in M.L. Knapp, *Essentials of Nonverbal Behavior.* New York: Holt, Rinehart & Winston, 1980.

HOCKER, J.L., AND WILMOT, W.W. *Interpersonal Conflict,* 2nd ed. Dubuque, IA: William C. Brown, 1985.

HOFHEINZ, R., JR., AND CALDER, K.E. *The Eastasia Edge.* New York: Basic Books, 1982.

HOFSTEDE, G. *Culture's Consequences: International Work-Related Values.* Abridged ed. Beverly Hills, CA: Sage Publications, 1984.

HOIJER, H. The Sapir-Whorf hypothesis. In *Intercultural Communication: A Reader.* L.A. Samovar and R.E. Porter, eds. Belmont, CA: Wadsworth Publishing Co., pp. 210–217, 1982.

HORNER, M. Toward an understanding of achievement related conflicts in women. *Journal of Social Issues.* 28, pp. 157–175, 1972.

HYMES, D. The scope of sociolinguistics. *Social Science Research Council Items.* Vol. 25, pp. 14–18, 1972.

ILLICH, I. *Toward a History of Needs.* New York: Pantheon, 1977.

JAMIESON, D.W., AND THOMAS, K.W. Power and conflict in student-teacher relationship. *Journal of Applied Behavioral Science.* Vol. 10, no 3, pp. 321–336, 1974.

JENSEN, J.V. Communicative functions of silence. *ETC* 30, pp. 249–257, 1973.

JENSEN, J.V. Perspective on nonverbal intercultural communication. In *Intercultural Communication: A Reader.* L.A. Samovar and R.E. Porter, eds. Belmont, CA: Wadsworth Publishing Co., pp. 260–276, 1982.

KAPLAN, C. Language and gender. Papers on Patriarchy. Lewes, Sussex: Women's Publishing Collective, 1976. Cited in C. Kramarae, *Women and Men Speaking.* Rowley, MA: Newbury House, 1981.

KENDON, A. Some functions of gaze direction in social interaction. *Acta Psychologica.* 26, pp. 22–63, 1967.

KEY, W.B. *Subliminal Seduction.* New York: Thomas Y. Cromwell, 1968.

KLUCKHOHN, C. *Mirror for Man: A Survey of Human Behavior and Social Attitudes.* Greenwich, CT: Fawcett Publications, 1964.

KNAPP, M.L. *Essentials of Nonverbal Communication.* New York: Holt, Rinehart & Winston, 1980.

KNOWLES, E.S. Convergent validity of personal space measures: consistent results with low intercorrelations. *Journal of Nonverbal Behavior.* 4, pp. 240–248, 1980.

KOHLBERG, L. A cognitive developmental analysis of children's sex role concepts and attitudes. In *The Development of Sex Differences.* E. Macoby, ed. Stanford, CA: Stanford University Press, pp. 82–172, 1966.

KRAMARAE, C. *Women and Men Speaking.* Rowley, MA: Newbury House, 1981.

KRAMER, E. The judgment of personal characteristics and emotions from nonverbal properties of speech. *Psychological Bulletin.* 60, pp. 408–420, 1963.

KROEBER, A.L., AND KLUCKHOHN, C. *Culture: A Critical Review of Concepts and Definitions.* New York: Random House, 1954.

LAKOFF, R. *Language and Woman's Place.* New York: Harper & Row, 1975.

LALLJEE, M.C. Disfluencies in normal English speech. Unpublished dissertation, Oxford University, 1971, quoted in M.L. Knapp, *Essentials of Nonverbal Communication.* New York: Holt, Rinehart & Winston, 1980.

LANDER, H. *Language and Culture.* New York: Oxford University Press, 1966.

LASS, N.J., HUGHES, K.R., BOWYER, M.D., WATERS, L.T., AND BROUNE, V.T. Speaker sex identification from voiced, whispered and filtered isolated vowels. *Journal of the Acoustical Society of America.* 59, pp. 361–374, 1976.

LAURENT, A. The cultural diversity of western conceptions of management. *Interna-*

tional Studies of Management and Organization. Vol. 13, no. 1-2, pp. 75–96, Spring-Summer 1983.

LEWIS, P.V. *Organizational Communication: The Essence of Effective Management.* 3rd ed. New York: John Wiley & Sons, 1987.

LIKERT, R., AND LIKERT, J.G. *New Ways of Managing Conflict.* New York: McGraw-Hill, 1976.

LIPS, H. *Women, Men, and the Psychology of Power.* Englewood Cliffs, NJ: Prentice-Hall, 1981.

LIVINGSTONE, J.M. *The International Enterprise.* New York: John Wiley & Sons, 1975.

LUCE, L.F., AND SMITH, E.C. Cross-cultural literacy: A national priority. In *Toward Internationalism: Readings in Cross-Cultural Communication.* 2nd ed. L.F. Luce and E.C. Smith eds. Cambridge, MA: Newbury House Publishers, pp. 3–9, 1987.

LYNN, D.B. *Parents and Sex-Role Identification.* Berkeley, CA: McCutchan, 1969.

MACOBY, E.E., AND JACKLIN, C.N. *The Psychology of Sex Differences.* Stanford, CA: Stanford University Press, 1974.

MAIER, N.R.F. *Problem Solving Discussions and Conferences: Leadership Methods and Skills.* New York: McGraw-Hill, 1963.

MAIER, N., AND SASHKIN, M. Specific leadership behaviors that promote problem solving. *Personnel Psychology.* 24, pp. 35–44, 1971.

MAIER, N., AND SOLEM, A.F. Improving solutions by turning choice situations into problems. *Personal Psychology.* Vol. 15, no. 2, pp. 151–157, 1962.

MANDELBAUM, D. (ed.). *Edward Sapir: Culture, Language and Personality.* Berkeley: University of California Press, 1962.

MEHRABIAN, A. *Nonverbal Communication.* Chicago: Aldine-Atherton, 1972.

MEHRABIAN, A. *Silent Messages: Implicit Communication of Emotions and Attitudes.* 2nd ed. Belmont, CA: Wadsworth Publishing Co., 1981.

MEISELS, M., AND GUARDO, C.J. Development of personal space schemata. *Child Development.* 40, pp. 1167–1178, 1969.

MILLER, G.R., AND STEINBERG, M. *Between People: A New Analysis of Interpersonal Communication.* Chicago: Science Research Associates, 1975.

MILLER, N., MARUYAMA, G., BEABER, R.J., AND VALONE, K. Speed of speech and persuasion. *Journal of Personality and Social Psychology.* 34, pp. 615–624, 1976.

MILLER, J.J., AND KILPATRICK, J.A. *Issues for Managers: An International Perspective.* Homewood, IL: Richard D. Irwin, 1987.

MISCHEL, W. Sex typing and socialization. In *Carmichael's Manual of Child Psychology.* 3rd ed. Vol. 2. P.H. Mussen, ed. New York: Wiley, 1970.

MORAIN, G.G. Kinesics and cross-cultural understanding. In *Toward Internationalism: Readings in Cross-Cultural Communication.* 2nd ed. L.F. Luce and E.C. Smith, eds. Cambridge, MA: Newbury House Publishers, pp. 117–142, 1987.

MORAN, R.T., AND HARRIS, P.R. *Managing Cultural Synergy.* Houston, TX: Gulf Publishing Co., 1982.

MORRIS, D., ET AL. *Gestures: Their Origins and Distribution.* Briarcliff Manor, NY: Stein & Day, 1979.

MULDE, A., HANLEY, T.D., AND PRIGGE, D.Y. Effects of phonological speech foreignness upon three dimensions of attitude of selected American listeners. *Quarterly Journal of Speech.* 60, pp. 411–420, 1974.

MULDER, M. Reduction of power differences in practice: The power distance reduction theory and its applications. In *European Contributions to organization Theory.* G. Hofstede and M.S. Kassem, eds. Assen, Netherlands: Van Gorcum, 1976.

MULDER, M. *The Daily Power Game.* Leyden: Martinus Nijhoff, 1977.

MURPHY, H.A., AND HILDEBRANDT, H.W. *Effective Business Communications.* 4th ed. New York: McGraw-Hill, 1984.

MYSAK, E.D. Pitch and duration characteristics of older males. *Journal of Speech and Hearing Research.* 2, pp. 46–54, 1959.

McCLELLAND, D. *Power: The Inner Experience.* New York: Irvington Publishers, 1975.

McCLONE, R.E., AND HOLLIEN, H. Vocal pitch characteristics of aged women. *Journal of Speech and Hearing Research.* 6, pp. 164–170, 1963.

NIYEKAWA-HOWARD, A. *A Psycholinguistic Study of the Whorfian Hypothesis Based on the Japanese Passive.* Honolulu: Educational Research & Development Center, University of Hawaii, 1968.

NOSTRAND, H.W. Describing and teaching the sociocultural context of a foreign language and literature. In *Trends in Foreign Language Teaching.* A. Valdman, ed. New York: McGraw-Hill, pp. 1–25, 1966.

O'REILLY, C.A., AND ROBERTS, K.H. Job satisfaction among whites and nonwhites. *Journal of Applied Psychology.* Vol. 19, no. 2, pp. 295–299, 1973.

OSBORN, A.F. *Applied Imagination.* New York: Scribners, 1957. In *The Communication Handbook: A Dictionary.* J. DeVito, ed. New York: Harper & Row, 1986.

OUCHI, W.G. *Theory Z.* Reading, MA: Addison-Wesley, 1981.

PEARCE, C.G., FIGGINS, R., AND GOLEN, S. *Principles of Business Communication.* New York: John Wiley & Sons, 1984.

PEARSON, J.C. *Gender and Communication.* Dubuque, IA: William C. Brown, 1985.

PHATAK, A.V. *International Dimensions of Management.* Boston: Kent Publishing Co., 1983.

PIKE, K.L. *Language in Relation to a Unified Theory of the Structure of Human Behavior.* 2nd rev. ed. The Hague: Mouton, 1971.

PORTER, R.E., AND SAMOVAR, L.A. Approaching intercultural communication. In *Intercultural Communication: A Reader.* L.A. Samovar and R.E. Porter, eds. Belmont, CA: Wadsworth Publishing Co., pp. 26–42, 1982.

PRUITT, D.G. *Negotiation Behavior.* New York: Academic Press, 1981.

PUTNAM, L. (ed.). Communication and conflict styles in organizations, *Management Communication Quarterly.* Vol. 1, no. 3, February 1988.

PUTNAM, L. Leadership and conflict management. *ACA Bulletin.* 61, pp. 42–49, 1987.

PUTNAM, L.L. Lady you're trapped: breaking out of conflict cycles. In *Women in Organizations: Barriers and Breakthroughs.* J.J. Pilotta, ed. Prospect Heights, IL: Waveland Press, 1983.

PUTNAM, L.L., AND WILSON, C.E. Communicative strategies in organizational conflicts: reliability and validity of a measurement scale. In *Communication Yearbook.* 6, M. Burgoon, ed. Beverly Hills, CA: Sage Publications, 1982.

REITZ, H.J. The relative importance of five categories of needs among industrial workers in eight countries. *Academy of Management Proceedings,* pp. 270–273, 1975.

RICKS, D.A., FU, M.Y.C., AND ARPAN, J.S. *International Business Blunders.* Columbus, OH: Grid, Inc., 1974.

ROGERS, C. *Client-centered Psychotherapy.* Boston: Houghton-Mifflin, 1951.

ROGERS, C. *On Becoming a Person.* Boston: Houghton-Mifflin, 1961.

ROGERS, C. Toward a modern approach to values. *Journal of Abnormal and Social Psychology.* Vol. 68, no. 2, pp. 160–167, 1964.

ROMNEY, A.K., AND D'ANDRADE, R.G. Transcultural studies in cognition. *American Anthropologist.* Vol. 66, no. 3, part 2, June 1964.

RONEN, S. *Comparative and Multinational Management.* New York: John Wiley & Sons, 1986.

ROSENTHAL, R., AND DePAULO, B.M. Sex differences in eavesdropping on nonverbal cues. *Journal of Personality and Social Psychology.* 37, pp. 273–285, 1979a.

ROSENTHAL, R., AND DePAULO, B.M. Sex differences in accommodation in nonverbal communication. In *Skill in Nonverbal Communication: Individual Differences*. R. Rosenthal, ed. Cambridge: Oelgeschager, Gunn and Hain, 1979b.

ROTHMAN, E. *Hands and Heart: A History of Courtship in America*. New York: Basic Books, 1984.

RUBEN, B.D. Human communication and cross-cultural effectiveness. *International and Intercultural Communication Annual*. Vol. 4, pp. 98–195, December 1977.

RUBEN, B.D. Guidelines for cross-cultural effectiveness. In *Toward Internationalism: Readings on Cross-Cultural Communication*. 2nd ed. L.F. Luce and E.C. Smith, eds. Cambridge, MA: Newbury House Publications, pp. 36–46, 1987.

RUBEN, L.B. *Worlds of Pain: Life in the Working-Class Family*. New York: Basic Books, 1976.

RUESCH, J., AND KEES, W. *Nonverbal Communication: Notes on the Visual Perception of Human Relations*. Berkeley: University of California Press, 1964.

RUGMAN, A.M., LECRAW, D.J., AND BOOTH, L.D. *International Business*. New York: McGraw-Hill, 1985.

RUHLY, S. *Orientations to Intercultural Communication*. Palo Alto, CA: SRA, 1976.

RYPCZYNSKI, W. *Taming the Tiger: The Struggle to Control Technology*. New York: Viking Penguin, Inc., 1983.

SADKER, M., AND SADKER, D. Sexism in the schoolroom of the '80s. *Psychology Today*. pp. 54–57, March 1985.

SAINT EXUPERY, A. DE. *Airman's Odyssey*. New York: Reynal, 1939.

SARBAUGH, L.E. *Intercultural Communication*. Rochelle Park, NJ: Hayden Book Co., 1979.

SCHOLES, R., AND KLAUS, C.H. *Elements of Writing*. New York: Oxford University Press, 1972.

SEELYE, H., ED. *Teaching Culture: Strategies for Intercultural Communication*. Lincolnwood, IL: National Textbook Co., 1984.

SHELDON, W.H. *The Variation of Human Physique*. New York: Harper & Row, 1940.

SHELDON, W.H. *The Varieties of Temperament*. New York: Harper & Row, 1942.

SIEBURG, E., AND LARSON, C. Dimensions of interpersonal response. Paper presented to the International Communication Association, Phoenix, AZ, 1971.

SIMMONS, G.J., AND MCCALL, J.L. *Identities and Interactions*. New York: The Free Press, 1966.

SINGER, M.R. *Intercultural Communication: A Perceptual Approach*. Englewood Cliffs, NJ: Prentice-Hall, 1987.

SLATER, J.R. *Beyond the Language Barrier: Principles for the Transcoding of Printed Linguistic-Iconic Texts*. Unpublished dissertation, New York University, 1987.

SMELTZER, L.R., AND WALTMAN, J.L. *Managerial Communication: A Strategic Approach*. New York: John Wiley & Sons, 1984.

SNOWDON, S. *The Global Edge: How Your Company Can Win in the International Marketplace*. New York: Simon & Schuster, 1986.

STALEY, C. Male-female use of expletives: a heck of a difference in expectations. *Anthropological Linguistics*. 20, pp. 367–380, 1978.

STARKWEATHER, J.A. Vocal communication of personality and human feelings. *Journal of Communication*. 11, 1961.

STEWART, C.J., AND CASH, W.B., JR. *Interviewing: Principles and Practices*. 5th ed. Dubuque, IA: William C. Brown, 1988.

STEWART, E.C. American assumptions and values: orientation to action. In *Toward Internationalism: Readings in Cross-Cultural Communication*. 2nd ed. L.F. Luce and E.C. Smith, eds. Cambridge, MA: Newbury House Publishers, pp. 51–72, 1987.

STOCKARD, J., AND JOHNSON, M.M. *Sex Roles: Sex Inequality and Sex Role Development*. Englewood Cliffs, NJ: Prentice Hall, 1980.

STUART, R.B. *Helping Couples Change: A Social Learning Approach to Marital Therapy.* New York: Guilford Press, 1980.

SWINGLE, P.G. *The Management of Power.* New York: Wiley & Sons, 1976.

TERPSTRA, V. *International Dimensions of Marketing.* Boston: Kent Publishing Co., 1982.

TERPSTRA, V., AND DAVID, K. *The Cultural Environment of International Business.* 2nd ed. Cincinnati: South-Western Publishing Co., 1985.

THOMAS, K.W. Conflict and conflict management. In *The Handbook of Industrial and Organizational Psychology.* M.D. Dunnette, ed. Chicago: Rand McNally, pp. 889–935, 1976.

THOMAS, K., AND KILMANN, R. Developing a forced-choice measure of conflict handling behavior: the 'mode' instrument. *Educational and Psychological Measurement.* 37, pp. 309–325, 1977.

THOMAS, K.W., AND KILMANN, R.H. *Thomas-Kilmann Conflict Mode Instrument.* Tuxedo, NY: XICOM, 1974.

TING-TOOMEY, S. An analysis of verbal communication patterns in high and low marital adjustment groups. *Human Communication Research.* 9, pp. 306–319, 1983.

TOULMIN, S. *The Uses of Argument.* Cambridge: Cambridge University Press, 1958.

TRIANDIS, H.C. *Interpersonal Behavior Across Cultures: Variations in Black and White Perceptions of the Social Environment.* Urbana: The University of Illinois Press, 1976.

TRUDGILL, P. *Sociolinguistics: An Introduction to Language and Society.* Harmondworth, Middlesex: Penguin Books, 1974.

TUCKER, R.W. *The Inequality of Nations.* New York: Basic Books, 1977.

VICTOR, D.A. Stamp: a formula for teaching business communication theory. *The Bulletin of the Association for Business Communication.* September, pp. 34–35, 1986.

VOGEL, E. Japan as Number One. Cambridge, MA: Harvard University Press, 1979.

WATSON, G., AND JOHNSON, D. *Social Psychology: Issues and Insights.* Philadelphia: Lippincott, 1972.

WATZLAWICK, P., BEAVIN, J.H., AND JACKSON, D.D. *Pragmatics of Human Communication: A Study of Interactional Patterns, Pathologies, and Paradoxes.* New York: W.W. Norton & Co., 1967.

Webster's New Collegiate Dictionary, Springfield, MA: G. & C. Merriam Co., 1981.

WEHR, P. *Conflict Resolution.* Boulder, Colorado: Westview Press, 1979.

WEST, C., AND ZIMMERMAN, D.H. Small insults: a study of interruptions in cross-sex conversations between unacquainted persons. In *Language, Gender and Society.* B. Thorne, C. Kramarae, and N. Henley, eds. Rowley, MA: Newbury House, pp. 102–117, 1983.

WHEELESS, V., AND DIERKS-STEWART, K. The psychometric properties of the Bem sex-role inventory. *Communication Quarterly.* 29, pp. 173–186, 1981.

WHORF, B.L. *Collected Papers on Metalinguistics.* Washington, DC: Department of State, Foreign Service Institute, 1952.

WILLIAMS, F. The psychological correlates of speech characteristics: on sounding disadvantaged. *Journal of Speech and Hearing Research.* 13, pp. 472–488, 1970.

WILLIAMS, J.E., AND BEST, D.L. *Measuring Sex Stereotypes: A Thirty Nation Study.* Beverly Hills, CA: Sage Publications, 1982.

WOLF, M.P., AND KUIPER, S. *Effective Communication in Business.* 8th ed. Cincinnati: South-Western, 1984.

WOLVIN, A.D., AND COAKLEY, C.G. *Listening.* Dubuque, IA: William C. Brown, 1982, 1985.

WOMACK, D. Cooperative behavior by female negotiators: experts or masochists. In *Advances in Gender Communication Research.* L.B. Nadler, M.K. Nadler, and W.R. Todd-Mancillas, eds. Lanham, MD: University Press of America, pp. 222–236, 1987.

ZAND, D.E. Trust and managerial problem solving. *Administrative Science Quarterly.* Vol. 17, no. 2, pp. 229–239, June 1972.

ZIMMERMAN, D., AND WEST, C. Sex roles, interruptions and silences in conversation. In *Language and Sex: Difference and Dominance.* B. Thorne and N. Henley, eds. Rowley, MA: Newbury House, 1975.

AUTHOR INDEX

SUBJECT INDEX